Big Data SMACK

A Guide to Apache Spark, Mesos, Akka, Cassandra, and Kafka

Raul Estrada
Isaac Ruiz

apress®

Big Data SMACK: A Guide to Apache Spark, Mesos, Akka, Cassandra, and Kafka

Raul Estrada
Mexico City
Mexico

Isaac Ruiz
Mexico City
Mexico

ISBN-13 (pbk): 978-1-4842-2174-7
DOI 10.1007/978-1-4842-2175-4

ISBN-13 (electronic): 978-1-4842-2175-4

Library of Congress Control Number: 2016954634

Managing Director: Welmoed Spahr
Acquisitions Editor: Susan McDermott
Developmental Editor: Laura Berendson
Technical Reviewer: Rogelio Vizcaino
Editorial Board: Steve Anglin, Pramila Balen, Laura Berendson, Aaron Black, Louise Corrigan, Jonathan Gennick, Robert Hutchinson, Celestin Suresh John, Nikhil Karkal, James Markham, Susan McDermott, Matthew Moodie, Natalie Pao, Gwenan Spearing
Coordinating Editor: Rita Fernando
Copy Editor: Kim Burton-Weisman
Compositor: SPi Global
Indexer: SPi Global
Cover Image: Designed by Harryarts - Freepik.com

Distributed to the book trade worldwide by Springer Science+Business Media New York, 233 Spring Street, 6th Floor, New York, NY 10013. Phone 1-800-SPRINGER, fax (201) 348-4505, e-mail orders-ny@springer-sbm.com, or visit www.springer.com. Apress Media, LLC is a California LLC and the sole member (owner) is Springer Science + Business Media Finance Inc (SSBM Finance Inc). SSBM Finance Inc is a Delaware corporation.

For information on translations, please e-mail rights@apress.com, or visit www.apress.com.

Apress and friends of ED books may be purchased in bulk for academic, corporate, or promotional use. eBook versions and licenses are also available for most titles. For more information, reference our Special Bulk Sales–eBook Licensing web page at www.apress.com/bulk-sales.

Any source code or other supplementary materials referenced by the author in this text is available to readers at www.apress.com. For detailed information about how to locate your book's source code, go to www.apress.com/source-code/.

Printed on acid-free paper

I dedicate this book to my mom and all the masters out there.
—Raúl Estrada

For all Binnizá people.
—Isaac Ruiz

Contents at a Glance

Contents

About the Authors

Raul Estrada has been a programmer since 1996 and a Java developer since the year 2000. He loves functional languages like Elixir, Scala, Clojure, and Haskell. With more than 12 years of experience in high availability and enterprise software, he has designed and implemented architectures since 2003. He has been enterprise architect for BEA Systems and Oracle Inc., but he also enjoys mobile programming and game development. Now he is focused on open source projects related to data pipelining like Apache Spark, Apache Kafka, Apache Flink, and Apache Beam.

Isaac Ruiz has been a Java programmer since 2001, and a consultant and an architect since 2003. He has participated in projects in different areas and varied scopes (education, communications, retail, and others). He specializes in systems integration, particularly in the financial sector. Ruiz is a supporter of free software and he likes to experiment with new technologies (frameworks, languages, and methods).

About the Technical Reviewer

Rogelio Vizcaino has been a programming professionally for ten years, and hacking a little longer than that. Currently he is a JEE and solutions architect on a consultancy basis for one of the major banking institutions in his country. Educated as an electronic systems engineer, performance and footprint are more than "desirable treats" in software to him. Ironically, the once disliked tasks in database maintenance became his mainstay skills through much effort in the design and development of both relational and non-relational databases since the start of his professional practice—and the good luck of finding great masters to work with during the journey. With most of his experience in the enterprise financial sector, Vizcaino's heart is with the Web. He keeps track of web-related technologies and standards, where he discovered the delights of programming back in the late 1990s. Vizcaino considers himself a programmer before an architect, engineer, or developer; "programming" is an all-encompassing term and should be used with pride. Above all, he likes to learn, to create new things, and to fix broken ones.

Acknowledgments

We want to say thanks to our acquisitions editor, Susan McDermott, who believed in this project from the beginning; without her help, it would not have started.

We also thank Rita Fernando and Laura Berendson; without their effort and patience, it would not have been possible to write this book.

We want to thank our technical reviewer, Rogelio Vizcaino; without him, the project would not have been a success.

We also want to thank all the heroes who contribute open source projects, specifically with Spark, Mesos, Akka, Cassandra and Kafka, and special recognition to those who develop the open source connectors between these technologies.

We also thank all the people who have educated us and shown us the way throughout our lives.

Introduction

During 2014, 2015, and 2016, surveys show that among all software developers, those with higher wages are the data engineers, the data scientists, and the data architects.

This is because there is a huge demand for technical professionals in data; unfortunately for large organizations and fortunately for developers, there is a very low offering.

Traditionally, large volumes of information have been handled by specialized scientists and people with a PhD from the most prestigious universities. And this is due to the popular belief that not all of us have access to large volumes of corporate data or large enterprise production environments.

Apache Spark is disrupting the data industry for two reasons. The first is because it is an open source project. In the last century, companies like IBM, Microsoft, SAP, and Oracle were the only ones capable of handling large volumes of data, and today there is so much competition between them, that disseminating designs or platform algorithms is strictly forbidden. Thus, the benefits of open source become stronger because the contributions of so many people make free tools more powerful than the proprietary ones.

The second reason is that you do not need a production environment with large volumes of data or large laboratories to develop in Apache Spark. Apache Spark can be installed on a laptop easily and the development made there can be exported easily to enterprise environments with large volumes of data. Apache Spark also makes the data development free and accessible to startups and little companies.

If you are reading this book, it is for two reasons: either you want to be among the best paid IT professionals, or you already are and you want to learn how today's trends will become requirements in the not too distant future.

In this book, we explain how dominate the SMACK stack, which is also called the Spark++, because it seems to be the open stack that will most likely succeed in the near future.

PART I

Introduction

CHAPTER 1

■ ■ ■

Big Data, Big Challenges

In this chapter, we expose the modern architecture challenges facing the SMACK stack (Apache Spark, Mesos, Akka, Cassandra, and Kafka). Also, we present dynamic processing environment problems to see which conditions are suitable and which are not.

This chapter covers the following:

- Why we need a pipeline architecture for big data
- The Lambda Architecture concept
- ETL and its dark side

Big Data Problems

We live in the information era, where almost everything is data. In modern organizations, there is a suitable difference between data engineers and data architects. Data engineers are experts who perfectly know the inner workings and handling of the data engines. The data architect well understands all the data sources—internal and external. Internal sources are usually owned systems. External sources are systems outside the organization. The first big data problem is that the number of data sources increases with time.

A few years ago, a big company's IT department could survive without data architects or data engineers. Today's challenge is to find good architects. The main purpose of architecture is always resilience. If the data architect doesn't have a data plan, then the data sources and the data size will become unmanageable.

The second problem is obtaining a data sample. When you are a data analyst (the person charged with the compilation and analysis of numerical information), you need data samples—that is, data from production environments. If the size of the data and/or the number of data sources increases, then obtaining data samples becomes a herculean task.

The third big data problem is that the validity of an analysis becomes obsolete as time progresses. Today, we have all the information. The true value of data is related to time. Within minutes, a recommendation, an analysis, or a prediction can become useless.

The fourth problem is related to the return on investment of an analysis. The analysis velocity is directly proportional to the return on investment. If the data analyst can't get data in a timely way, then analysis costs increase and the earnings decrease.

Electronic supplementary material The online version of this chapter (doi:10.1007/978-1-4842-2175-4_1) contains supplementary material, which is available to authorized users.

© Raul Estrada and Isaac Ruiz 2016
R. Estrada and I. Ruiz, *Big Data SMACK*, DOI 10.1007/978-1-4842-2175-4_1

Infrastructure Needs

Modern companies require a scalable infrastructure. The costs of your data center are always in accordance with your business size. There is expensive hardware and costly software. And nowadays, when it comes to open source software, people's first thoughts are the high costs of consulting or the developer's price tag. But there is good news: today, big data solutions are not exclusive to large budgets.

Technologies must be distributed. Nowadays, when we talk about *distributed software*, we are no longer talking about multiple processors; instead, we are talking about multiple data centers. This is the same system, geographically dispersed.

If your business grows, your data should fit those needs. This is scalability. Most people are afraid of the term *big data*, and spend valuable economic resources to tackle a problem that they don't have. In a traditional way, your business growth implies your data volumes' growth. Here, the good news is scale linearly with cheap hardware and inexpensive software.

Faster processing speed is not related to processor cycles per second, but the speed of all your enterprise process. The now is everything, opportunities are unique, and few situations are repeatable.

When we talk about complex processing, we are not talking about the "Big O" of an algorithm. This is related to the number of actors involved in one process.

The data flow is constant. The days when businesses could store everything in warehouses are gone. The businesses that deliver responses the next day are dying. The *now* is everything. Data warehouses are dying because stored data becomes rotten, and data caducity is shorter every day. The costs associated with a warehouse are not affordable today.

And finally, there is visible and reproducible analysis. As we have mentioned, data analysts need fresh and live data to satisfy their needs. If data becomes opaque, the business experiences a lack of management.

ETL

ETL stands for *extract, transform, load*. And it is, even today, a very painful process. The design and maintenance of an ETL process is risky and difficult. Contrary to what many enterprises believe, they serve the ETL and the ETL doesn't serve anyone. It is not a requirement; it is a set of unnecessary steps.

Each step in ETL has its own risk and introduces errors. Sometimes, the time spent debugging the ETL result is longer than the ETL process itself. ETL always introduces errors. Everyone dedicated to ETL knows that having no errors is an error. In addition, everyone dedicated to ETL knows that applying ETL onto sensitive data is playing with the company's stability.

Everybody knows that when there is a failure in an ETL process, data duplication odds are high. Expensive debugging processes (human and technological) should be applied after an ETL failure. This means looking for duplicates and restoring information.

The tools usually cost millions of dollars. Big companies know that ETL is good business for them, but not for the client. The human race has invested a lot of resources (temporal and economic) in making ETL tools.

The ETL decreases throughput. The performance of the entire company decreases when the ETL process is running, because the ETL process demands resources: network, database, disk space, processors, humans, and so forth.

The ETL increases complexity. Few computational processes are as common and as complicated. When a process requires ETL, the consultants know that the process will be complex, because ETL rarely adds value to a business's "line of sight" and requires multiple actors, steps, and conditions.

ETL requires intermediary files writing. Yes, as if computational resources were infinite, costless, and easily replaceable. In today's economy, the concept of big intermediary files is an aberration that should be removed.

The ETL involves parsing and reparsing text files. Yes, the lack of appropriate data structures leads to unnecessary parsing processes. And when they finish, the result must be reparsed to ensure the consistency and integrity of the generated files.

Finally, the ETL pattern should be duplicated over all our data centers. The number doesn't matter; the ETL should be replicated in every data center.

The good news is that no ETL pipelines are typically built on the SMACK stack. ETL is the opposite of high availability, resiliency, and distribution. As rule of thumb, if you write a lot of intermediary files, you suffer ETL; as if your resources—computational and economic—were infinite.

The first step is to remove the extract phase. Today we have very powerful tools (for example, Scala) that can work with binary data preserved under strongly typed schemas (instead of using big text dumps parsed among several heterogeneous systems). Thus, it is an elegant weapon for a more civilized big data age.

The second step is to remove the load phase. Today, your data collection can be done with a modern distributed messaging system (for example, Kafka) and you can make the distribution to all your clients in real time. There is no need to batch "load."

Lambda Architecture

Lambda Architecture is a data processing architecture designed to handle massive quantities of data by taking advantage of both batch and stream processing methods. As you saw in previous sections, today's challenge is to have the batch and streaming at the same time.

One of the best options is Spark. This wonderful framework allows batch and stream data processing in the same application at the same time. Unlike many Lambda solutions, SMACK satisfies these two requirements: it can handle a data stream in real time and handle despair data models from multiple data sources.

In SMACK, we persist in Cassandra, the analytics data produced by Spark, so we guarantee the access to historical data as requested. In case of failure, Cassandra has the resiliency to replay our data before the error. Spark is not the only tool that allows both behaviors at the same time, but we believe that Apache Spark is the best.

Hadoop

Apache Hadoop is an open-source software framework written in Java for distributed storage and the distributed processing of very large data sets on computer clusters built from commodity hardware.

There are two main components associated with Hadoop: Hadoop MapReduce and Hadoop Distributed File System (HDFS). These components were inspired by the Google file system.

We could talk more about Hadoop, but there are lots of books specifically written on this topic. Hadoop was designed in a context where size, scope, and data completeness are more important than speed of response.

And here you face with a crucial decision: if the issue that you need to solve is more like data warehousing and batch processing, Apache Hadoop could be your solution. On the other hand, if the issue is the speed of response and the amount of information is measured in speed units instead of data size units, Apache Spark is your solution.

Data Center Operation

And we take this space to briefly reflect on how the data center operation has changed.

Yesterday, everything scaled up; today, everything scales out. A few years ago, the term *data center* meant proprietary use of specialized and expensive supercomputers. Today's challenge is to be competitive using commodity computers connected with a non-expensive network.

The total cost of ownership determines all. Business determines the cost and size of the data center. Modern startups always rise from a small data center. Buying or renting an expensive data center just to see if your startup is a good idea has no meaning in the modern economy.

The M in SMACK is a good solution to all your data center needs. With Apache Mesos, you can "abstract" all the resources from all the interconnected small computers to build a supercomputer with the linear sum of each machine's resources: CPU cores, memory, disk, and network.

The Open Source Reign

A few years ago, dependency on a vendor was a double-edged sword. On one hand, large companies hired proprietary software firms to later blame the manufacturer for any failure in their systems. But, on the other hand, this dependence—all the processes, development, and maintenance—became slow and all the issues were discussed with a contract in hand.

Many large companies don't implement open source solutions for fear that no one else can provide the same support as large manufacturers. But weighing both proposals, the vendor lock-in and the external bug fixing is typically more expensive than open source solutions.

In the past, the big three-letter monopolies dictated the game rules. Today, the rules are made "by and for" the developers, the transparency is guaranteed by APIs defined by the same community. Some groups—like the Apache Software Foundation and the Eclipse Foundation—provide guides, infrastructure, and tools for sustainable and fair development of these technologies.

Obviously, nothing is free in this life; companies must invest in training their staff on open source technologies.

The Data Store Diversification

Few people see this, but this is the beginning of the decline of the relational databases era. Since 2010, and the emergence of NoSQL and NoETL, there has been tough criticism of traditional systems, which is redefining the leader board.

Due to modern business needs, having everything stored in a relational database will go from being the standard way to the old-fashioned and obsolete way. Simple daily problems like recording the data, multiple store synchronization, and expensive store size are promoting NoSQL and NoETL solutions.

When moving data, gravity and location matter. Data gravity is related to the costs associated with moving a huge amount of data from one point to another. Sometimes, the simple everyday task of restoring a backup can be a daunting task in terms of time and money.

Data allocation is a modern concept related to moving the computation resources where the data is located, rather than moving the data to where the computation is. It sounds simple, but due to the hardware (re)evolution, the ability to perform complex calculations on new and powerful client machines doesn't impact customer perception on the performance of the entire system.

DevOps (development operations) is a term coined by Andrew Clay Shafer and Patrick Debois at the Agile Conference in 2008.[1] Since then, DevOps has become a movement, a culture, and a lifestyle where software developers and information technology professionals charged with data center operation can live and work in harmony. How is this achieved? Easy: by dissolving the differences between them.

Today DevOps is one of the most profitable IT specializations. Modern tools like Docker and Spark simplify the movement between testing and production environments. The developers can have production data easily and the testing environments are almost mirrored with production environments.

As you will see in Chapter 7, today's tendency is containerize the development pipeline from development to production.

---

[1]http://ieeexplore.ieee.org/xpl/mostRecentIssue.jsp?punumber=4599439

Is SMACK the Solution?

Even today, there are very few companies fully using SMACK. That is, many major companies use a flavor of SMACK—just use one, two, or three letters of the SMACK stack. As previously mentioned, Spark has many advantages over Hadoop. Spark also solves problems that Hadoop cannot. However, there are some environments where Hadoop has deep roots and where workflow is completely batch based. In these instances, Hadoop is usually a better choice.

Several SMACK letters have become a requirement for some companies that are in pilot stages and aim to capitalize all the investment in big data tools and training. The purpose of this book is to give you options. The goal is not to make a full pipeline architecture installation of all the five technologies.

However, there are many alternatives to the SMACK stack technologies. For example, Yarn may be an alternative to Mesos. For batch processing, Apache Flink can be an alternative to Spark. The SMACK stack axiom is to build an end-to-end pipeline and have the right component in the correct position, so that integration can be done quickly and naturally, instead of having expensive tools that require a lot of effort to cohabit among them.

CHAPTER 2

■ ■ ■

Big Data, Big Solutions

In Chapter 1, we answered the *Why?*. In this chapter, we will answer the *How?*. When you understand the Why, the answer to the How happens in only a matter of time.

This chapter covers the following topics:

- Traditional vs. modern (big) data

- SMACK in a nutshell

- **S**park, the engine

- **M**esos, the container

- **A**kka, the model

- **C**assandra, the storage

- **K**afka, the broker

Traditional vs. Modern (Big) Data

Is time quantized? Is there an indivisible amount of time that cannot be divided? Until now, the correct answer to these questions was "Nobody knows." The only certain thing is that on a human scale, life doesn't happen in batch mode.

Many systems are monitoring a continuous stream of events: weather events, GPS signals, vital signs, logs, device metrics.... The list is endless. The natural way to collect and analyze this information is as a stream of data.

Handling data as streams is the correct way to model this behavior, but until recently, this methodology was very difficult to do well. The previous rates of messages were in the range of thousands of messages per second—the new technologies discussed in this book can deliver rates of millions of messages per second.

The point is this: streaming data is not a matter for very specialized computer science projects; stream-based data is becoming the rule for data-driven companies.

Table 2-1 compares the three approaches: traditional data, traditional big data, and modern big data.

© Raul Estrada and Isaac Ruiz 2016
R. Estrada and I. Ruiz, *Big Data SMACK*, DOI 10.1007/978-1-4842-2175-4_2

Table 2-1. *Traditional Data, Traditional Big Data, and Modern Big Data Approaches*

CONCEPT	TRADITIONAL DATA	TRADITIONAL BIG DATA	MODERN BIG DATA
Person	• IT oriented	• IT oriented	• Business oriented
Roles	• Developer	• Data engineer	• Business user
		• Data architect	• Data scientist
Data Sources	• Relational	• Relational	• Relational
	• Files	• Files	• Files
	• Message queues	• Message queues	• Message queues
		• Data service	• Data service
			• NoSQL
Data Processing	• Application server	• Application server	• Application server
	• ETL	• ETL	• ETL
		• Hadoop	• Hadoop
			• Spark
Metadata	• Limited by IT	• Limited by model	• Automatically generated
			• Context enriched
			• Business oriented
			• Dictionary based
User interface	• Self-made	• Self-made	• Self-made
	• Developer skills required	• Developer skills required	• Built by business users
			• Tools guided
Use Cases	• Data migration	• Data lakes	• Self-service
	• Data movement	• Data hubs	• Internet of Things
	• Replication	• Data warehouse offloading	• Data as a Service
Open Source Technologies	• Fully embraced	• Minimal	• TCO rules
Tools Maturity	• High	• Medium	• Low
	• Enterprise	• Enterprise	• Evolving
Business Agility	• Low	• Medium	• Extremely high
Automation level	• Low	• Medium	• High
Governance	• IT governed	• Business governed	• End-user governed
Problem Resolution	• IT personnel solved	• IT personnel solved	• Timely or die
Collaboration	• Medium	• Low	• Extremely high
Productivity/Time to Market	• Slower	• Slower	• Highly productive

(continued)

Table 2-1. (*continued*)

CONCEPT	TRADITIONAL DATA	TRADITIONAL BIG DATA	MODERN BIG DATA
Integration Analysis	• Minimal	• Medium	• Faster time to market • Modeled by analytical transformations
Real-time	• Minimal real time	• Minimal real time	• In real time or die
Data Access	• Primarily batch	• Batch	• Micro batch

Modern technologies and architectures allow you to build systems more easily and efficiently, and to produce a better model of the way business processes take place. We will explain the real value of a streaming architecture. The possibilities are vast.

Apache Spark is not a replacement for Hadoop. Spark is a computing engine, whereas Hadoop is a complete stack for storage, cluster management, and computing tools. Spark runs well over Hadoop.

Hadoop is a ten-year-old technology. Today, we see the rising of many deployments that are not on Hadoop, including deployments on NoSQL stores (like Cassandra) and deployments directly against cloud storage (e.g., Amazon S3). In this aspect, Spark is reaching a broader audience than Hadoop.

SMACK in a Nutshell

If you poll several IT people, we agree on a few things, including that we are always searching for a new acronym.

SMACK, as you already know, stands for Spark, Mesos, Akka, Cassandra, and Kafka. They are all open source technologies and all are Apache software projects, except Akka. The SMACK acronym was coined by Mesosphere, a company that, in collaboration with Cisco, bundled these technologies together in a product called Infinity, which was designed to solve some big data challenges where the streaming is fundamental.[1]

Big data architecture is required in the daily operation of many companies, but there are a lot of sources talking about each technology separately.

Let's discuss the full stack and how to make the integration.

This book is a cookbook on how to integrate each technology in the most successful big data stack. We talk about the five main concepts of big data architecture and how to integrate/replace/reinforce every technology:

- Spark: The engine

- Mesos: The container

- Akka: The model

- Cassandra: The storage

- Kafka: The message broker

Figure 2-1 represents the reference diagram for the whole book.

---

[1]https://mesosphere.com/

Figure 2-1. *SMACK at a glance*

Apache Spark vs. MapReduce

MapReduce is a programming model for processing large data sets with a parallel and distributed algorithm on a cluster.

As we will see later, in functional programming, there are two basic methods: map(), which is dedicated filtering and sorting, and reduce(), which is dedicated to doing an operation. As an example, to serve a group of people at a service window, you must first queue (map) and then attend them (reduce).

The term MapReduce was coined in 1995, when the Message Passing Interface was used to solve programming issues, as we will discuss later. Obviously, when Google made the implementation, it had only one use case in mind: web search.

It is important to note that Hadoop born in 2006 and grew up in an environment where MapReduce reigned. MapReduce was born with two characteristics that mark its life: high latency and batch mode; both make it incapable to withstand modern challenges.

As you can see in Table 2-2, Spark is different.

Table 2-2. *Apache Spark /MapReduce Comparison*

CONCEPT	Apache Spark	MapReduce
Written in	Scala/Akka	Java
Languages Supported	Java, Scala, Python, and R are first-class citizens.	Everything should be written using Java.
Storage Model	Keeps things in memory	Keeps things in disk. Takes a long time to write things to disk and read them back, making it slow and laborious.
I/O Model	Keeps things in memory without I/O. Operates on the same data quickly.	Requires a lot of I/O activity over disk.
Recovery	Runs the same task in seconds or minutes. Restart is not a problem.	Records everything in disk, allowing restart after failure
Knowledge	The abstraction is high; codification is intuitive.	Could write MapReduce jobs intelligently, avoiding overusing resources, but requires specialized knowledge of the platform.
Focus	Code describes how to process data. Implementation details are hidden.	Apache Hive programming goes into code to avoid running too many MapReduce jobs.
Efficiency	Abstracts all the implementation to run it as efficiently as possible.	Programmers write complex code to optimize each MapReduce job.
Abstraction	Abstracts things like a good high-level programming language. It is a powerful and expressive environment.	Code is hard to maintain over time.
Libraries	Adds libraries for machine learning, streaming, graph manipulation, and SQL.	Programmers need third-party tools and libraries, which makes work complex.
Streaming	Real-time stream processing out of the box.	Frameworks like Apache Storm needed; increased complexity.
Source Code Size	Scala programs have dozens of lines of code (LOC).	Java programs have hundreds of LOC.
Machine Learning	Spark ML	If you want to do machine learning, you have to separately integrate Mahout, H2O, or Onyx. You have to learn how it works, and how to build it on.
Graphs	Spark GraphX	If you want to do graph databases, you have to select from Giraph, TitanDB, Neo4J, or some other technologies. Integration is not seamless.

Apache Spark has these advantages:

- Spark speeds up application development 10 to 100 times faster, making applications portable and extensible.

- Scala can read Java code. Java code can be rewritten in Scala in a much smaller form factor that is much easier to read, repurpose, and maintain.

- When the Apache Spark core is improved, all the machine learning and graphs libraries are improved too.

- Integration is easier: the applications are easier to maintain and costs go down.

If an enterprise bets on one foundation, Spark is the best choice today.
Databricks (a company founded by the Apache Spark creators) lists the following use cases for Spark:

- ETL and data integration

- Business intelligence and interactive analytics

- Advanced analytics and machine learning

- Batch computation for high performance

- Real-time stream processing

Some of the new use cases are just the old use cases done faster; although some use cases are totally new. There are some scenarios that just can't be done with acceptable performance on MapReduce.

The Engine

It is important to recall that Spark is better at OLAP (online analytical processing), which are batch jobs and data mining. Spark is not suitable for OLTP (online transaction processing), such as numerous atomic transactions; for this type of processing, we strongly recommend Erlang (a beautiful language inspired in the actor's model).
Apache Spark has five main components:

- Spark Core

- Spark SQL

- Spark Streaming

- Spark MLib

- Spark GraphX

Each Spark library typically has an entire book dedicated to it. In this book, we try to simply tackle the Apache Spark essentials to meet the SMACK stack.
The role of Apache Spark on the SMACK stack is to act as the processor and provide real-time data analysis. It addresses the aggregation and analysis layers.
There are few open source alternatives to Spark. As we've mentioned, Apache Hadoop is the classic approach. The strongest modern adversary is the Apache Flink project, which is good to keep in mind.

The Model

Akka is a model, a toolkit, and a runtime for building distributed, resilient, and highly concurrent message-driven applications on the Java virtual machine. In 2009, the Akka toolkit was released as open source. Language bindings exist for both Java and Scala. We need to first analyze Akka in order to understand the Spark architecture. Akka was designed based on the actor concurrency models:

- Actors are arranged hierarchically
- Asynchronous message (data) passing
- Fault tolerant
- Customizable failure and detection strategies
- Hierarchical supervision
- Adaptive, predictive
- Parallelized
- Load balance

There are many Akka competitors; we make a special mention of Reactor. The actor model is the foundation of many frameworks and languages. The main languages that are based on the actor model (called *functional languages*) are Lisp, Scheme, Erlang, Haskell, and recently, Scala, Clojure, F#, and Elixir (a modern implementation of Erlang).

The Broker

Apache Kafka is a publish/subscribe message broker redesigned as a distributed commit log. In SMACK, Kafka is the data ingestion point, mainly on the application layer. Kafka takes data from applications and streams and processes them into the stack. Kafka is a distributed messaging system with high throughput. It handles massive data load and floods. It is the valve that regulates the pressure.

Apache Kafka inspects incoming data volume, which is fundamental for partitioning and distribution among the cluster nodes. Apache Kafka's features include the following:

- Automatic broker failover
- Very high performance distributed messaging
- Partitioning and Distribution across the cluster nodes
- Data pipeline decoupling
- A massive number of consumers are supported
- Massive data load handling

Kafka is the champion among a lot of competitors in MOM (message-oriented middleware). In the MQ family, this includes ActiveMQ, ZeroMQ, IronMQ, and RabbitMQ. The best of all is RabbitMQ, which is made with Erlang.

The best alternative to Kafka is Apache Storm, which has a lot of integration with Apache Hadoop. Keep it in mind. Apache Kafka is here to stay.

The Storage

Apache Cassandra is a distributed database. It is the perfect choice when you need to escalate and need hyper-high availability with no sacrifice in performance. Cassandra was originally used on Facebook in 2008 to handle large amounts of data. It became a top-level Apache project in 2010. Cassandra handles the stack's operational data. Cassandra can also be used to expose data to the application layer.

The following are the main features of Apache Cassandra:

- Extremely fast and scalable

- Multi data center, no single point of failure

- Survives when multiple nodes fault

- Easy to operate

- Flexible data modeling

- Automatic and configurable replication

- Ideal for real-time ingestion

- Has a great Apache based community

There are a lot of Cassandra competitors, including DynamoDB (powered by Amazon; it's contending in the NoSQL battlefield), Apache HBase (the best-known database implementation of Hadoop), Riak (made by the Basho samurais; it's a powerful Erlang database), CouchBase, Apache CouchDB, MongoDB, Cloudant, and Redis.

The Container

Apache Mesos is a distributed systems kernel that is easy to build and effective to run. Mesos is an abstraction layer over all computer resources (CPU, memory, storage) on the machines (physical or virtual), enabling elastic distributed systems and fault tolerance. Mesos was designed with the Linux kernel principles at a higher abstraction level. It was first presented as Nexus in 2009. In 2011, it was relaunched by Matei Zaharia under its current name. Mesos is the base of three frameworks:

- Apache Aurora

- Chronos

- Marathon

In SMACK, Mesos orchestrates components and manages resources. It is the secret for horizontal cluster scalation. Usually, Apache Mesos is combined with Kubernetes (the competitor used by the Google Cloud Platform) or with Docker (as you will see, more than a competitor, it is a complement to Mesos). The equivalent in Hadoop is Apache Yarn.

Summary

This chapter, like the previous one, was full of theory. We reviewed the fundamental SMACK diagram as well as Spark's advantages over traditional big data technologies such as Hadoop and MapReduce. We also visited every technology in the SMACK stack, briefly presented each tool's potential, and most importantly, we discussed the actual alternatives for each technology. The upcoming chapters go into greater depth on each of these technologies. We will explore the connectors and the integration practices, and link techniques, as well as describe alternatives to every situation.

PART II

Playing SMACK

CHAPTER 3

■ ■ ■

The Language: Scala

The main part of the SMACK stack is Spark, but sometimes the S is for Scala. You can develop in Spark in four languages: Java, Scala, Python, and R. Because Apache Spark is written in Scala, and this book is focused on streaming architecture, we are going to show examples in only the Scala language.

Other Apache Spark books present their examples in the four languages, but for the SMACK stack, simply discussing Scala is enough to develop a robust streaming pipeline. It is important to mention that all the Java programs run in Scala.

If you came here without previous Scala knowledge, welcome to the crash course. It is always good to learn a new programming language. We are not going to study Scala as the first programming language, however. This chapter is organized as a series of exercises in the language. If you already know Scala, try to follow the exercises to improve your knowledge.

As said by many, programming is just about algorithms and data structures. This chapter covers all the Scala data structures. The next chapter covers the algorithms—that is, the Akka actor model.

Functional Programming

Our goal in this chapter is not to learn Scala, but to reach the fully functional thinking in all of its pure expression. It is an open secret that each SMACK technology is independent and autonomous from the others. However, each could be developed (replaced) in Java or Scala.

The truth is that each and every one of the SMACK technologies can be developed ad hoc. Yes, the sun shines for everyone in the streaming pipeline world. You can develop from scratch any SMACK technology or replace one as your project needs.

How to write an entire Apache Akka project is beyond this book's scope, but you should understand how it works to make good architectural decisions.

You need to be clear on these rules:

- Scala collections and Java collections are different

- Spark collections and Scala collections are different

There are three fundamentals (among many others) in functional programming:

- Predicates

- Literal functions

- Implicit loops

Predicate

A predicate is a multiple parameter function with just one boolean value as a return.

© Raul Estrada and Isaac Ruiz 2016
R. Estrada and I. Ruiz, *Big Data SMACK*, DOI 10.1007/978-1-4842-2175-4_3

This is an example (with body definition):

```
def isEven (i: Int) = if (i % 2 == 0) true else false
```

Here is another example (without body definition):

```
def isPrime (p: Long)
```

Note that the function has no parameters, but this is weird. If a function doesn't receive an input, then this implies it is obtaining its data from a global variable or a shared context; both are strongly discouraged (even prohibited) in functional programming. Yes, we know that it could take a random number or take the system time to make its decisions, but these are special cases.

Literal Functions

In functional programming, functions are first-class citizens. In the 21st century it may sound archaic, but programming languages that discriminate against functions still exist, usually because they are low-level languages.

The rule of thumb is to think of it as algebra. In algebra, functions can be composed; you can make operations with functions and pass functions as other functions parameters. If you have problems with algebra, then sorry, this book (and programming) is not for you.... Just kidding. In this case, you can think of functions as traditional object-oriented programming (OOP) objects. So following that idea, you define a higher-order function in mathematics and computer science as a function that does at least one of the following:

- Takes functions as arguments (as parameters)

- Returns a function as a result

For example, the isEven function could be rewritten as this:

```
(i: Int) => i % 2 == 0
```

In this code, the => symbol should be thought of as a *transformer*.

This is a high-order function because it returns a function. Simple, isn't it?

Yes, in mathematics, as in life, definitions are difficult but necessary to support and generalize our theories. With examples, everything is clear.

Implicit Loops

As a final step, the isEven function could be rewritten as this:

```
_ % 2 == 0
```

The _ symbol denotes the parameter, or the thing (object, function, entity) to be used as input. Combined with the filter method, over a list, we find expressions like these:

```
scala> val oneToTen = List.range(1, 10)
oneToTen: List[Int] = List(1, 2, 3, 4, 5, 6, 7, 8, 9)
scala> val evens = nums.filter(_ % 2 == 0)
evens: List[Int] = List(2, 4, 6, 8)
```

The third line contains an implicit loop. Yes, in functional programming we try to avoid loops. If your code has a lot of fors and whiles, it could probably be simplified.

Functional is elegant and concise, but of course, there are some memory tricks that can be issued and solved through structured programming. Throughout history, code readability has proved to be more effective in economic terms (time and money) than hardware optimization, which has become cheaper.

Collections Hierarchy

At the top of the Scala collections hierarchy there is the Traversable class (as shown in Figure 3-1). All Traversable trait children have the implementation for this method:

```
def foreach[U](f: Elem => U)
```

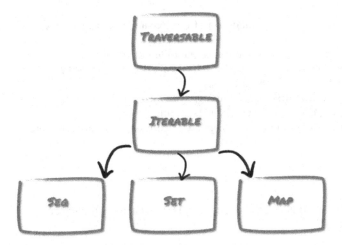

Figure 3-1. *The Scala collection's top hierarchy*

The Iterable trait has implementation in terms of an iterator:

```
def foreach[U](f: Elem => U): Unit = {
  val ite = iterator
  while (ite.hasNext) f(ite.next())
}
```

As you can see, the Iterable trait has three children: Seq, Set, and Map.

Sequences

The Seq trait represents sequences.

As shown in Figure 3-2, Seq has three children: IndexedSeq, LinearSeq, and Buffer.

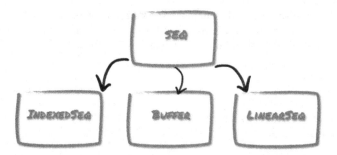

Figure 3-2. *The Seq children*

A *sequence* is an iterable that has a length and whose elements start from zero and have fixed index positions.

LinearSeq and IndexedSeq don't add any new operations, but each has different performance.

LinearSeq is the list. As you know from functional programming, it has head, tail, and isEmpty operations. It is very efficient with apply, length, and update operations.

IndexedSeq is the array. As you know from structured programming, it has the index operations. So, if you have an array of rooms, and you write Room(101), you access the 101st room.

Buffer is an important mutable sequence. Buffers allow you to update existing elements and to insert, remove, and add new elements at the end.

Maps

A *map* is an iterable consisting of pairs. Each pair consists of a key and a value (also called *mappings* or *associations*). The Map family is shown in Figure 3-3.

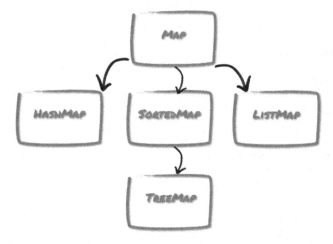

Figure 3-3. *The Map family*

Scala offers an implicit conversion that lets you write *key* -> *value* as an alternate syntax for the (key, value).

For example, Map("uno" -> 1, "dos" -> 2, "tres" -> 3) is the same as Map(("uno", 1), ("dos", 2), ("tres", 3)), but is easier to read.

Sets

A *set* is an iterable that contains no duplicate elements. As you can see in Figure 3-4, the Set hierarchy is similar to the Map family.

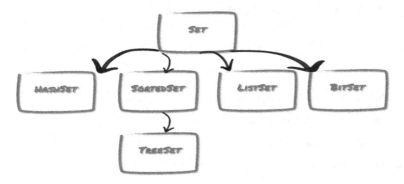

Figure 3-4. *The Set family*

Choosing Collections

Many programmers argue that the Scala type system is difficult and cumbersome. In fact, as you saw, you have to choose only one of these three types:

- Sequence
- Map
- Set

The actual decision is to choose between the mutable and immutable versions.

Sequences

There are only two sequences: the LinearSeq (list) and the IndexedSeq (array). The true effort is to learn the names used, not the hierarchy itself (see Table 3-1).

Table 3-1. *The Sequence Collections*

	Immutable	Mutable
IndexedSeq	Vector	ArrayBuffer
LinearSeq	List	ListBuffer

Immutable Sequences

LinearSeq

- **List**: The list as we know from the functional world.
- **Queue**: The FIFO data structure of the traditional computer science books.
- **Stack**: The LIFO data structure of the traditional computer science books.
- **Stream**: Infinite, lazy and persistent; our everyday flow.

IndexedSeq

- **Range**: A limited list of integers.
- **String**: The well-known and limited char sequence.
- **Vector**: Immutable, indexed, the sedan model of the lists.

Mutable Sequences

LinearSeq

- **LinkedList**: Those traditionally used as an introduction to the C/C++ pointers.
- **DoubleLinkedList**: LinkedList with the "previous" method implemented.
- **ListBuffer**: The List version of the indexed Array.
- **MutableList**: A list for those non-functional rebels.
- **Queue**: The FIFO for non-functional guys.
- **Stack**: The LIFO for non-functional fellas.

IndexedSeq

- **Array**: A list which length is constant and every element is not.
- **ArrayBuffer**: An indexed array that always fits memory needs.
- **ArrayStack**: LIFO implementation when performance matters.
- **StringBuilder**: Efficient string manipulation for those with a limited memory budget.

Maps

You have to choose either a mutable map or a sorted map.

Mutable maps

- **HashMap**: A map whose internal implementation is a hash table.
- **LinkedHashMap**: Elements are returned as they were inserted.
- **ListMap**: Elements are returned as the inverse of how they were inserted.
- **Map**: The map as everybody knows it; key-value pairs.

Immutable maps

- **HashMap**: A map whose internal implementation is a tree.
- **ListMap**: Elements are returned as the inverse of how they were inserted.
- **Map**: The map as everybody knows it; key-value pairs.
- **SortedMap**: The keys are stored in a sorted order.
- **TreeMap**: A sorted map; the red-black tree of the traditional computer science books.

Sets

You have to choose either a mutable set or a sorted set.

Mutable sets

- **BitSet**: Used to save memory, but only integers are allowed.
- **HashSet**: A set implemented using a hash table.
- **LinkedHashSet**: The elements are returned as they were inserted.
- **TreeSet**: The AVL tree of the traditional computer science books.
- **Set**: The mutable vanilla set.
- **SortedSet**: The mutable TreeSet, but ordered.

Immutable sets

- **BitSet**: To save (more) memory, only integers are allowed.
- **HashSet**: A set implemented using a tree.
- **ListSet**: A set for the public; a list for those who knows it.
- **TreeSet**: An immutable set implemented using a tree.
- **Set**: The immutable vanilla set.
- **SortedSet**: The immutable TreeSet but ordered.

Traversing

foreach is the standard method for traversing collections in Scala. Its complexity is O(n); that is, the computation time has a linear relation with the number of elements in the input. We also have the traditional for and the iterators, as in Java.

foreach

In Scala, the foreach method takes a function as argument. This function must have only one parameter and it doesn't return anything (this is called a *procedure*). It operates in every element of the collection, one at a time. The parameter type of the function must match the type of every element in the collection.

```
scala> val zahlen = Vector("Eins", "Zwei", "Drei")
zahlen: scala.collection.immutable.Vector[String] = Vector(Eins, Zwei, Drei)

scala> zahlen.foreach(s => print(s))
EinsZweiDrei
```

This function takes one character and prints it:

```
scala> def printAChar(c: Char) { print(c) }
printAChar: (c: Char)Unit
```

The function is applied to a string (a sequence of chars):

```scala
scala> "SMACK".foreach( c => printAChar(c) )
SMACK
```

The type inference is a useful tool in these modern times:

```scala
scala> "SMACK".foreach( printAChar )
SMACK
```

This is same as the preceding example but with a literal function:

```scala
scala> "SMACK".foreach( (c: Char) => print(c) )
SMACK
```

This is same as the preceding example but uses a type inference and literal functions:

```scala
scala> "SMACK".foreach( print )
SMACK
```

This example uses an implicit loop:

```scala
scala> "SMACK: Spark Mesos Akka Cassandra Kafka".split(" ")
Array[String] = Array(SMACK:, Spark, Mesos, Akka, Cassandra, Kafka)
```

for

As in all modern functional programming languages, we can explore all the elements of a collection with a for loop.

Remember, foreach and for are not designed to produce new collections. If you want a new collection, use the for/yield combo.

As we stated earlier, if it's iterable, then it's traversable (inheritance 101):

```scala
scala> val smack = Traversable("Spark", "Mesos", "Akka", "Cassandra", "Kafka")
smack: Traversable[String] = List(Spark, Mesos, Akka, Cassandra, Kafka)

scala> for (f <- smack) println(f)
Spark
Mesos
Akka
Cassandra
Kafka

scala> for (f <- smack) println( f.toUpperCase )
SPARK
MESOS
AKKA
CASSANDRA
KAFKA
```

To build a new collection, use the for/yield construct:

```
scala> val smack = Array("Spark", "Mesos", "Akka", "Cassandra", "Kafka")
smack: Array[java.lang.String] = Array(Spark, Mesos, Akka, Cassandra, Kafka)

scala> val upSmack = for (s <- smack) yield s.toUpperCase
upSmack: Array[java.lang.String] = Array(SPARK, MESOS, AKKA, CASSANDRA, KAFKA)
```

This for/yield construct is called *for comprehension*.

Now, let's iterate a map with a for loop:

```
scala> val smack = Map("S" ->"Spark", "M" -> "Mesos", "A" -> "Akka", "C" ->"Cassandra", "K"
-> "Kafka")
smack: scala.collection.immutable.Map[String,String] = Map(A -> Akka, M -> Mesos, C ->
Cassandra, K -> Kafka, S -> Spark)

scala> for ((k,v) <- smack) println(s"letter: $k, means: $v")
letter: A, means: Akka
letter: M, means: Mesos
letter: C, means: Cassandra
letter: K, means: Kafka
letter: S, means: Spark
```

Iterators

To iterate a collection in Java, you use hasNext() and next(). In Scala, however, they don't exist, because there are the map and foreach methods.

You only use iterators in Scala when reading very large streams; a file is the most common example. As a rule of thumb, you use iterators when it's not convenient to load all the data structure in memory.

Once it has been used, an iterator remains "exhausted," as shown in the following:

```
scala> val iter = Iterator("S","M","A","C","K")
iter: Iterator[String] = non-empty iterator

scala> iter.foreach(println)
S
M
A
C
K
scala> iter.foreach(println)
```

As you can see, the last line didn't produce any output, because the iterator is exhausted.

Mapping

Another way to transform collections different from the for/yield is by using the map method call with a function as argument, as follows:

```
scala> val smack = Vector("spark", "mesos", "akka", "cassandra", "kafka")

smack: scala.collection.immutable.Vector[String] = Vector(spark, mesos, akka, cassandra, kafka)
```

```
// the long way
scala> val cap = smack.map(e => e.capitalize)
cap: scala.collection.immutable.Vector[String] = Vector(Spark, Mesos, Akka, Cassandra,
Kafka)

// the short way
scala> val cap = smack.map(_.capitalize)
cap: scala.collection.immutable.Vector[String] = Vector(Spark, Mesos, Akka, Cassandra,
Kafka)

//producing a Vector of Int
scala> val lens = smack.map(_.size)
lens: scala.collection.immutable.Vector[Int] = Vector(5, 5, 4, 9, 5)

//producing a Vector of XML elements
scala> val elem = smack.map(smack => <li>{smack}</li>)
elem: scala.collection.immutable.Vector[scala.xml.Elem] = Vector(<li>spark</li>, <li>mesos</
li>, <li>akka</li>, <li>cassandra</li>, <li>kafka</li>)
```

Unfortunately, Scala has type inference; that is, there is no a general rule for the collection type returned after a mapping operation.

You can say that you are a seasoned Scala functional programmer if you can identify the comprehension to be used: for/yield or map.

```
scala> val smack = List("spark", "mesos", "akka", "cassandra", "kafka")
smack: List[String] = List(spark, mesos, akka, cassandra, kafka)

// capitalize with map
scala> val m = smack.map(_.capitalize)
m: List[String] = List(Spark, Mesos, Akka, Cassandra, Kafka)

// capitalize with for/yield
scala> val y = for (s <- smack) yield s.capitalize
y: List[String] = List(Spark, Mesos, Akka, Cassandra, Kafka)
```

Flattening

In functional programming, the *flattening process* occurs when you convert a list of lists (also called *sequence of sequences* or *multilist*) into one list. The following is an example:

```
scala> val allies = List(List("Java","Scala"), List("Javascript","PHP"))
allies: List[List[String]] = List(List(Java, Scala), List(Javascript, PHP))

scala> val languages = allies.flatten
languages: List[String] = List(Java, Scala, Javascript, PHP)
```

The power of (functional) programming is the expressive power and simplicity. Here we capitalize, flat, and sort all in one sentence:

```
scala> val jargon = allies.flatten.map(_.toUpperCase).sorted
jargon: List[String] = List(JAVA, JAVASCRIPT, PHP, SCALA)
```

When you work with connected nodes, flattening helps with the network:

```
val webFriends = List("Java", "JS")
val javaFriends = List("Scala", "Clojure", "Ceylon")
val jsFriends = List("PHP", "Ceylon")

val friendsOfFriends = List( javaFriends, jsFriends)

scala> val uniqueFriends = friendsOfFriends.flatten.distinct
uniqueFriends: List[String] = List(Scala, Clojure, Ceylon, PHP)
```

As you may guess, flattening a string produces a list of its chars:

```
scala> val stuff = List("SMACK", "Scala")
stuff: List[String] = List(SMACK, Scala)

scala> stuff.flatten
List[Char] = List(S, M, A, C, K, s, c, a, l, a)
```

If a collection contains elements of type None, flattening removes them.
If a collection contains elements of type Some, flattening strips them:

```
scala> val boxes = Vector(Some("Something"), None, Some(3.14), None)
boxes: scala.collection.immutable.Vector[Option[Any]] = Vector(Some(Something), None,
Some(3.14), None)

scala> boxes.flatten
res1: scala.collection.immutable.Vector[Any] = Vector(Something, 3.14)
```

Filtering

In functional programming, filtering traverses a collection and builds a new collection with elements that match specific criteria. This criteria must be a predicate. You apply the predicate to each collection element, for example:

```
scala> val dozen = List.range(1, 13)
dozen: List[Int] = List(1, 2, 3, 4, 5, 6, 7, 8, 9, 10, 11, 12)

scala> val multiplesOf3 = dozen.filter(_ % 3 == 0)
multiplesOf3: List[Int] = List(3, 6, 9, 12)

scala> val languages = Set("Java", "Scala", "Clojure", "Ceylon")
languages: scala.collection.immutable.Set[String] = Set(Java, Scala, Clojure, Ceylon)

scala> val c = languages.filter(_.startsWith("C"))
c: scala.collection.immutable.Set[String] = Set(Clojure, Ceylon)

scala> val s = languages.filter(_.length < 6)
s: scala.collection.immutable.Set[String] = Set(Java, Scala)
```

Filtering has the following two rules:

1. The filter doesn't modify the collection. You must keep the result in a new one.

2. Only the elements whose predicate returns true are kept.

Extracting

In this section, we are going to examine the methods to extract subsequences. The following are examples.

```
// We declare an array of Int from 1 to 9
scala> val magic = (0 to 9).toArray
magic: Array[Int] = Array(0, 1, 2, 3, 4, 5, 6, 7, 8, 9)

// Without the first N elements
scala> val d = magic.drop(3)
d: Array[Int] = Array(3, 4, 5, 6, 7, 8, 9)

// Without the elements matching a predicate
scala> val dw = magic.dropWhile(_ < 4)
dw: Array[Int] = Array(4, 5, 6, 7, 8, 9)

// Without the last N elements
scala> val dr = magic.dropRight(4)
dr: Array[Int] = Array(0, 1, 2, 3, 4, 5)

// Just the first N elements
scala> val t = magic.take(5)
t: Array[Int] = Array(0, 1, 2, 3, 4)

// Just the first elements matching a predicate (from the left)
scala> val tw = magic.takeWhile(_ < 4)
tw: Array[Int] = Array(0, 1, 2, 3)

// Just the last N elements
scala> val tr = magic.takeRight(3)
tr: Array[Int] = Array(7, 8, 9)

// the subsequence between the index A and B
scala> val sl = magic.slice(1,7)
sl: Array[Int] = Array(1, 2, 3, 4, 5, 6)
```

The List methods are used to achieve functional purity.

```
// head, the first element
scala> val h = magic.head
h: Int = 0

// the head boxed (to prevent errors)
scala> val hb = magic.headOption
hb: Option[Int] = Some(0)
```

```
// the list without the last element
scala> val in = magic.init
in: Array[Int] = Array(0, 1, 2, 3, 4, 5, 6, 7, 8)

// the last element
scala> val ta = magic.last
ta: Int = 9

// the last boxed (to prevent errors)
scala> val lo = magic.lastOption
lo: Option[Int] = Some(9)

// all the list without the first element (known as tail)
scala> val t = magic.tail
t: Array[Int] = Array(1, 2, 3, 4, 5, 6, 7, 8, 9)
```

Splitting

For those fans of the database perspective, there are methods to discriminate lists. We split samples into two groups, as follows.

```
// Here, a sample list
scala> val sample = List(-12, -9, -3, 12, 18, 15)
sample: List[Int] = List(-12, -9, -3, 12, 18, 15)

// lets separate our sample in two groups
scala> val teens = sample.groupBy(_ > 10)
teens: scala.collection.immutable.Map[Boolean,List[Int]] = Map(false -> List(-12, -9, -3),
true -> List(12, 18, 15))

// to access the generated groups
scala> val t = teens(true)
t: List[Int] = List(12, 18, 15)

scala> val f = teens(false)
f: List[Int] = List(-12, -9, -3)

// partition does the same as groupBy but it returns a List with two Lists
scala> val teens = sample.partition(_ > 10)
teens: (List[Int], List[Int]) = (List(12, 18, 15),List(-12, -9, -3))

// span the list, in one list with the longest index who meets the predicate
scala> val negs = sample.span(_ < 0)
negs: (List[Int], List[Int]) = (List(-12, -9, -3),List(12, 18, 15))

// splitAt generates two lists, one before the index at N, and the rest
scala> val splitted = sample.splitAt(2)
splitted: (List[Int], List[Int]) = (List(-12, -9),List(-3, 12, 18, 15))

// partition can assign the result to a Tuple
scala> val (foo, bar) = sample.partition(_ > 10)
foo: List[Int] = List(12, 18, 15)
bar: List[Int] = List(-12, -9, -3)
```

Unicity

If you want to remove duplicates in a collection, only use unique elements. The following are some examples.

```scala
scala> val duplicated = List("A", "Y", "Y", "X", "X", "Z")
duplicated: List[String] = List(A, Y, Y, X, X, Z)

// The first option is using distinct
scala> val u = duplicated.distinct
u: List[String] = List(A, Y, X, Z)

// the second is is converting the Collection to a Set, duplicates not allowed
scala> val s = duplicated.toSet
s: scala.collection.immutable.Set[String] = Set(A, Y, X, Z)
```

Merging

For merging and subtracting collections, use ++ and --. The following show some of examples.

```scala
// The ++= method could be used in any mutable collection
scala> val nega = collection.mutable.ListBuffer(-30, -20, -10)
nega: scala.collection.mutable.ListBuffer[Int] = ListBuffer(-30, -20, -10)

// The result is assigned to the original collection, and it is mutable
scala> nega ++= Seq(10, 20, 30)
res0: nega.type = ListBuffer(-30, -20, -10, 10, 20, 30)

scala> val tech1 = Array("Scala", "Spark", "Mesos")
tech1: Array[String] = Array(Scala, Spark, Mesos)

scala> val tech2 = Array("Akka", "Cassandra", "Kafka")
tech2: Array[String] = Array(Akka, Cassandra, Kafka)

// The ++ method merge two collections and return a new variable
scala> val smack = tech1 ++ tech2
smack: Array[String] = Array(Scala, Spark, Mesos, Akka, Cassandra, Kafka)
```

We have the classic Set operations from Set Theory.

```scala
scala> val lang1 = Array("Java", "Scala", "Ceylon")
lang1: Array[String] = Array(Java, Scala, Ceylon)

scala> val lang2 = Array("Java", "JavaScript", "PHP")
lang2: Array[String] = Array(Java, JavaScript, PHP)

// intersection, the elements in both collections
scala> val inter = lang1.intersect(lang2)
inter: Array[String] = Array(Java)
// union, the elements in both collections
```

```
scala> val addition = lang1.union(lang2)
addition: Array[String] = Array(Java, Scala, Ceylon, Java, JavaScript, PHP)

// to discriminate duplicates we use distinct
scala> val substraction = lang1.union(lang2).distinct
substraction: Array[String] = Array(Java, Scala, Ceylon, JavaScript, PHP)
```

The diff method results depend on which sequence it's called on (in set theory, A-B is different from B-A):

```
// difference, the elements in one set that are not in the other
scala> val dif1 = lang1 diff lang2
dif1: Array[String] = Array(Scala, Ceylon)

scala> val dif2 = lang2 diff lang1
dif2: Array[String] = Array(JavaScript, PHP)
```

Lazy Views

In functional programming, we call something "lazy" when it doesn't appear until it is needed. A lazy view is a version of a collection computed and returned when it is actually needed.

By contrast, in Java, all the memory is allocated immediately when the collection is created.

The difference between these two lines could save a lot of memory:

```
scala> 0 to 25
res0: scala.collection.immutable.Range.Inclusive = Range(0, 1, 2, 3, 4, 5, 6, 7, 8, 9, 10,
11, 12, 13, 14, 15, 16, 17, 18, 19, 20, 21, 22, 23, 24, 25)

scala> (0 to 25).view
res1: scala.collection.SeqView[Int,scala.collection.immutable.IndexedSeq[Int]] = SeqView(...)
```

To force the memory allocation of a view, use the force instruction:

```
scala> val v = (0 to 25).view
v: scala.collection.SeqView[Int,scala.collection.immutable.IndexedSeq[Int]] = SeqView(...)

scala> val f = v.force
f: scala.collection.immutable.IndexedSeq[Int] = Vector(0, 1, 2, 3, 4, 5, 6, 7, 8, 9, 10, 11,
12, 13, 14, 15, 16, 17, 18, 19, 20, 21, 22, 23, 24, 25)
```

Mixing views with the map method significantly improves the performance of your programs. In the following example, increasing the bounds causes your CPU to struggle.

```
scala> (0 to 100).map { _ * 3 }
res0: scala.collection.immutable.IndexedSeq[Int] = Vector(0, 3, 6, 9, 12, 15, 18, 21, 24,
27, 30, 33, 36, 39, 42, 45, 48, 51, 54, 57, 60, 63, 66, 69, 72...

scala> (0 to 100).view.map { _ * 3 }
res1: scala.collection.SeqView[Int,Seq[_]] = SeqViewM(...)
```

Good programmers (functional or SQL) know well the views benefits:

- Performance (the reason that you're reading this book)

- The data structure is similar to database views

Database views were created to allow modifications on big result sets and tables without compromising the performance.

```
// lets create an array
scala> val bigData = Array("B", "I", "G", "-", "D", "A", "T", "A")
bigData: Array[String] = Array(B, I, G, -, D, A, T, A)

// and a view over the first elements
scala> val view = bigData.view.slice(0, 4)
view: scala.collection.mutable.IndexedSeqView[String,Array[String]] = SeqViewS(...)

// we modify the VIEW
scala> view(0) = "F"
scala> view(1) = "A"
scala> view(2) = "S"
scala> view(3) = "T"

// voilá, our original array was modified
scala> bigData
res0: Array[String] = Array(F, A, S, T, D, A, T, A)
```

Sorting

To sort, you use the sorted method with the <, <=, >, and >= operators. The following are some examples.

```
// sorting Strings
scala> val foo = List("San Francisco", "London", "New York", "Tokio").sorted
foo: List[String] = List(London, New York, San Francisco, Tokio)

// sorting numbers
scala> val bar = List(10, 1, 8, 3.14, 5).sorted
bar: List[Double] = List(1.0, 3.14, 5.0, 8.0, 10.0)

// ascending
scala> List(10, 1, 8, 3.14, 5).sortWith(_ < _)
res0: List[Double] = List(1.0, 3.14, 5.0, 8.0, 10.0)

// descending
scala> List(10, 1, 8, 3.14, 5).sortWith(_ > _)
res0: List[Double] = List(10.0, 8.0, 5.0, 3.14, 1.0)

// ascending alphabetically
scala> List("San Francisco", "London", "New York", "Tokio").sortWith(_ < _)
res0: List[String] = List(London, New York, San Francisco, Tokio)
```

```
// descending alphabetically
scala> List("San Francisco", "London", "New York", "Tokio").sortWith(_ > _)
res0: List[String] = List(Tokio, San Francisco, New York, London)

// ascending by length
scala> List("San Francisco", "London", "New York", "Tokio").sortWith(_.length < _.length)
res0: List[String] = List(Tokio, London, New York, San Francisco)

// descending by length
scala> List("San Francisco", "London", "New York", "Tokio").sortWith(_.length > _.length)
res0: List[String] = List(San Francisco, New York, London, Tokio)
```

Streams

Just as views are the lazy version of collections, streams are the lazy version of lists. Here we taste some stream power:

```
scala> val torrent = (0 to 900000000).toStream
torrent: scala.collection.immutable.Stream[Int] = Stream(0, ?)

scala> torrent.head
res0: Int = 0

scala> torrent.tail
res1: scala.collection.immutable.Stream[Int] = Stream(1, ?)

scala> torrent.take(3)
res2: scala.collection.immutable.Stream[Int] = Stream(0, ?)

scala> torrent.filter(_ < 100)
res3: scala.collection.immutable.Stream[Int] = Stream(0, ?)

scala> torrent.filter(_ > 100)
res4: scala.collection.immutable.Stream[Int] = Stream(101, ?)

scala> torrent.map{_ * 2}
res5: scala.collection.immutable.Stream[Int] = Stream(0, ?)

scala> torrent(5)
res6: Int = 5
```

Arrays

Scala is a strong typed language. It determines the array type if it's not specified.

```
// in numeric, the biggest data type determines the Collection type
scala> Array(6.67e-11, 3.1415, 333F, 666L)
res0: Array[Double] = Array(6.67E-11, 3.1415, 333.0, 666.0)
```

```
// we can force manually the type
scala> Array[Number] (6.67e-11,  3.1415,  333F,  666L)
res0: Array[Number] = Array(6.67E-11, 3.1415, 333.0, 666)
```

There are several ways to create and initialize arrays:

```
// from Range
scala> val r = Array.range(0, 16)
r: Array[Int] = Array(0, 1, 2, 3, 4, 5, 6, 7, 8, 9, 10, 11, 12, 13, 14, 15)

// from Range with step
scala> val rs = Array.range(-16, 16, 3)
rs: Array[Int] = Array(-16, -13, -10, -7, -4, -1, 2, 5, 8, 11, 14)

// with fill
scala> val f = Array.fill(3)("ha")
f: Array[String] = Array(ha, ha, ha)

// with tabulate
scala> val t = Array.tabulate(9)(n => n * n)
t: Array[Int] = Array(0, 1, 4, 9, 16, 25, 36, 49, 64)

// from List
scala> val a = List("Spark", "Mesos", "Akka", "Cassandra", "Kafka").toArray
a: Array[String] = Array(Spark, Mesos, Akka, Cassandra, Kafka)

// from String
scala> val s = "ELONGATION".toArray
s: Array[Char] = Array(E, L, O, N, G, A, T, I, O, N)

// Scala Arrays corresponds to Java Arrays
scala> val bigData = Array("B", "I", "G", "-", "D", "A", "T", "A")
bigData: Array[String] = Array(B, I, G, -, D, A, T, A)

scala> bigData(0) = "F"
scala> bigData(1) = "A"
scala> bigData(2) = "S"
scala> bigData(3) = "T"
scala> bigData
bigData: Array[String] = Array(F, A, S, T, D, A, T, A)
```

ArrayBuffers

An ArrayBuffer is an array with dynamic size. The following are some examples.

```
// initialization with some elements
val cities = collection.mutable.ArrayBuffer("San Francisco", "New York")

// += to add one element
cities += "London"
```

```
// += to add multiple elements
cities += ("Tokio", "Beijing")

// ++= to add another collection
cities ++= Seq("Paris", "Berlin")

// append, to add multiple elements
cities.append("Sao Paulo", "Mexico")
```

Queues

The queue follows the first-in, first-out (FIFO) data structure. The following are some examples.

```
// to use it we need to import it from collection mutable
scala> import scala.collection.mutable.Queue
import scala.collection.mutable.Queue

// here we create a Queue of Strings
scala> var smack = new Queue[String]
smack: scala.collection.mutable.Queue[String] = Queue()

// += operator, to add an element
scala> smack += "Spark"
res0: scala.collection.mutable.Queue[String] = Queue(Spark)

// += operator, to add multiple elements
scala> smack += ("Mesos", "Akka")
res1: scala.collection.mutable.Queue[String] = Queue(Spark, Mesos, Akka)

// ++= operator, to add a Collection
scala> smack ++= List("Cassandra", "Kafka")
res2: scala.collection.mutable.Queue[String] = Queue(Spark, Mesos, Akka, Cassandra, Kafka)

// the Queue power: enqueue
scala> smack.enqueue("Scala")
scala> smack
res3: scala.collection.mutable.Queue[String] =
Queue(Spark, Mesos, Akka, Cassandra, Kafka, Scala)

// its counterpart, dequeue
scala> smack.dequeue
res4: String = Spark

// dequeue remove the first element of the queue
scala> smack
res5: scala.collection.mutable.Queue[String] = Queue(Mesos, Akka, Cassandra, Kafka, Scala)

// dequeue, will take the next element
scala> val next = smack.dequeue
next: String = Mesos
```

```
// we verify that everything run as the book says
scala> smack
res6: scala.collection.mutable.Queue[String] = Queue(Akka, Cassandra, Kafka, Scala)
```

The dequeueFirst and dequeueAll methods dequeue the elements matching the predicate.

```
scala> val smack = Queue("Spark", "Mesos", "Akka", "Cassandra", "Kafka")
smack: scala.collection.mutable.Queue[String] = Queue(Spark, Mesos, Akka, Cassandra, Kafka)

// remove the first element containing a k
scala> smack.dequeueFirst(_.contains("k"))
res0: Option[String] = Some(Spark)

scala> smack
res1: scala.collection.mutable.Queue[String] = Queue(Mesos, Akka, Cassandra, Kafka)

// remove all the elements beginning with A
scala> smack.dequeueAll(_.startsWith("A"))
res2: scala.collection.mutable.Seq[String] = ArrayBuffer(Akka)

scala> smack
res3: scala.collection.mutable.Queue[String] = Queue(Mesos, Cassandra, Kafka)
```

Stacks

The stack follows the last-in, first-out (LIFO) data structure. The following are some examples.

```
// to use it we need to import it from collection mutable
scala> import scala.collection.mutable.Stack
import scala.collection.mutable.Stack

// here we create a Stack of Strings
scala> var smack = Stack[String]()
smack: scala.collection.mutable.Stack[String] = Stack()

// push, to add elements at the top
scala> smack.push("Spark")
res0: scala.collection.mutable.Stack[String] = Stack(Spark)
scala> smack.push("Mesos")
res1: scala.collection.mutable.Stack[String] = Stack(Mesos, Spark)

// push, to add multiple elements
scala> smack.push("Akka", "Cassandra", "Kafka")
res2: scala.collection.mutable.Stack[String] = Stack(Kafka, Cassandra, Akka, Mesos, Spark)

// pop, to take the last element inserted
scala> val top = smack.pop
top: String = Kafka
scala> smack
res3: scala.collection.mutable.Stack[String] = Stack(Cassandra, Akka, Mesos, Spark)
```

```
// top, to access the last element without extract it
scala> smack.top
res4: String = Cassandra

// "Cassandra" is still on the top
scala> smack
res5: scala.collection.mutable.Stack[String] = Stack(Cassandra, Akka, Mesos, Spark)

// size, the Seq method to know the number of elements
scala> smack.size
res6: Int = 4

// isEmpty, another Seq method
scala> smack.isEmpty
res7: Boolean = false

// clear, to empty all the stack suddenly
scala> smack.clear
scala> smack
res9: scala.collection.mutable.Stack[String] = Stack()
```

Ranges

Ranges are most commonly used with loops, as shown in the following examples.

```
// to, to make a range from a to b (upper limit is included)
scala> 0 to 6
res0: scala.collection.immutable.Range.Inclusive = Range(0, 1, 2, 3, 4, 5, 6)

// until, to make a range from 0 to 7 (upper limit not included)
scala> 0 until 6
res1: scala.collection.immutable.Range.Inclusive = Range(0, 1, 2, 3, 4, 5)

// by, to specify a step (in this case, every 3)
scala> 0 to 21 by 3
res2 scala.collection.immutable.Range = Range(0, 3, 6, 9, 12, 15, 18, 21)

// to, also function with chars
scala> 'a' to 'k'
res3: scala.collection.immutable.NumericRange.Inclusive[Char] = NumericRange(a, b, c, d, e,
f, g, h, i, j, k)

// a Range toList
scala> val l = (0 to 16).toList
l: List[Int] = List(0, 1, 2, 3, 4, 5, 6, 7, 8, 9, 10, 11, 12, 13, 14, 15, 16)

// a Range toArray
scala> val a = (0 to 16).toArray
a: Array[Int] = Array(0, 1, 2, 3, 4, 5, 6, 7, 8, 9, 10, 11, 12, 13, 14, 15, 16)
```

```
// a Range toSet
scala> val s = (0 to 10).toSet
s: scala.collection.immutable.Set[Int] = Set(0, 5, 10, 1, 6, 9, 2, 7, 3, 8, 4)

// Array has a range method (upper limit excluded)
scala> val a = Array.range(0, 17)
a: Array[Int] = Array(0, 1, 2, 3, 4, 5, 6, 7, 8, 9, 10, 11, 12, 13, 14, 15, 16)

// Vector has a range method (upper limit excluded)
scala> val v = Vector.range(0, 10)
v: collection.immutable.Vector[Int] = Vector(0, 1, 2, 3, 4, 5, 6, 7, 8, 9)

// List has a range method (upper limit excluded)
scala> val l = List.range(0, 17)
l: List[Int] = List(0, 1, 2, 3, 4, 5, 6, 7, 8, 9, 10, 11, 12, 13, 14, 15, 16)

// A list with numbers in a range with a step of 5
scala> val l = List.range(0, 50, 5)
l: List[Int] = List(0, 5, 10, 15, 20, 25, 30, 35, 40, 45)

// An ArrayBuffer with characters in a range
scala> val ab = collection.mutable.ArrayBuffer.range('a', 'f')
ab: scala.collection.mutable.ArrayBuffer[Char] = ArrayBuffer(a, b, c, d, e)

// An old fashioned for loop using a range
scala> for (i <- 1 to 5) println(i)
1
2
3
4
5
```

Summary

Since all the examples in this book are in Scala, we need to reinforce it before beginning our study. This chapter provided a review of Scala. We studied the fundamental parts of the language. Programming is about data structures and algorithms. In this chapter, we discussed the Scala type system (the data structures) and the principal concepts of functional programming.

The use of object-oriented programming (OOP) in past decades was an era of reusable software components. Things no longer work that way. Now components interoperate by exchanging immutable data structures (lists, maps, and sets), which is more like functional programming.

In the next chapter, we review an actor model implementation called Akka. To fully understand the examples, you need to know the Scala programming language.

CHAPTER 4

■ ■ ■

The Model: Akka

Welcome to the chapter on the SMACK stack model. The A stands for Akka. If the previous chapter's objective was to develop functional thinking, this chapter's objective is to develop actor model thinking.

The chapter on Scala was focused on moving your mind from a structured programming paradigm to functional programming thinking. This chapter shifts from the object-oriented paradigm to actors-based programming.

This chapter has three parts:

- Actor model

- Actor communication

- Actor lifecycle

The actor model is fundamental to understanding the SMACK operation. So, by the end of this chapter, we hope that you can model in terms of actors.

The Actor Model

The Sámi people were the first to inhabit northern Scandinavia. Until the Middle Age, its culture and way of life (fishing, hunting, and trading) dominated the north of Sweden, Norway, Finland, and the Kola Peninsula in Russia. In Sámi mythology, the goddess Akka represented beauty and goodness in the world. According to Sámi people, Akka's representation on Earth is a beautiful mountain in Laponia, located in northern Sweden.

In the platform's context, the letters A and K stand for *actor kernel*. It is for this reason that the platform is called Akka and its symbol is the Akka mountain (see Figure 4-1).

Figure 4-1. *The original and modern Akka logos, representing the Akka mountain*

© Raul Estrada and Isaac Ruiz 2016
R. Estrada and I. Ruiz, *Big Data SMACK*, DOI 10.1007/978-1-4842-2175-4_4

The actor model is a mathematical model developed by Carl Hewitt, Peter Bishop, and Richard Steiger at MIT in 1973 and presented in a paper called "A Universal Modular Actor Formalism for Artificial Intelligence".[1]

So, you may argue that if the actor model is more than 40 years old, why have we been dealing with another paradigm all of this time? The answer is not simple. When the actor model was developed, hardware (and memory) was very expensive. Today, it's just the opposite: hardware is dirt cheap and programmers are expensive.

To land this idea, consider computer science history. If hardware is very expensive, then to program, you have to optimize and deal with low-level concepts and implementations related to the hardware. So you have to think in terms of interruptions, assembly language, and pointers to (physical) memory locations.

As programming language has a higher level, we can ignore the details related to hardware and start talking in terms that have nothing to do with implementation but with abstraction. Think in concepts as a recursive call, or function composition, which is hard to do if you have to deal with low-level hardware implementations.

Threads and Labyrinths

Between 1980 and 2003, we experienced the rise and dominance of object-oriented languages. These years were the dark ages of functional programming. Functional languages were spoken only in academic and scientific environments, barely related to industry.

An interesting problem arose with object-oriented programming: the implementation of concurrency and parallelism. These two concepts are the Achilles' heel of structured and object-oriented programming. Imagine an implementation of threads in C ++ or Java; complexity is vast and proneness to error is very large.

Concurrency is not easy; making more than one thing with a program is related to dealing with race conditions, semaphores, mutexes, locks, shared data, and all the stuff related to multithreading. This includes basic issues to determine precisely what a program with several threads is doing, or when a variable is being accessed from multiple threads, or what its value is at a given point in time, or how to know if there are two threads in standby, and if this condition is going to release them (and when) or if it is a deadlock. Unfortunately, thread-based concurrency gives more challenges than solutions.

Today there is a lot of technical debt in the proprietary thread implementations of concurrency issues. No one wants to touch huge systems because the code is complex and the chances of a change breaking everything are very high.

In this context, functional programming experienced rebirth. With the release of Scala in 2003, F# in 2005, Clojure in 2007, and Elixir in 2012, the actor model approach was declared the winner in solving concurrency issues.

Actors 101

Actors are objects. An actor is an object that sends and receives messages. According to the actor specification, the order of the received messages is not relevant; but in Akka, there is an implementation called a *mailbox*, which is a stack where messages are consumed.

What the actor does with a received message depends on how you solve a specific problem. The actor could handle the message internally, it could send a message to another actor, it could create another actor, or it could take an action with the message. An Akka actor is a high-level abstraction.

The following are the main comparison points between OOP and actors:

- **Unit**. In OOP, the smallest processing unit is the object; in the actor model, it is the actor. We already know that in Akka, the actors are objects but an actor is a more bounded representation of reality than an object.

---

[1]Carl Hewitt, Peter Bishop, and Richard Steiger, A Universal Modular Actor Formalism for Artificial Intelligence (http://dl.acm.org/citation.cfm?id=1624804, 1973).

- **Encapsulation**. In both models, the smallest processing unit encapsulates state and behavior. In OOP, the state is determined by the value of the attributes in a given time, and behavior is ruled by the class methods. In the actor model, the state is determined by the messages; if there are no messages in the mailbox, the actor will wait indefinitely for messages.

- **Access**. In OOP, executing object methods from outside of the object is allowed (but not recommended), as well as access and modify object fields from outside of the object. In the actor model, access to the actor's methods or fields is strictly prohibited; all the communication must be done through messages.

- **Globals**. In OOP, for example, there is the Singleton pattern, which is a class with a single instance. Global variables and class variables exist, but they are discouraged. In the actor model, global variables don't exist. A shared global state doesn't exist either.

- **Messages**. In OOP, the messages between Objects could be mutable. In the actor model, the messages between actors are strictly immutable.

- **Exceptions**. In OOP exists the traditional and well-known try-catch approach, which is the most complex way to handle exceptions because you have to manage all the possible values of the variables involved. In the actor model, the "let it crash" approach exists; if something fails, let it fail. The exception scenario could affect only the actor involved, not the complete environment.

- **Concurrency** and **parallelism**. In OPP, the most used approach is the thread model, which is a complex solution to the problem. In the actor model, you don't have to worry about concurrency and parallelism, because if everything follows the actor convention, there is no problem with parallelism.

The following are the Lightbend recommendations for the actor model:

- Think of actors as employees. Think of each actor model as a company.

- Think of the actor's siblings as people in the same hierarchical level.

- Think of the actor's children as the employee's subordinates.

- An actor has one (and only one) supervisor—the actor who created it.

- Actor model success is the delegation to subordinates.

The Akka implementation of the actor model has these peculiarities:

- When you create an actor, Akka provides an ActorRef.

- Actors run in real Java threads. Some actors could share the same thread.

- There are three mailbox types: Unbounded, Bounded, and Priority.

- Actors can scan their mailboxes to look for specific messages.

- There is a "dead letter" mailbox with all the actors' terminated messages.

The Lightbend Reactive Platform (`www.lightbend.com`) is a family of five members, described as follows:

- **Scala**: The programming language. The Reactive Platform fully supports both Java and Scala, so you can choose what is best for you.

- **Akka**: Message-driven runtime. At the center of the Reactive Platform is Akka, a message-driven middleware or runtime with Scala and Java APIs.

- **Spark:** Apache Spark, which is written in Scala and Akka, is a fast data engine to fuel Reactive applications.

- **Lagom:** Reactive microservices framework. An opinionated framework for building web microservices.

- **Play:** Just-hit-reload web framework. The Play Framework is the just-hit-reload web development framework with Scala and Java APIs.

We have always said that Apache Spark is the Scala "killer app."

In this book, we only cover Scala, Akka, and Spark, but if you are an enthusiastic web service developer or web developer, don't pass on the opportunity to explore Lagom and Play, respectively, more deeply.

Installing Akka

Well, enough theory, let's get our feet wet.

The first thing you have to do is go to `http://akka.io/downloads/`, as shown in Figure 4-2.

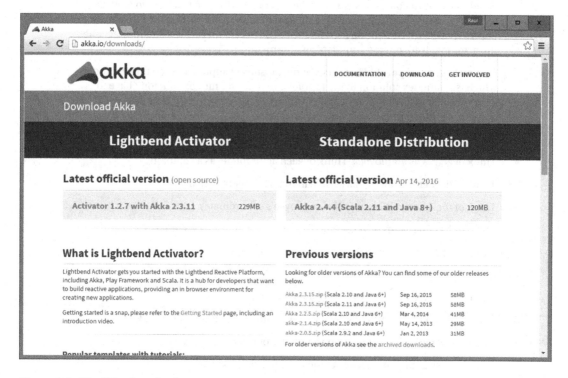

Figure 4-2. *The Akka download page*

Then download the Lightbend Activator according to your platform and operating system. Lightbend is the company behind Akka; it builds and maintains the Akka message-driven runtime. Follow the installation instructions from the web page.

After downloading and extracting the package, go to the directory (in this example, we use version 1.3.10):

```
%> cd activator-dist-1.3.10/bin
```

Then, execute the activator shell:

```
%> activator ui
```

Now go to http://127.0.0.1:8888. You'll see a web page like the one shown in Figure 4-3.

Figure 4-3. *Lightbend Activator main page*

Now select the Hello Akka! application and click the "Create app" button, as shown in Figure 4-4.

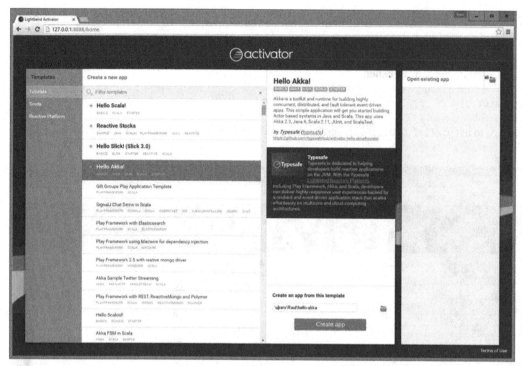

Figure 4-4. *Creating an Akka application from a template*

Now open your IDE. In this case, we used the IntelliJ IDEA Community Edition, as shown in Figure 4-5.

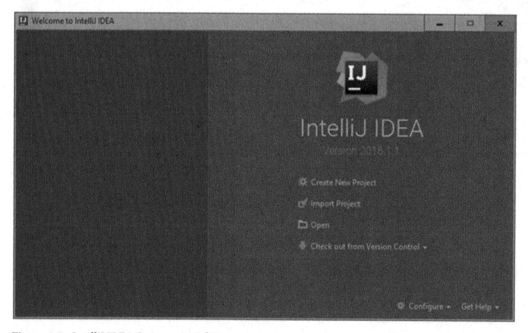

Figure 4-5. *IntelliJ IDEA Community Edition*

Select Open. Enter the directory in which you created the project (see Figure 4-6).

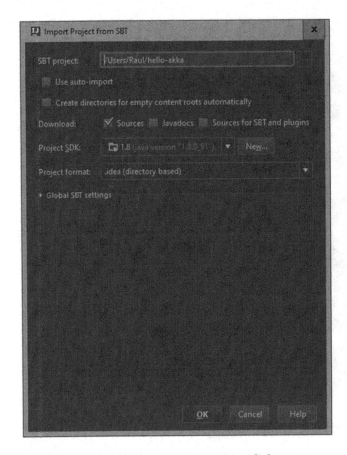

Figure 4-6. *IntelliJ IDEA open existing project dialog*

We select both modules inside our project (see Figure 4-7).

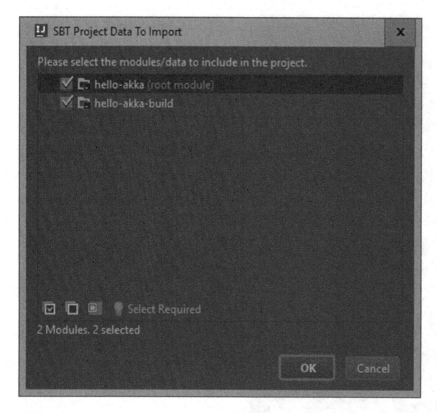

Figure 4-7. IntelliJ IDEA import SBT project dialog

Now you have a fully functional Hello World! Akka project (see Figure 4-8).

Figure 4-8. *Hello World! Akka project on IntelliJ IDEA*

As you can see in Figure 4-9, the Lightbend Activator is a full web IDE.

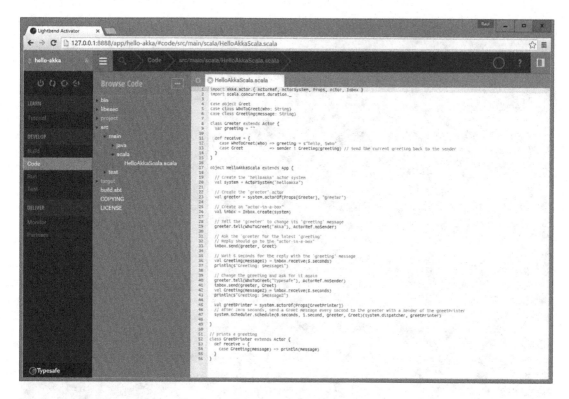

Figure 4-9. *Lightbend Activator, the Typesafe web IDE*

You can build, code, run, and test your Akka applications from your browser.

As you can see in Figure 4-10, there are a lot of project templates to play with. The Akka world is vast, and it's beyond the scope of this book to cover the entire Reactive universe.

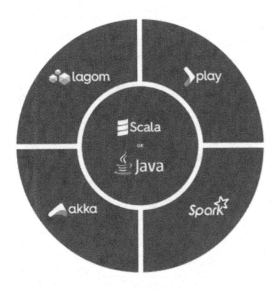

Figure 4-10. *Lightbend Reactive Platform*

Akka Actors

It is essential to recall that before Scala version 2.10, there was a scala.actors package. The Scala actors library was deprecated in March 2013 and replaced by Akka. Scala actor models prior to version 2.10 should no longer be used.

Actors

For our first example, we use a multilanguage greeter; that is, we enter a particular language and the program responds by replying "Good day," in the language specified.

```
import akka.actor.Actor
import akka.actor.ActorSystem
import akka.actor.Props

class GreeterActor extends Actor {
  def receive = {
    case "en" => println("Good day")
    case "es" => println("Buen dia")
    case "fr" => println("Bonjour")
    case "de" => println("Guten Tag")
    case "pt" => println("Bom dia")
    case _ => println(":(")
  }
}
```

```scala
object Main extends App {

  // build the ActorSystem
  val actorSystem = ActorSystem("MultilangSystem")

  // instantiate the actor
  val greeter = actorSystem.actorOf(Props[GreeterActor], name = "GreeterActor")

  // send the actor some messages
  greeter ! "en"
  greeter ! "es"
  greeter ! "fr"
  greeter ! "de"
  greeter ! "pt"
  greeter ! "zh-CN"

  // shut down the actor system
  actorSystem.shutdown
}
```

When we run this program, the output is as follows:

```
$ sbt run
[info] Running Main
Good day
Buen dia
Bonjour
Guten Tag
Bom dia
:(
Process finished with exit code 0
```

Here is the step-by-step explanation:

- When using Akka actors, you need to import the akka.actor._ package. You at least need these classes: Actor, ActorSystem, and Props.

- You must define a class of type Actor. In this case, we called it GreeterActor. You can use any name that you want.

- The actor main performance must be defined under the actor receive() method.

- The structure of the receive()method is typical in functional programming; it is called a *match expression*. The lines should always go from the most specific case to the most general case. The most specific case is at the top and the more general case is at the bottom.

- The last line in the match expression should be (as good practice; not required) the default case; it says what to do if the pattern didn't find a match.

- Recall that the underscore operator (_) in Scala means whatever. If the message doesn't find a match, an UnhandledMessage exception is thrown, which represents poor programming practices.

- You create a `Main` object that extends a Scala app to give your actor a scenario that displays their histrionic abilities.

- You first need an actor system. Any name with alphanumeric characters is good; hyphens are allowed but not as the first character.

- To liven up your actor, invoke the `actorOf` method in the actor system. The actor will start asynchronously.

- If you want to interact, send messages with the `!` operator.

- To finish the play, you must call the `shutdown` method in the actor system.

Actor System

Imagine the actor system as a theater company, an actors union, or a circus:

- There is a hierarchy; each actor always has a supervisor and an actor can have siblings and children.

- Actors belonging to the same system of actors share dispatchers, deployments, and addresses.

- The actor system is the meeting point where the actors are created and searched.

- Internally, the actor system is a thread controller; the actor system decides when to create threads for an application.

- If the system does not turn off the actors (with the `shutdown` method), the application will not end. As long as the actor system is running, the application will continue running.

Actor Reference

Imagine the actor reference as the actor agent; that is, someone who represents them and receives letters from his fans:

- The actor system's `actorOf` method has two main tasks: start the actor asynchronously and return the ActorRef requested.

- The ActorRef is a handler, so you cannot directly access the actor and break the actor system encapsulation rules.

- The ActorRef follows the facade pattern over the actor; that is, it serves as a way to communicate with the actor without directly accessing the actor. Thus, you never access actor variables and methods directly, as dictated by the encapsulation principles.

- The ActorRef is immutable; you cannot change it because it is only a reference.

- An actor has one (and only one) ActorRef. An ActorRef refers to one (and only one) actor. It is a one-to-one relationship.

- To comply with the Akka actor model, the ActorRef is serializable and server independent, so you can distribute, copy, and pass references (to the actors' fans) across the network.

Actor Communication

Actor communication is always more easily explained by example. Just remember that to send a message to an actor, you use the ! operator.

The ! operator always works with ActorRefs; never between Actor class instances.

In Akka, when you send a message to an actor with the ! operator, the actor that receives the message also receives a reference to the actor that sent the message; this reference is accessed by the sender variable. And it helps to send the actor invoker response messages. Recall that *sender* is a reserved word; use it wisely.

```scala
import akka.actor._

case object SendANewCat
case object LiveALife
case object BackToHeaven
case object LifeSpended {
  var remaining = 0// a default value
}

class God(indulged: ActorRef) extends Actor {

  def receive = {
    case SendANewCat =>
      println("GOD: Go!, you have seven lives")
      indulged ! LiveALife
    case LifeSpended =>
      if ( LifeSpended.remaining == 0){
        println("GOD: Time to Return!")
        indulged ! BackToHeaven
        context.stop(self)
      }
      else {
        println("GOD: one live spent, " + LifeSpended.remaining + " remaining.")
        indulged ! LiveALife
      }
    case _ => println("GOD: Sorry, I don't understand")
  }
}

class Cat extends Actor {
  var lives = 7 // All the cats born with 7 lives

  def receive = {
    case LiveALife =>
      println("CAT: Thanks God, I still have " + lives + " lives")
      lives -= 1
      LifeSpended.remaining = lives
      sender ! LifeSpended
    case BackToHeaven =>
      println("CAT: No more lives, going to Heaven")
      context.stop(self)
    case _ => println("CAT: Sorry, I don't understand")
  }
}
```

```
object CatLife extends App {
  val system = ActorSystem("CatLifeSystem")
  val sylvester = system.actorOf(Props[Cat], name = "Sylvester")
  val catsGod = system.actorOf(Props(new God(sylvester)), name = "CatsGod")

  // God sends a Cat
  catsGod ! SendANewCat

  system.terminate()
}
```

Running our example, we get this output:

```
GOD: Go!, you have seven lives
CAT: Thanks God, I still have 7 lives
GOD: one live spent, 6 remaining.
CAT: Thanks God, I still have 6 lives
GOD: one live spent, 5 remaining.
CAT: Thanks God, I still have 5 lives
GOD: one live spent, 4 remaining.
CAT: Thanks God, I still have 4 lives
GOD: one live spent, 3 remaining.
CAT: Thanks God, I still have 3 lives
GOD: one live spent, 2 remaining.
CAT: Thanks God, I still have 2 lives
GOD: one live spent, 1 remaining.
CAT: Thanks God, I still have 1 lives
GOD: Time to Return!
CAT: No more lives, going to Heaven
Process finished with exit code 0
```

Here is an actor communication example analysis:

- It is always advisable to model messages as classes within your application; in our example, we have four objects that we use as a message:

  - SendANewCat case object

  - LiveALife case object

  - BackToHeaven case object

  - LifeSpended case object

- CatLife is the application in which we have the main application. The first line creates the actor system and calls it CatLifeSystem.

- On the next line, we create an ActorRef for the Cat class. An ActorRef to a cat actor is loaded in the sylvester variable.

- We then create the god actor. Note that the constructor receives a reference to his indulged cat. This was used to show the relationship between the actors; we could have declared a constructor with no arguments, but this was only for demonstration purposes.

- Then, we send a message to god requesting a new cat.

- When the god actor receives the message, it starts the cat's life, until we reach the life limit, then we stop this actor context.

- The context object is available to all actors in the actor system. It is used to stop the actors together.

- It is important to recall that cat, god, and indulged are ActorRefs and are not Actor class instances. An actor should never be accessed directly; always through messages.

- If we access the actors directly, the environment becomes unreliable in making high concurrency and parallelism. The message system and encapsulation always ensure that we are doing a parallelizable and concurrent environment because there are no shared variables or locks. All transactions are ACID.

Actor Lifecycle

In addition to the constructor, an actor has the following lifecycle methods, which are all described in Table 4-1:

- receive
- preStart
- postStop
- preRestart
- postRestart

Table 4-1. *Actor Lifecycle Methods*

Method	Description
constructor	Called when a class is instantiated, as in Java.
preStart	Called immediately after the actor started.
postStop	Called immediately after the actor stopped. Typically for cleaning work.
preRestart	Called immediately after the actor restarted. Usually, a restart causes an exception. The preRestart receives Throwable and the message as parameters; the old object receives these parameters.
postRestart	Called immediately after the actor restarted. Usually, a restart causes an exception. The postRestart receives a Throwable as parameter; the new object receives this parameter.

In the following example code, The Hulk (the green superhero) is used to show the lifecycle methods:

```scala
import akka.actor._
case object GetAngry

class Hulk extends Actor {
  println("in the Hulk constructor")

  override def preStart {
    println("in the Hulk preStart")
  }

  override def postStop {
    println("in the Hulk postStop")
  }

  override def preRestart(reason: Throwable, message: Option[Any]) {
    println("in the Hulk preRestart")
    println(s" preRestart message: ${message.getOrElse("")}")
    println(s" preRestart reason: ${reason.getMessage}")
    super.preRestart(reason, message)
  }

  override def postRestart(reason: Throwable) {
    println("in the Hulk postRestart")
    println(s" postRestart reason: ${reason.getMessage}")
    super.postRestart(reason)
  }

  def receive = {
    case GetAngry => throw new Exception("ROAR!")
    case _ => println("Hulk received a message...")
  }
}

object LifecycleTest extends App {
  val system = ActorSystem("LifeCycleSystem")
  val hulk = system.actorOf(Props[Hulk], name = "TheHulk")
  println("sending Hulk a message")
  hulk ! "hello Hulk"
  Thread.sleep(5000)
  println("making Hulk get angry")
  hulk ! GetAngry
  Thread.sleep(5000)
  println("stopping Hulk")
  system.stop(hulk)
  println("shutting down Hulk system")
  system. terminate()
}
```

The following is the output when the program is run:

```
[info] Running LifecycleTest
sending Hulk a message
in the Hulk constructor
in the Hulk preStart
Hulk received a message...
making Hulk get angry
in the Hulk preRestart
[ERROR] [01/01/2015 01:01:01.964] [LifeCycleSystem-akka.actor.default-dispatcher-6]
[akka://LifeCycleSystem/user/TheHulk] ROAR!
java.lang.Exception: ROAR!
        at Hulk$$anonfun$receive$1.applyOrElse(chapter04_03.scala:31)
        at akka.actor.Actor$class.aroundReceive(Actor.scala:480)
        at Hulk.aroundReceive(chapter04_03.scala:6)
        at akka.actor.ActorCell.receiveMessage(ActorCell.scala:525)
        at akka.actor.ActorCell.invoke(ActorCell.scala:494)
        at akka.dispatch.Mailbox.processMailbox(Mailbox.scala:257)
        at akka.dispatch.Mailbox.run(Mailbox.scala:224)
        at akka.dispatch.Mailbox.exec(Mailbox.scala:234)
 preRestart message: GetAngry
 preRestart reason: ROAR!
in the Hulk postStop
in the Hulk constructor
in the Hulk postRestart
 postRestart reason: ROAR!
in the Hulk preStart
```

As an exercise, make the trace source code vs. the program output.

Starting Actors

You have already seen how to create actors from the actor system. To create actors from another actor, you must use the following context:

```
class GodWanabe extends Actor {
        val = context.actorOf creature (Props [Creature] name = "Creature")
        // Add the code for its creation ...
}
```

Let's look at the actor lifecycle control between actors with an example based on characters from *The Simpsons*. Mr. Burns is the boss and has a nuclear power plant. He hires two employees, Homer Simpson and Frank Grimes, but then only fires Frank Grimes.

```
import akka.actor._

case class Hire(name: String)
case class Name(name: String)

class Boss extends Actor {
  def receive = {
```

```
    case Hire(name) =>
      // here the boss hire personnel
      println(s"$name is about to be hired")
      val employee = context.actorOf(Props[Employee], name = s"$name")
      employee ! Name(name)
    case _ => println(s"The Boss can't handle this message.")
  }
}

class Employee extends Actor {
  var name = "Employee name"

  override def postStop {
    println(s"I'm ($name) and Mr. Burns fired me: ${self.path}")
  }

  def receive = {
    case Name(name) => this.name = name
    case _ => println(s"The Employee $name can't handle this message.")
  }
}

object StartingActorsDemo extends App {
  val actorSystem = ActorSystem("StartingActorsSystem")
  val mrBurns = actorSystem.actorOf(Props[Boss], name = "MrBurns")

  // here the boss hires people
  mrBurns ! Hire("HomerSimpson")
  mrBurns ! Hire("FrankGrimes")

  // we wait some office cycles
  Thread.sleep(4000)

  // we look for Frank and we fire him
  println("Firing Frank Grimes ...")
  val grimes = actorSystem.actorSelection("../user/MrBurns/FrankGrimes")

  // PoisonPill, an Akka special message
  grimes ! PoisonPill
  println("now Frank Grimes is fired")
}
```

The following is the output when we run this program:

```
[info] Running StartingActorsDemo
HommerSimpson is about to be hired
FrankGrimes is about to be hired
Firing Frank Grimes ...
now Frank Grimes is fired
I'm (FrankGrimes) and Mr. Burns fired me: akka://StartingActorsSystem/user/MrBurns/FrankGrimes
Process finished with exit code -1
```

Let's analyze the starting actors example code:

1. Create and use the Name and Hire utility classes to send messages between actors.

2. When the employee actor receives the Name message, assigns it to the name variable.

3. When the boss receives a Hire message, it uses the context.actorOf method to hire new employees.

4. As usual, the main program creates the actor system.

5. The main program then creates the boss actor using the actor system reference.

6. The main program sends the boss two Hire messages, with HomerSimpson and FrankGrimes as names.

7. After a pause (4 seconds), look for Frank Grimes in the actor system, then send him the PoisonPill message, which is an Akka actor system special message that asynchronously sends the stop signal to an actor. Use the postStop method to print a message after PoisonPill.

Stopping Actors

As you saw previously, there are four ways to stop an actor:

- Calling system.stop(ActorRef) from the ActorSystem level

- Calling context.stop(ActorRef) from inside an actor

- Sending an actor the PoisonPill message

- Programming a gracefulStop

Table 4-2 summarizes the ways to stop an actor.

Table 4-2. *Ways to Stop an Actor*

Message	Characteristics
stop	When the stop method is received, the actor processes only the current message (if any). All the messages are discarded: the queued messages in the actor's mailbox and the newly arriving.
PoisonPill	Once the PoisonPill message is received, it is queued in the actor's mailbox as any normal message. Once the PoisonPill message is processed, the actor stops.
gracefulStop	This method allows actors to end gracefully, waiting for the timeout signal. If you need a specific set of instructions before stopping the actor, this is the right way

Some aspects to consider when stopping actors:

- The stop message is asynchronous. The stop method could return *before* the actor is actually stopped; use it wisely.

- The shutdown process has two subprocesses. First, it suspends the actor's mailbox. Second, it sends the stop message to all the actor children; the father actor has to wait for all its children to stop.

- When you can't process any more messages, these messages are sent to the dead letters mailbox. You can access them with the deadLetters method in the actor system.

- When an actor is stopped, the postStop lifecycle method is invoked. Normally it is used to clean up resources.

Here is an example of code using system.stop:

```
import akka.actor._

class Scapegoat extends Actor {
  def receive = {
    case s:String => println("Message received: " + s)
    case _ => println("What?")
  }
}

object StopExample extends App {
  val system = ActorSystem("StopExample")
  val sg = system.actorOf(Props[Scapegoat], name = "ScapeGoat")
  sg ! "ready?"

  // stop our crash dummy
  system.stop(sg)
  system.terminate()
}
```

Killing Actors

The following code shows how to kill actors. It is a very violent way; discretion is advised. Normally, if you want to stop an actor gracefully, you use the methods described earlier.

```
import akka.actor._

class ScapeGoat extends Actor {
  def receive = {
    case s:String => println("Message received: " + s)
    case _ => println("Uh?")
  }

  override def preStart {
    println("In preStart method")
  }
```

```
  override def postStop {
    println("In postStop method")
  }

  override def preRestart(reason: Throwable, message: Option[Any]) {
    println("In preRestart method")
  }

  override def postRestart(reason: Throwable) {
    println("In postRestart method")
  }
}

object Abbatoir extends App {
  val system = ActorSystem("Abbatoir")
  val sg = system.actorOf(Props[ScapeGoat], name = "ScapeGoat")
  sg ! "say goodbye"

  // finish him!
  sg ! Kill
  system. terminate()
}
```

This is the code output:

```
In preStart method
Message received: say goodbye
In postStop method
Process finished with exit code 0
```

Shutting down the Actor System

As you have already seen in the examples, this is the method to shut down the actor system:

```
system.terminate()
```

Because of its importance, we dedicated this section to this method. Remember, if you don't call the shutdown method in your application, the program will run indefinitely.

Actor Monitoring

This code shows how an actor asks to be notified when a child actor dies:

```
import akka.actor._

class Child extends Actor {
  def receive = {
    case _ => println("Child received a message")
  }
}
```

```scala
class Dad extends Actor {
  // Dad actor create a child actor
  val child = context.actorOf(Props[Child], name = "Son")
  context.watch(child)

  def receive = {
    case Terminated(child) => println("This will not end here -_-")
    case _ => println("Dad received a message")
  }
}

object ChildMonitoring extends App {

  val system = ActorSystem("ChildMonitoring")

  // we create a Dad (and it will create the Child)
  val dad = system.actorOf(Props[Dad], name = "Dad")

  // look for child, then we kill it
  val child = system.actorSelection("/user/Dad/Son")

  child ! PoisonPill
  Thread.sleep(3000)

  println("Revenge!")
  system. terminate()
}
```

Running this code produces the following result:

```
This will not end here
Revenge!
Process finished with exit code 0
```

Through the watch() method, an actor knows when a subordinate stops. This is very useful because it lets the supervisor handle the situation.

Note that when an exception occurs within an actor, the actor does not kill himself. In Akka, an exception makes an actor restart automatically.

Looking up Actors

In the previous example, you saw how to find a specific actor:

```scala
val child = system.actorSelection("/user/Dad/Son")
```

The actorSelection method is available under the actor system and within each actor instance through the context variable.

You can also look for actors with a relative path; for example, from siblings:

```scala
// From an actor brother
val bro = context.actorSelection("../myBrother")
```

The `actorSelection` method in the actor system can be used to find actors:

```
val child = system.actorSelection("akka://MonitoringTest/user/Dad/Son")
val child = system.actorSelection(Sec("user", "Dad", "Son"))
```

With the `actorSelection` method, you can also look for a sibling:

```
val child = system.actorSelection(Sec("..." "Son"))
```

Actor Code of Conduct

At this point, you have seen everything that you need to write actors. To achieve concurrent programming, it is important to maintain a performance style; that is, a code of ethics among actors. If you keep this code of ethics, the source code will be easy to debug and won't have typical multithreaded programming problems, such as deadlocks and race conditions. In this section, we present the fundamental principles for a good performance.

Actors Do Not Block Each Other

A written good actor does not block others while processing a message. When an actor blocks another actor, the first actor cannot attend to a request. If the actor is locked while working on the first request, you cannot attend to the second request. The worst case scenario is when actors block each other; this is known as *deadlock*: the first actor is waiting for the second one to do something and the second one is waiting for the first one to do something.

Rather than block messages, the code of an actor must prioritize messages as they arrive so that a lock is never generated. Normally, when you do not know how to handle a lock, good practices indicate that it is the right time to delegate. You always have to delegate; an actor should not block a message on itself.

Another good practice is to never use `Thread.sleep`, and to try to avoid the `Thread` class in your programs. The actor programming replaces any thread operation. If you need an actor to wait to perform a task, ideally the actor should be delegated to another lighter actor the time handling. The use of the `Thread` class causes more problems than it remedies.

When you need an actor to perform an answer waiting operation, the original actor, let's call it Actor A, must attend requests—that is its primary function. So if it requires a standby condition, you must generate an Actor B to standby for the answer and do nothing more. This way, Actor A is free to meet requests, which is its primary function.

Communication is only via Messages

The key to understanding how the actor model addresses the difficulties of the shared data and lock model is to provide a space where operations are safe. This sequential space is within each option in the `receive` method. In other words, the actors allow you to program multithreaded programs through single-threaded programs that communicate with each other through asynchronous messages. This multithread abstraction model works as long as the only form of communication among the stakeholders is through sending messages.

For example, let's say that there are two actors: GoodPerformer and BadPerformer. Suppose that GoodPerformer sends a good and nice message to BadPerformer, and as a courtesy, GoodPerformer sends a reference to himself in the message. Well, suppose that BadPerformer misuses this reference and invokes methods on GoodPerformer instead of sending messages to GoodPerformer through the ! operator. This is where the drama begins, because the invoked methods may read an instance of GoodPerformer being used by another thread. Or worse, the method invoked can modify GoodPerformer's own variables and decompose its state.

If you continued this lack of privacy, BadPerformer would write synchronization methods on GoodPerformer's variables, which would become "shared data," not only between them, but among all who could invoke them. This shared data and locks models have brought ruin to many systems.

On the other hand, if for practical purposes you need to share state—for example, maintain code clarity with other non-functional programmers, you can achieve this state in Scala. The difference between Erlang and Scala is that Erlang *never* lets you communicate in a way different from sending messages between actors. Scala designers did this to preserve the hybrid state language. We can pass endless hours in discussion on whether this is correct or not.

■ **Note** We are not saying that you, the reader, should be involved in one of these discussions (of course not, programmers never enter these discussions). Although now you may be vowing to never share status or provoke lock conditions. But, we share this example in case you are involved in an argument with purist programmers.

Imagine that you would need the shared mutable map data structure. That is, it is mutable because you need to insert a pair (key, value) on the map to obtain the value of a given key, get a key set having specific value, and so forth—common operations on a mutable map. The actor model states that you must build a wrapper on the map; that is, an actor contains the map and manages all requests. Only the actor can access the map, no one else, and that actor only receives and responds to messages, nothing more.

Everything is going well so far, but practical programmers will tell you that for this type of challenge, there is the ConcurrentHashMap class on Java Concurrency utilities. One of its benefits is that it allows you to send status change messages to multiple actors (a broadcast), which greatly simplifies life and makes the code more understandable; however, it does not meet the actor model. Another difference is that the responses of actors are an asynchronous model; the ConcurrentHashMap response model is synchronous, simple, and immediate as most understand them.

Messages must be Immutable

Because the Akka actor model provides a single-threaded model, you never need to worry about whether the objects used in the implementation of these methods are thread-safe. In the actor model, this is called the *share nothing model*; data is confined in a thread instead of being shared by many threads.

But there is one exception to "share nothing," which is when the message that you send is shared data among several actors; as a result, you have to worry whether messages are thread-safe. In general, they should always be thread-safe.

In all good practices you want to avoid unnecessary complexity. The best and simplest way to ensure that objects in messages are thread-safe is to ensure the use of immutable objects within messages. Instances of any class having only val fields, which themselves only refer to immutable objects, are immutable. Besides val, you can use all the immutable classes offered by Scala, such as tuples, strings, lists, immutable sets, immutable maps, and so on.

Suppose an actor sends a mutable and unsynchronized object as a message (at this point, you could say that it's like cussing). And after that, this object is never read nor written again. It might work, but you are invoking misfortune, because in the future, some code maintainer could debug and see that this object is shared, and may try to improve scalability, or worse, try to reuse and modify the values for reuse, which could lead to a bug, which can lead to concurrency disaster.

In general, the best way to arrange your data is to keep all unsynchronized, mutable objects fully contained within the actors, and therefore accessed only by the owner actor. Whenever objects are transferred between actors (not messages), you must 100% guarantee what those objects are doing at any point in time and anywhere in the system.

In the actor model, whenever you want to modify a variable that is not your own, you must at least send a message to the variable owner to warn that you are making changes. Moreover, you must wait for confirmation that the values can be modified.

If you still want to continue sending objects between actors but without messages, a good alternative is to send a copy of the object. This at least guarantees that the original object will not be modified by a foreign entity. A very good example is when you have arrays indiscriminately sent among objects; two array methods are really good: `arr.clone` (to send a copy) and `arr.toList` (to send a copy as a list, which is also immutable).

Messages must be Self-Contained

When you return the value of a method, the caller has the advantage of knowing what it was doing before invoking this method, and can take the return value and continue what it was doing.

With actors, things are not so simple. When an actor makes a request, the answer may not be immediate; it may take a long time. So as conditions are non-blocking, the actor can continue doing other work while it waits for the response. The problem is that when the answer arrives, how do you know what was the actor doing when it made the invocation?

One commonly used method to simplify the logic of the actors in a program includes sending redundant information in messages. If the request is an immutable object, you can cheaply include a reference to the request in the response. This makes the message larger, but simplifies the actor logic.

Another way to increase redundancy in messages is by building a case class for each type of message. While such a wrapper is not strictly necessary in many cases, it makes actor programs easier to understand. Code with case classes are always easier to understand than code using tuples, for example.

Summary

You learned how to build scalable, robust, concurrent programs using the Akka actor model, avoiding the problems of traditional approaches based on synchronized access and shared and mutable states.

You reviewed Akka's main concepts:

- Actor model
- Actor communication
- Actor lifecycle

You also explored the actor Code of Conduct.

In the following chapters, you will need Scala/Akka power to code SMACK pipeline applications.

CHAPTER 5

Storage: Apache Cassandra

Congratulations! You are almost halfway through this journey. You are at the point where it is necessary to meet the component responsible for information persistence; the sometimes neglected "data layer" will take on a new dimension when you have finished this chapter. It's time to meet Apache Cassandra, a NoSQL database that provides high availability and scalability without compromising performance.

Note   We suggest that you have your favorite terminal ready to follow the exercises. This will help you become familiar with the tools faster.

Once Upon a Time...

Before you start, let's do a little time traveling to ancient Greece to meet *the other* Cassandra. In Greek mythology, there was a priestess who was chastised for her treason to the god Apollo. She asked for the gift of prophecy in exchange for a carnal encounter; however, she failed to fulfill her part of the deal. For this, she received this punishment: she would have the gift of prophecy, but no one would ever believe her prophecies. *A real tragedy*. This priestess's name was Cassandra.

Perhaps the modern Cassandra, the Apache project, has come to claim the ancient Cassandra. With modern Cassandra, it is probably best to believe what she tells you and do not be afraid to ask.

Modern Cassandra

Modern Cassandra represents the persistence layer in our reference implementation.

First, let's have a short overview of NoSQL, and then continue to the installation and learn how to integrate Cassandra on the map.

NoSQL Everywhere

Fifteen years ago, nobody imagined the amount of information that a modern application would have to manage; the *Web* was only beginning to take its shape today. Computer systems were becoming more powerful, defying the Moore's law,[1] not only in large data centers but also in desktop computers, warning us that the *free lunch is over.* [2]

---

[1] https://en.wikipedia.org/wiki/Moore%27s_law.
[2] http://www.gotw.ca/publications/concurrency-ddj.htm.

© Raul Estrada and Isaac Ruiz 2016
R. Estrada and I. Ruiz, *Big Data SMACK*, DOI 10.1007/978-1-4842-2175-4_5

In this scenario, those who drove the change had to be innovative in the way that they looked for alternatives to a relational database management system (RDBMS). Google, Facebook, and Twitter had to experiment with creating their own data models—each with different architectures—gradually building what is known today as NoSQL.

The diversity of NoSQL tools is so broad that it is difficult to make a classification. But there was one audacious guy who did, and he proposed that a NoSQL tool must meet the following characteristics:

- Non-relational

- Open source

- Cluster-friendly

- Twenty-first-century web

- Schemaless

That guy was Martin Fowler and he exposes this in his book with Pramod J. Sadalage, *NoSQL Distilled* (Addison-Wesley Professional, 2012).[3]

At the GOTO conference in 2013,[4] Fowler presented the "Introduction to NoSQL," a very educational presentation well worth checking out.

But how is that NoSQL improves data access performance over traditional RDBMS? It has much to do with the way NoSQL handles and abstracts data; that is, how it has defined the data model.

Following Martin Fowler's comments, if you use this criterion, you can classify NoSQL (as shown in Figure 5-1) with distinct types according to this data model: document, column-family, graph, key-value.

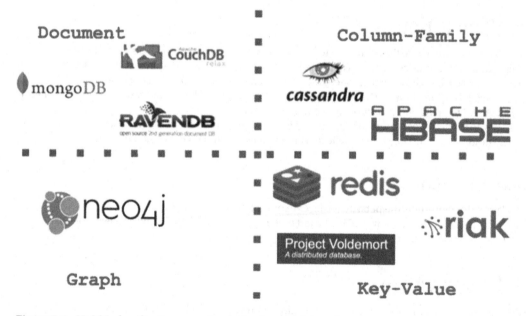

Figure 5-1. *NoSQL classification according to the data model used*

[3]http://martinfowler.com/books/nosql.html
[4]https://www.youtube.com/watch?v=qI_g07C_Q5I

Another NoSQL-specific feature is that the data model does not require a data schema, which allows a greater degree of freedom and faster data access.

As seen in Figure 5-2, the data models can be grouped as aggregated-oriented and schemaless.

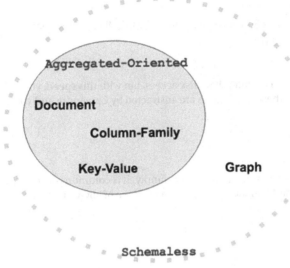

Figure 5-2. *Another data model classification*

The amount of data to be handled and the need of a mechanism to ease the development are indicators of when to use NoSQL. Martin Fowler recommends that you use these two major criteria for when to start using NoSQL, as shown in Figure 5-3.

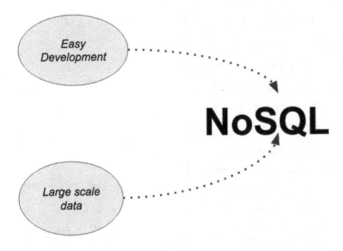

Figure 5-3. *A simple way to determine when to use NoSQL*

Finally, you must remember that there is no silver bullet, and although the rise of SQL is not large, you must be cautious in choosing when to use it.

The Memory Value

Many of the advantages of NoSQL are based on the fact that a lot of data management is performed in memory, which gives excellent performance to data access.

■ **Note**   The processing performance of main memory is 800 times faster than HDD, 40 times faster than a common SSD, and seven times faster than the fastest SSD.[5]

Surely, you already know that the memory access is greater than disk access, but with this speed, you want to do everything in memory. Fortunately, all of these advantages are abstracted by Cassandra and you just have to worry about what and how to store.

Key-Value and Column

There are two particular data models that to discuss: key-value and column-family. It is common practice that NoSQL use several data models to increase its performance. Cassandra makes use of key-value and column-family data models.

Key-Value

The simplest data model is key-value. You have probably already used this paradigm within a programming language. In a nutshell, it is a hash table.

Given a key, you can access the content (value), as demonstrated in Figure 5-4.

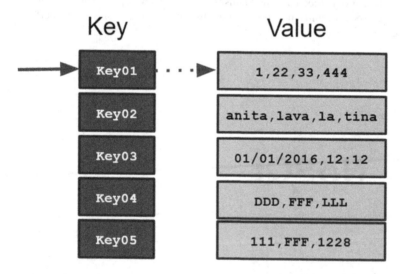

Figure 5-4. *You can imagine this data model as a big hash. The key allows access to certain <content>. This <content> can be different types of data, which makes it a much more flexible structure.*

---

[5]Ki Sun Song, "Introduction to In-Memory Data Grid; Main Features." http://www.cubrid.org/blog/dev-platform/introduction-to-in-memory-data-grid-main-features/

Column-Family

An important part of this data model is that the storage and fetch processes are made from columns and not from rows. Also, a lot of the data model is done in memory, and you already know how important that is.

What's a column? It is a tuple containing key-value pairs. In the case of several NoSQL, this tuple is formed by three pairs: name/key, value, and one timestamp.

In this model, several columns (the family) are grouped by a key called a *row-key*. Figure 5-5 shows this relationship.

Column family

Row Key	key: xxxxx	key: xxxxx	key: xxxxx	.....	key: xxxxx
	value: yyyyy	value: yyyyy	value: yyyyy		value: yyyyy
	timestamp: tttttt	timestamp: tttttt	timestamp: tttttt		timestamp: tttttt

Figure 5-5. A key (row-key) can access the column family. This group exemplifies the data model column-family

The main advantage of this model is that it substantially improves write operations, which improves their performance in distributed environments.[6]

Why Cassandra?

Cassandra implements "no single points of failure," which is achieved with redundant nodes and data. Unlike legacy systems based on master-slave architectures, Cassandra implements a masterless "ring" architecture (see Figure 5-6).

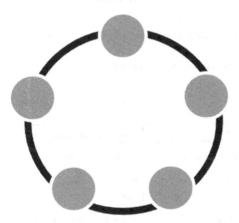

Figure 5-6. When all nodes have the same role, having data redundancy is much easier to maintain a replication, which always help maintain the availability of data.

---

[6]Comparative study of NoSQL document, column store databases, and evaluation of Cassandra. http://airccse.org/journal/ijdms/papers/6414ijdms02.pdf

With this architecture, all nodes have an identical role: there is no master node. All nodes communicate with each other using a scalable and distributed protocol called gossip.[7]

This architecture, together with the protocol, collectively cannot have a single point of failure. It offers true continuous availability.

The Data Model

At this point, you can say that the Cassandra data model is based primarily on managing columns. As mentioned earlier, some NoSQL combine multiple data models, as is the case with Cassandra (see Figure 5-7).

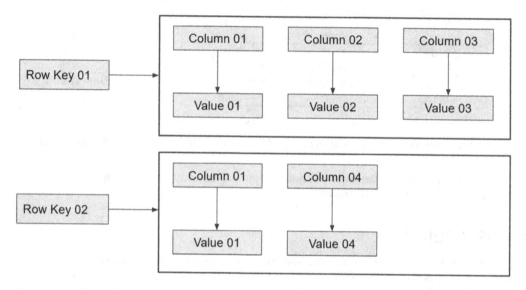

Figure 5-7. *Cassandra uses a model of combined data; key-value uses this to store and retrieve the columns*

Cassandra has some similarity to an RDBMS; these similarities facilitate use and adoption, although you must remember that they do not work the same way.

Table 5-1 provides some comparisons that help us better understand Cassandra's concepts.

Table 5-1. *Cassandra Data Model and RDBMS Equivalences*

	Definition	RDBMS Equivalent
Schema/Keyspace	A collection of column families.	Schema/database
Table/Column-Family	A set of rows.	Table
Row	An ordered set of columns.	Row
Column	A key/value pair and timestamp.	Column (name, value)

---

[7]https://docs.datastax.com/en/cassandra/2.1/cassandra/architecture/architectureGossipAbout_c.html

Figure 5-8 illustrates the relationships among these concepts.

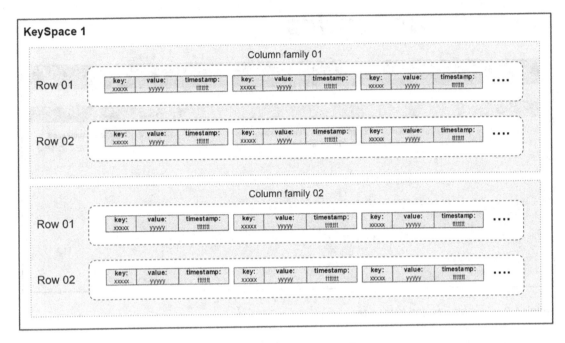

Figure 5-8. *Relationships among column, row, column-family, and keyspace*

Cassandra 101

Installation

This section explains how to install Apache Cassandra on a local machine. The following steps were performed on a Linux machine. At the time of this writing, the stable version is 3.4, released on March 8, 2016.

Prerequisites

Apache Cassandra requires Java version 7 or 8, preferably the Oracle/Sun distribution. The documentation indicates that it is also compatible with OpenJDK, Zing, and IBM distributions.

File Download

The first step is to download the `.zip` file distribution downloaded from `http://cassandra.apache.org/download/`.

On the Apache Cassandra project home page (see Figure 5-9 and `http://cassandra.apache.org`), the project logo reminds us of the seeing ability of the mythological character.

Tick-Tock Cassandra Server Releases

Cassandra is moving to a monthly release process called Tick-Tock. **Even-numbered** releases (e.g. 3.2) contain new features; **odd-numbered** releases (e.g. 3.3) contain bug fixes only. If a critical bug is found, a patch will be released against the most recent bug fix release. Read more about tick-tock here.

The latest tick-tock release is 3.4, released on 2016-03-08.

- apache-cassandra-3.4-bin.tar.gz [PGP] [MD5] [SHA1]
- Debian installation instructions

The previous tick-tock bugfix release is 3.3, released on 2016-02-09.

- apache-cassandra-3.3-bin.tar.gz [PGP] [MD5] [SHA1]
- Debian installation instructions

Figure 5-9. *Cassandra project home page*

Locate the following file:

apache-cassandra-3.4-bin.tar.gz

It's important to validate file integrity. You do not want it to fail while it's running. This particular file has the following values to validate its integrity:

[MD5] e9f490211812b7db782fed09f20c5bb0
[SHA1]7d010b8cc92d5354f384b646b302407ab90be1f0

It's easy to make this validation. Any flavor of Linux gives the md5 and sha1sum commands, as shown in the following:

```
%> md5sum apache-cassandra-3.4-bin.tar.gz
e9f490211812b7db782fed09f20c5bb0  apache-cassandra-3.4-bin.tar.gz

%> sha1sum apache-cassandra-3.4-bin.tar.gz
7d010b8cc92d5354f384b646b302407ab90be1f0  apache-cassandra-3.4-bin.tar.gz

%> ls -lrt apache-cassandra-3.4-bin.tar.gz
-rw-r--r--. 1 rugi rugi 34083682 Mar  7 22:06 apache-cassandra-3.4-bin.tar.gz
```

Once you have validated the file's integrity, you can unzip it and continue.

Start

Starting Apache Cassandra is easy; you only execute the following:

```
./cassandra -f
INFO  18:06:58 Starting listening for CQL clients on localhost/127.0.0.1:9042 (unencrypted)...
INFO  18:06:58 Not starting RPC server as requested. Use JMX (StorageService->startRPCServer())
or nodetool (enablethrift) to start it
INFO  18:07:07 Scheduling approximate time-check task with a precision of 10 milliseconds
INFO  18:07:07 Created default superuser role 'cassandra'
```

With this command, your server Apache Cassandra is ready to receive requests. You must always keep in mind that Apache Cassandra runs with a client-server approach. You have launched the server; the server is responsible for receiving requests from clients and then giving them answers. So now you need to validate that clients can send requests.

The next step is to use the CLI validation tool, an Apache Cassandra client.

Validation

Now, let's execute the CLI tool.

```
%> ./cqlsh
Connected to Test Cluster at 127.0.0.1:9042.
[cqlsh 5.0.1 | Cassandra 3.4 | CQL spec 3.4.0 | Native protocol v4]
Use HELP for help.
cqlsh>
```

The first step is to create a keyspace, an analogy with relational databases in which you define the database, per se.

```
%>CREATE KEYSPACE mykeyspace WITH REPLICATION = { 'class' : 'SimpleStrategy', 'replication_factor' : 1 };
```

Once the keyspace is defined, indicate that you will use it.

```
USE mykeyspace;
```

This is a familiar sentence, isn't?

Apache Cassandra, like other NoSQL frameworks, tries to use analogies with the SQL statements that you already know.

And if you have already defined the database, do you remember what is next? Now you create a test table.

```
%> CREATE TABLE users (  user_id int PRIMARY KEY,  fname text,  lname text);
```

And, having the table, inserting records is simple, as you can see in the following:

```
%>INSERT INTO users (user_id,  fname, lname)  VALUES (1745, 'john', 'smith');
%>INSERT INTO users (user_id,  fname, lname)  VALUES (1744, 'john', 'doe');
%>INSERT INTO users (user_id,  fname, lname)  VALUES (1746, 'john', 'smith');
```

You make a simple query, like this:

```
%>SELECT * FROM users;
```

And, you should have the following results (or similar, if you already modified the data with the inserts):

```
 user_id | fname | lname
---------+-------+-------
    1745 |  john | smith
    1744 |  john |   doe
    1746 |  john | smith
```

With Apache Cassandra, you can create indexes on the fly:

```
CREATE INDEX ON users (lname);
```

To facilitate searches on specific fields, do this:

```
SELECT * FROM users WHERE lname = 'smith';
```

This is the result:

```
 user_id | fname | lname
---------+-------+-------
    1745 |  john | smith
    1746 |  john | smith
```

And that's it. This is enough to validate that communication between your CLI and your Cassandra server is working properly.

Here is the complete output from the previous commands:

```
{16-03-21 14:05}localhost:~/opt/apache/cassandra/apache-cassandra-3.4/bin rugi% cd /home/
                         rugi/opt/apache/cassandra/apache-cassandra-3.4/bin
{16-03-21 14:05}localhost:~/opt/apache/cassandra/apache-cassandra-3.4/bin rugi% ./cqlsh
Connected to Test Cluster at 127.0.0.1:9042.
[cqlsh 5.0.1 | Cassandra 3.4 | CQL spec 3.4.0 | Native protocol v4]
Use HELP for help.
cqlsh> CREATE KEYSPACE mykeyspace WITH REPLICATION = { 'class' : 'SimpleStrategy',
                                      'replication_factor' : 1 };
cqlsh> USE mykeyspace;
cqlsh:mykeyspace> CREATE TABLE users (  user_id int PRIMARY KEY,  fname text,  lname text);
cqlsh:mykeyspace> INSERT INTO users  (user_id,  fname, lname)  VALUES (1745, 'john', 'smith');
cqlsh:mykeyspace> INSERT INTO users  (user_id,  fname, lname)  VALUES (1744, 'john', 'doe');
cqlsh:mykeyspace> INSERT INTO users  (user_id,  fname, lname)  VALUES (1746, 'john', 'smith');

cqlsh:mykeyspace> SELECT * FROM users;
 user_id | fname | lname
---------+-------+-------
    1745 |  john | smith
    1744 |  john |   doe
    1746 |  john | smith
(3 rows)
```

```
cqlsh:mykeyspace> CREATE INDEX ON users (lname);
cqlsh:mykeyspace> SELECT * FROM users WHERE lname = 'smith';
user_id | fname | lname
---------+-------+-------
   1745 |  john | smith
   1746 |  john | smith
(2 rows)

cqlsh:mykeyspace> exit
{16-03-21 15:24}localhost:~/opt/apache/cassandra/apache-cassandra-3.4/bin rugi%
```

You should have two terminals open: one with the server running and the other one with CLI running. If you check the first one, you will see how CLI is processing the requests. Figure 5-10 shows the server running.

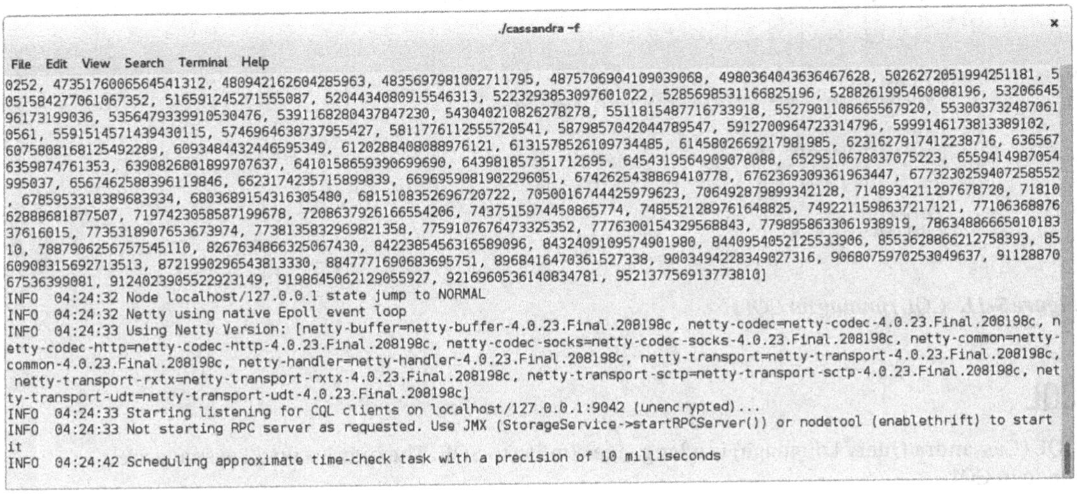

Figure 5-10. *Cassandra server running*

Figure 5-11 is a screenshot of running the test commands described earlier.

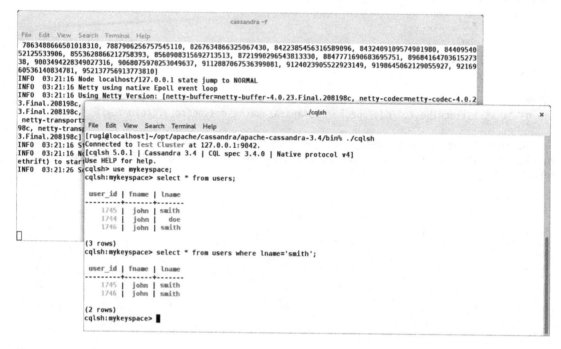

Figure 5-11. *CQL running on CQLs*

CQL

CQL (Cassandra Query Language) is a language similar to SQL. The queries on a keyspace are made in CQL.

CQL Shell

There are several ways to interact with a keyspace; in the previous section, you saw how to do it using a shell called *CQL shell* (CQLs). Later you will see other ways to interact with the keyspace.

CQL shell is the primary way to interact with Cassandra; Table 5-2 lists the main commands.

Table 5-2. *Shell Command Summary*

Command	Description
cqlsh	Starts the CQL interactive terminal.
CAPTURE	Captures the command output and appends it to a file.
CONSISTENCY	Shows the current consistency level; or given a level, sets it.
COPY	Imports and exports CSV (comma-separated values) data to and from Cassandra.
DESCRIBE	Provides information about the connected Cassandra cluster or about the data objects stored in the cluster.
EXPAND	Formats the output of a query vertically.
EXIT	Terminates cqlsh.
PAGING	Enables or disables query paging.
SHOW	Shows the Cassandra version, host, or tracing information for the current cqlsh client session.
SOURCE	Executes a file containing CQL statements.
TRACING	Enables or disables request tracing.

For more detailed information on shell commands, you should visit the following web page:

http://docs.datastax.com/en/cql/3.1/cql/cql_reference/cqlshCommandsTOC.html

Let's try some of these commands. First, activate the shell, as follows;

```
{16-04-15 23:54}localhost:~/opt/apache/cassandra/apache-cassandra-3.4/bin rugi% ./cqlsh
Connected to Test Cluster at 127.0.0.1:9042.
[cqlsh 5.0.1 | Cassandra 3.4 | CQL spec 3.4.0 | Native protocol v4]
Use HELP for help.
```

The describe command can work in specific tables, in all the keyspaces, or in one specific keyspace:

```
cqlsh> describe keyspaces

system_schema   system        system_distributed
system_auth     mykeyspace    system_traces

cqlsh> describe mykeyspace

CREATE KEYSPACE mykeyspace WITH replication = {'class': 'SimpleStrategy', 'replication_
factor': '1'}  AND durable_writes = true;

CREATE TABLE mykeyspace.users (
    user_id int PRIMARY KEY,
    fname text,
    lname text
```

```
) WITH bloom_filter_fp_chance = 0.01
    AND caching = {'keys': 'ALL', 'rows_per_partition': 'NONE'}
    AND comment = ''
    AND compaction = {'class': 'org.apache.cassandra.db.compaction.SizeTieredCompactionStrategy',
                               'max_threshold': '32', 'min_threshold': '4'}
    AND compression = {'chunk_length_in_kb': '64',
                           'class': 'org.apache.cassandra.io.compress. LZ4Compressor'}
    AND crc_check_chance = 1.0
    AND dclocal_read_repair_chance = 0.1
    AND default_time_to_live = 0
    AND gc_grace_seconds = 864000
    AND max_index_interval = 2048
    AND memtable_flush_period_in_ms = 0
    AND min_index_interval = 128
    AND read_repair_chance = 0.0
    AND speculative_retry = '99PERCENTILE';
CREATE INDEX users_lname_idx ON mykeyspace.users (lname);
```

The show command is also simple to test to see the version number:

```
cqlsh> show version
[cqlsh 5.0.1 | Cassandra 3.4 | CQL spec 3.4.0 | Native protocol v4]
cqlsh>
```

As you can see, these commands are very easy to use.

CQL Commands

CQL is very similar to SQL, as you have already seen in the first part of this chapter. You have created a keyspace, made inserts, and created a filter.

CQL, like SQL, is based on sentences/statements. These sentences are for data manipulation and work with their logical container, the keyspace. As in SQL statements, they must end with a semicolon (;).

Table 5-3 lists all the language commands.

Table 5-3. *CQL Command Summary*

Command	Description
ALTER KEYSPACE	Changes the property values of a keyspace.
ALTER TABLE	Modifies the column metadata of a table.
ALTER TYPE	Modifies a user-defined type. Cassandra 2.1 and later.
ALTER USER	Alters existing user options.
BATCH	Writes multiple DML statements.
CREATE INDEX	Defines a new index on a single column of a table.
CREATE KEYSPACE	Defines a new keyspace and its replica placement strategy.
CREATE TABLE	Defines a new table.
CREATE TRIGGER	Registers a trigger on a table.
CREATE TYPE	Creates a user-defined type. Cassandra 2.1 and later.
CREATE USER	Creates a new user.
DELETE	Removes entire rows or one or more columns from one or more rows.
DESCRIBE	Provides information about the connected Cassandra cluster or about the data objects stored in the cluster.
DROP INDEX	Drops the named index.
DROP KEYSPACE	Removes the keyspace.
DROP TABLE	Removes the named table.
DROP TRIGGER	Removes registration of a trigger.
DROP TYPE	Drops a user-defined type. Cassandra 2.1 and later.
DROP USER	Removes a user.
GRANT	Provides access to database objects.
INSERT	Adds or updates columns.
LIST PERMISSIONS	Lists permissions granted to a user.
LIST USERS	Lists existing users and their superuser status.
REVOKE	Revokes user permissions.
SELECT	Retrieves data from a Cassandra table.
TRUNCATE	Removes all data from a table.
UPDATE	Updates columns in a row.
USE	Connects the client session to a keyspace.

For more detailed information of CQL commands, you can visit the following web page:

http://docs.datastax.com/en/cql/3.1/cql/cql_reference/cqlCommandsTOC.html

Let's play with some of these commands.

```
{16-04-16 6:19}localhost:~/opt/apache/cassandra/apache-cassandra-3.4/bin rugi% ./cqlsh
Connected to Test Cluster at 127.0.0.1:9042.
```

```
[cqlsh 5.0.1 | Cassandra 3.4 | CQL spec 3.4.0 | Native protocol v4]
Use HELP for help.
```

Use the keyspace created at beginning, as follows:

```
cqlsh> use mykeyspace;
```

The DESCRIBE command can be applied to almost any object to discover the keyspace tables.

```
cqlsh:mykeyspace> describe tables users
```

Or in a specific table.

```
cqlsh:mykeyspace> describe users

CREATE TABLE mykeyspace.users (
    user_id int PRIMARY KEY,
    fname text,
    lname text
) WITH bloom_filter_fp_chance = 0.01
    AND caching = {'keys': 'ALL', 'rows_per_partition': 'NONE'}
    AND comment = ''
    AND compaction = {'class': 'org.apache.cassandra.db.compaction.SizeTieredCompactionStrategy',
                              'max_threshold': '32', 'min_threshold': '4'}
    AND compression = {'chunk_length_in_kb': '64',
                           'class': 'org.apache.cassandra.io.compress.LZ4Compressor'}
    AND crc_check_chance = 1.0
    AND dclocal_read_repair_chance = 0.1
    AND default_time_to_live = 0
    AND gc_grace_seconds = 864000
    AND max_index_interval = 2048
    AND memtable_flush_period_in_ms = 0
    AND min_index_interval = 128
    AND read_repair_chance = 0.0
    AND speculative_retry = '99PERCENTILE';
CREATE INDEX users_lname_idx ON mykeyspace.users (lname);
cqlsh:mykeyspace> exit
```

Beyond the Basics

You already know that Apache Cassandra runs on a client-server architecture. The client-server architecture is used by nearly everyone every day; it is the base of what you know as the Internet.

Client-Server

By definition, the client-server architecture allows distributed applications, since the tasks are divided into two main parts:

- The service providers: the servers
- The service petitioners: the clients

In this architecture, several clients are allowed to access the server. The server is responsible for meeting requests and it handles each one according its own rules. So far, you have only used one client, managed from the same machine—that is, from the same data network.

Figure 5-12 shows our current client-server architecture in Cassandra.

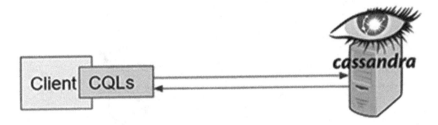

Figure 5-12. *The native way to connect to a Cassandra server is via CQLs.*

CQL shell allows you to connect to Cassandra, access a keyspace, and send CQL statements to the Cassandra server. This is the most immediate method, but in daily practice, it is common to access the keyspaces from different execution contexts (other systems and other programming languages).

Other Clients

You require other clients, different from CQLs, to do it in the Apache Cassandra context. You require connection *drivers*.

Drivers

A *driver* is a software component that allows access to a keyspace to run CQL statements.

Figure 5-13 illustrates accessing clients through the use of a driver. A driver can access a keyspace and also allows the execution of CQL sentences.

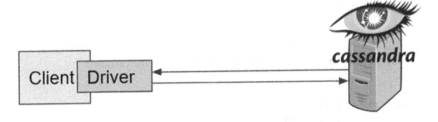

Figure 5-13. *To access a Cassandra server, a driver is required*

Fortunately, there are a lot of these drivers for Cassandra in almost any modern programming language. You can see an extensive list at http://wiki.apache.org/cassandra/ClientOptions.

Currently, there are different drivers to access a keyspace in almost all modern programming languages. Typically, in a client-server architecture, there are clients accessing the server from different clients, which are distributed in different networks, therefore, Figure 5-13 may now look like what's shown in Figure 5-14.

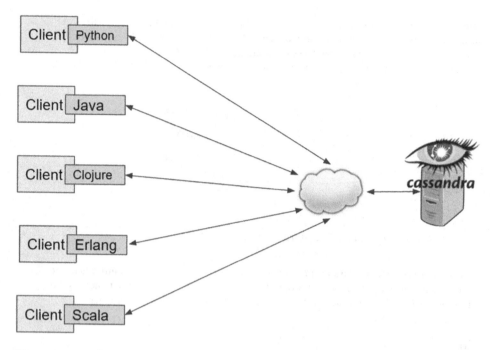

Figure 5-14. *Different clients connecting to a Cassandra server through the cloud*

The Figure 5-14 illustrates that given the distributed characteristics that modern systems require, the clients actually are in different points and access the Cassandra server through public and private networks.

Your implementation needs will dictate the required clients.

All languages offer a similar API through the driver. Consider the following code snippets in Java, Ruby, and Node.

Java

The following snippet was tested with JDK 1.8.x.

Get Dependence

With java, it is easiest is to use Maven. You can get the driver using the following Maven artifact:

```
<dependency>
    <groupId>com.datastax.cassandra</groupId>
    <artifactId>cassandra-driver-core</artifactId>
    <version>3.0.2</version>
</dependency>
```

Snippet

The following is the Java snippet:

```java
import com.datastax.driver.core.Cluster;
import com.datastax.driver.core.ResultSet;
import com.datastax.driver.core.Row;
import com.datastax.driver.core.Session;
import java.util.Iterator;

...

    public static void main(String[] args) {
        Cluster cluster = Cluster.builder().addContactPoint("127.0.0.1").build();
        Session session = cluster.connect("mykeyspace");
        ResultSet results = session.execute("SELECT * FROM users");
        StringBuilder line = new StringBuilder();

        for (Iterator<Row> iterator = results.iterator(); iterator.hasNext();) {
            Row row = iterator.next();
            line.delete(0, line.length());
            line.append("FirstName = ").
                    append(row.getString("fname")).
                    append(",").append(" ").
                    append("LastName = ").
                    append(row.getString("lname"));
            System.out.println(line.toString());
        }
    }
}
```

Ruby

The snippet was tested with Ruby 2.0.x.

Get Dependence

In Ruby, obtaining the driver is as simple as installing a gem.

```
%>gem install cassandra-driver
```

Snippet

The following is the Ruby snippet:

```ruby
require 'cassandra'

node = '127.0.0.1'
cluster = Cassandra.cluster(hosts: node)
keyspace = 'mykeyspace'
session  = cluster.connect(keyspace)
session.execute("SELECT fname, lname FROM users").each do |row|
        p "FirstName = #{row['fname']}, LastName = #{row['lname']}"
end
```

Node

The snippet was tested with Node v5.0.0.

Get Dependence

With Node, it could not be otherwise; the driver is obtained with npm.

```
%>npm install cassandra-driver
%>npm install async
```

Snippet

The following is the Node snippet:

```
var cassandra = require('cassandra-driver');
var async = require('async');

var client = new cassandra.Client({contactPoints: ['127.0.0.1'], keyspace: 'mykeyspace'});
client.stream('SELECT fname, lname FROM users', [])
  .on('readable', function () {
                var row;
                    while (row = this.read()) {
                            console.log('FirstName =  %s , LastName= %s', row.fname,
                            row.lname);
                                }
                })
  .on('end', function () {
            //todo
            })
  .on('error', function (err) {
                // todo
            });
</code>
```

These three snippets did the same thing: made a connection to the Cassandra server, got a reference to the keyspace, made a single query, and displayed the results. In conclusion, the three snippets generated the same result:

```
"FirstName = john, LastName = smith"
"FirstName = john, LastName = doe"
"FirstName = john, LastName = smith"
```

You can see more examples that use other languages on the following web page:

```
http://www.planetcassandra.org/apache-cassandra-client-drivers/
```

Apache Spark-Cassandra Connector

Now that you have a clear understanding on how connecting to a Cassandra server is done, let's talk about a very special client. Everything that you have seen previously has been done to get to this point. You can now see what Spark can do since you know Cassandra and you know that you can use it as a storage layer to improve the Spark performance.

What do you need to achieve this connection? A client. This client is special because it is designed specifically for Spark, not for a specific language. This special client is called the Spark-Cassandra Connector (see Figure 5-15).

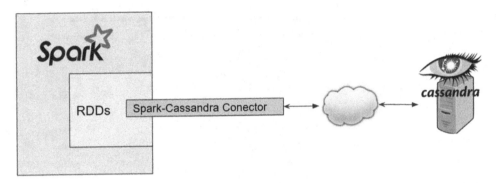

Figure 5-15. *The Spark-Cassandra Connector is a special type of client that allows access to keyspaces from a Spark context*

Installing the Connector

The Spark-Cassandra connector has its own GitHub repository. The latest stable version is the master, but you can access a special version through a particular *branch*.

Figure 5-16 shows the Spark-Cassandra Connector project home page, which is located at `https://github.com/datastax/spark-cassandra-connector`.

Figure 5-16. *The Spark-Cassandra Connector on GitHub*

At the time of this writing, the most stable connector version is 1.6.0. The connector is basically a .jar file loaded when Spark starts. If you prefer to directly access the .jar file and avoid the build process, you can do it by downloading the official maven repository. A widely used repository is located at http://mvnrepository.com/artifact/com.datastax.spark/spark-cassandra-connector_ .10/1.6.0-M2.

Generating the .jar file directly from the Git repository has one main advantage: all the necessary dependencies of the connector are generated. If you choose to download the jar from the official repository, you must also download all of these dependencies.

Fortunately, there is a third way to run the connector, which is by telling the spark-shell that you require certain packages for the session to start. This is done by adding the following flag:

```
./spark-shell --packages datastax:spark-cassandra-connector:1.6.0-M2-s_2.10
```

The nomenclature of the package is the same used with Gradle, Buildr, or SBT:

```
GroupID: datastax
ArtifactID: spark-cassandra-connector
Version: 1.6.0-M2-s_2.10
```

In the preceding lines of code, you are telling the shell that you require that artifact, and the shell will handle all the units. Now let's see how it works.

Establishing the Connection

The connector version used in this section is 1.6.0 because it is the latest stable version of Apache Spark as of this writing.

First, validate that the versions are compatible. Access the Spark shell to see if you have the correct version.

```
{16-04-18 1:10}localhost:~/opt/apache/spark/spark-1.6.0-bin-hadoop2.6/bin rugi% ./spark-shell
log4j:WARN No appenders could be found for logger (org.apache.hadoop.metrics2.lib.
MutableMetricsFactory).
log4j:WARN Please initialize the log4j system properly.
log4j:WARN See http://logging.apache.org/log4j/1.2/faq.html#noconfig for more info.
Using Spark's repl log4j profile: org/apache/spark/log4j-defaults-repl.properties
To adjust logging level use sc.setLogLevel("INFO")
Welcome to


      / __/__  ___ _____/ /__
     _\ \/ _ \/ _ `/ __/  '_/
    /___/ .__/\_,_/_/ /_/\_\   version 1.6.0
       /_/


Using Scala version 2.10.5 (Java HotSpot(TM) 64-Bit Server VM, Java 1.8.0_60)
Type in expressions to have them evaluated.
Type :help for more information.
....
scala>
```

Next, try a simple task:

```
scala> sc.parallelize( 1 to 50 ).sum()
res0: Double = 1275.0
scala>
```

Stop the shell (exit command). Now at start time, indicate the package that you require (the connector). The first time, the shell makes downloading dependencies:

```
{16-06-08 23:18}localhost:~/opt/apache/spark/spark-1.6.0-bin-hadoop2.6/bin rugi% >./spark-
shell --packages datastax:spark-cassandra-connector:1.6.0-M2-s_2.10
Ivy Default Cache set to: /home/rugi/.ivy2/cache
The jars for the packages stored in: /home/rugi/.ivy2/jars
:: loading settings :: url = jar:file:/home/rugi/opt/apache/spark/spark-1.6.0-bin-hadoop2.6/
lib/spark-assembly-1.6.0-hadoop2.6.0.jar!/org/apache/ivy/core/settings/ivysettings.xml
datastax#spark-cassandra-connector added as a dependency
:: resolving dependencies :: org.apache.spark#spark-submit-parent;1.0
        confs: [default]
        found datastax#spark-cassandra-connector;1.6.0-M2-s_2.10 in spark-packages
        found joda-time#joda-time;2.3 in local-m2-cache
        found com.twitter#jsr166e;1.1.0 in central
        found org.scala-lang#scala-reflect;2.10.5 in central
```

```
---------------------------------------------------------------
|               |       |       modules        ||   artifacts    |
|     conf      | number| search|dwnlded|evicted|| number|dwnlded|
---------------------------------------------------------------
|    default    |  16   |   2   |   2   |   0   ||  16   |   2   |
---------------------------------------------------------------
```
:: retrieving :: org.apache.spark#spark-submit-parent
       confs: [default]
       2 artifacts copied, 14 already retrieved (5621kB/32ms)
log4j:WARN No appenders could be found for logger (org.apache.hadoop.metrics2.lib.
MutableMetricsFactory).
log4j:WARN Please initialize the log4j system properly.
log4j:WARN See http://logging.apache.org/log4j/1.2/faq.html#noconfig for more info.
Using Spark's repl log4j profile: org/apache/spark/log4j-defaults-repl.properties
To adjust logging level use sc.setLogLevel("INFO")
Welcome to

      ____   __
     / __/__ ___ _____/ /__
    _\ \/ _ \/ _ `/ __/ '_/
   /___/ .__/_,_/_/ /_/_\   version 1.6.0
      /_/

Using Scala version 2.10.5 (Java HotSpot(TM) 64-Bit Server VM, Java 1.8.0_60)
Type in expressions to have them evaluated.
Type :help for more information.
16/06/08 23:18:59 WARN Utils: Your hostname, localhost.localdomain resolves to a loopback
address: 127.0.0.1; using 192.168.1.6 instead (on interface wlp7s0)
16/06/08 23:18:59 WARN Utils: Set SPARK_LOCAL_IP if you need to bind to another address
Spark context available as sc.
16/06/08 23:19:07 WARN ObjectStore: Version information not found in metastore. hive.
metastore.schema.verification is not enabled so recording the schema version 1.2.0
16/06/08 23:19:07 WARN ObjectStore: Failed to get database default, returning
NoSuchObjectException
SQL context available as sqlContext.

scala>
```

The connector is loaded and ready for use.
First, stop the Scala executor from the shell:

```
sc.stop
```

Next, import the required classes for communication:

```
import com.datastax.spark.connector._, org.apache.spark.SparkContext, org.apache.spark.
SparkContext._, org.apache.spark.SparkConf
```

Then, set a variable with the required configuration to connect:

```
val conf = new SparkConf(true).set("spark.cassandra.connection.host", "localhost")
```
```

Finally, connect to the well-known keyspace and table that were created at the beginning of this chapter:

```
val sc = new SparkContext(conf)
val test_spark_rdd = sc.cassandraTable("mykeyspace", "users")
```

Given the context and keyspace, it is possible to consult the values with the following statement:

```
test_spark_rdd.foreach(println)
```

Here is the complete sequence of the five lines of code:

```
scala> sc.stop

scala> import com.datastax.spark.connector._, org.apache.spark.SparkContext, org.apache.
spark.SparkContext._, org.apache.spark.SparkConf
import com.datastax.spark.connector._
import org.apache.spark.SparkContext
import org.apache.spark.SparkContext._
import org.apache.spark.SparkConf

scala> val conf = new SparkConf(true).set("spark.cassandra.connection.host", "localhost")
conf: org.apache.spark.SparkConf = org.apache.spark.SparkConf@68b5a37d

scala> val sc = new SparkContext(conf)
sc: org.apache.spark.SparkContext = org.apache.spark.SparkContext@3d872a12

scala> val test_spark_rdd = sc.cassandraTable("mykeyspace", "users")
```

The connection is established and is already accessible through test_spark_rdd to make operations in our table within our keyspace; for example, to show values.

```
scala> test_spark_rdd.foreach(println)
CassandraRow{user_id: 1745, fname: john, lname: smith}
CassandraRow{user_id: 1744, fname: john, lname: doe}
CassandraRow{user_id: 1746, fname: john, lname: smith}
```

More Than One Is Better

Up to this moment, unknowingly, you have been working with a cluster of Cassandra. A cluster with a single node, but a cluster. Let's check it. ;)

To check, use the nodetool utility, which is administered as a cluster of the Cassandra nodetool via CLI. You can run the following to see the full list of commands:

```
CASSANDRA_HOME/bin>./nodetool
```

Among the list, you see the status command.

```
status          Print cluster information (state, load, IDs, ...)
```

You can run nodetool with the status command.

```
CASSANDRA_HOME/bin>./nodetool   status
Datacenter: datacenter1
========================
Status=Up/Down
|/ State=Normal/Leaving/Joining/Moving
--  Address     Load        Tokens        Owns (effective)  Host
ID                                Rack
UN  127.0.0.1  122.62 KiB   256       100.0%      3e7ccbd4-8ffb-4b77-bd06-110d27536cb2  rack1
```

You can see that you run a cluster with a single node.

cassandra.yaml

When you have a cluster of more than one node, you modify the cassandra.yaml file. In this file, the necessary settings of each node within a cluster are made. When you have only one node, there's nothing to change. The file is located in the CASSANDRA_HOME/conf folder.

The file has several options; you can see each option in detail in the documentation.[8] For a basic configuration, however, there are few options that are required.

Table 5-4 describes the fields to create our cluster. The descriptions were taken from the afore mentioned documentation.

Table 5-4. *Minimum Configuration Options for Each Node in the Cluster*

Option	Description
cluster_name	The name of the cluster.
seed_provider	The addresses of the hosts deemed as contact points. Cassandra nodes use the -seeds list to find each provider and learn the topology of the ring.
seed_provider - class_name	The class within Cassandra that handles the seed logic. It can be customized, but this is typically not required.
seed_provider- parameters - seeds	A comma-delimited list of IP addresses used by gossip for bootstrapping new nodes joining a cluster.
listen_address	The IP address or hostname that Cassandra binds to in order to connect to other Cassandra nodes.
rpc_address	The listen address for client connections (Thrift RPC service and native transport).
broadcast_rpc_address	The RPC address to broadcast to drivers and other Cassandra nodes.
endpoint_snitch	Set to a class that implements the IEndpointSnitch interface.

---

[8]http://docs.datastax.com/en/cassandra/3.0/cassandra/configuration/configCassandra_yaml.html

Setting the Cluster

In this example, assume that Cassandra is installed on the following machines:

```
107.170.38.238 (seed)
107.170.112.81
107.170.115.161
```

The documentation recommends having more than one seed, but because you have only three nodes in this exercise, leave only a single seed. All machines have Ubuntu 14.04 and JDK 1.8 (HotSpot) ready.

The following steps assume that you are starting a clean installation in each machine, so, if a machine is running Cassandra, you must stop and delete all data. We recommend that you start with clean installations. If there is a firewall between the machines, it is important to open specific ports.[9]

Machine01

Our first machine has the address 107.170.38.238 and it is the seed. It starts first when you finish setting up the three machines.

Locate the CASSANDRA HOME/conf/cassandra.yaml file and make the following modifications. All nodes in the cluster must have the same cluster_name.

```
cluster_name: 'BedxheCluster'
num_tokens: 256
seed_provider:
    - class_name: org.apache.cassandra.locator.SimpleSeedProvider
      parameters:
          - seeds: "107.170.38.238"
listen_address: 107.170.38.238
rpc_address: 0.0.0.0
broadcast_rpc_address: 1.2.3.4
endpoint_snitch: RackInferringSnitch
```

Machine02

Our second machine has the address 107.170.112.81. Its setting only changes the value of listen_address.

```
cluster_name: 'BedxheCluster'
num_tokens: 256
seed_provider:
    - class_name: org.apache.cassandra.locator.SimpleSeedProvider
      parameters:
          - seeds: "107.170.38.238"
listen_address: 107.170.112.81
rpc_address: 0.0.0.0
broadcast_rpc_address: 1.2.3.4
endpoint_snitch: RackInferringSnitch
```

---

[9]http://docs.datastax.com/en/cassandra/3.0/cassandra/configuration/secureFireWall.html

Machine03

Our third machine has the address 107.170.115.161. Its setting also only changes the value of listen_address.

```
cluster_name: 'BedxheCluster'
num_tokens: 256
seed_provider:
    - class_name: org.apache.cassandra.locator.SimpleSeedProvider
      parameters:
          - seeds: "107.170.38.238"
listen_address: 107.170.115.161
rpc_address: 0.0.0.0
broadcast_rpc_address: 1.2.3.4
endpoint_snitch: RackInferringSnitch
```

You have now finished the configuration of the nodes.

■ **Note** This configuration was simple. It was used for illustrative purposes. Configuring a cluster to a production environment requires studyng several factors and experimenting a lot. Therefore, we recommend using this setting because it is a simple exercise to begin learning the options.

Booting the Cluster

You first started Cassandra in the seed node (removing the -f flag, Cassandra starts the process and passes the background).

```
MACHINE01/CASSANDRA_HOME/bin%>./cassandra
After you started cassandra in the other two nodes.
MACHINE02/CASSANDRA_HOME/bin%>./cassandra
MACHINE03/CASSANDRA_HOME/bin%>./cassandra
```

Now, if you execute nodetool in any of the machines, you see something like the following.

```
CASSANDRA_HOME/bin>./nodetool status
Datacenter: 170
===============
Status=Up/Down
|/ State=Normal/Leaving/Joining/Moving
```

--	Address	Load	Tokens	Owns (effective)	Host ID	Rack
UN	107.170.38.238	107.95 KiB	256	68.4%	23e16126-8c7f-4eb8-9ea0-40ae488127e8	38
UN	107.170.115.161	15.3 KiB	256	63.7%	b3a9970a-ff77-43b2-ad4e-594deb04e7f7	115
UN	107.170.112.81	102.49 KiB	256	67.9%	ece8b83f-d51d-43ce-b9f2-89b79a0a2097	112

Now, if you repeat the creation of the keyspace example in the seed node, you will see how the keyspace is available in the other nodes. And conversely, if you apply a change to the keyspace in any node, it is immediately reflected in the others.

Execute the following in machine01 (the seed machine):

```
MACHINE01_CASSANDRA_HOME/bin%> ./cqlsh

cqlsh>CREATE KEYSPACE mykeyspace WITH REPLICATION = { 'class' : 'SimpleStrategy',
                                                      'replication_factor' : 1 };

cqlsh>USE mykeyspace;
cqlsh>CREATE TABLE users (user_id int PRIMARY KEY,  fname text,  lname text);
cqlsh>INSERT INTO users (user_id,  fname, lname)  VALUES (1745, 'john', 'smith');
cqlsh>INSERT INTO users (user_id,  fname, lname)  VALUES (1744, 'john', 'doe');
cqlsh>INSERT INTO users (user_id,  fname, lname)  VALUES (1746, 'john', 'smith');
```

Execute the following in machine02 or machine03:

```
CASSANDRA_HOME/bin%>./cqlsh
cqlsh> use mykeyspace;
cqlsh:mykeyspace> select * from users;

 user_id | fname | lname
---------+-------+-------
    1745 |  john | smith
    1744 |  john |   doe
    1746 |  john | smith

(3 rows)
```

That's it. You have a cluster of three nodes working properly.

Putting It All Together

The best way to assimilate all of these concepts is through examples, so in later chapters, we show concrete examples of the use of this architecture.

As you can see, beginning to use Cassandra is very simple; the similarity to SQL in making queries helps to manipulate data from the start. Perhaps now that you know the advantages of Cassandra, you want to know who is using it. There are three companies in particular that have helped increase the popularity of Cassandra: SoundCloud,[10] Spotify,[11] and Netflix.[12]

A lot of the stuff that exists online about Cassandra makes references to these companies, but they are not the only ones. The following two web pages offer more extensive lists of companies that are committed to Cassandra, and using some part of their data management in interesting use cases.

- http://www.planetcassandra.org/companies/

- http://www.planetcassandra.org/apache-cassandra-use-cases/

Beyond the advantages Cassandra, as the ring model and distributed data management within the cluster, its main advantage is the level of integration with Spark, and in general, with the rest of the technologies in this book.

Surely, you'll use Cassandra in an upcoming project.

---

[10]How SoundCloud Uses Cassandra. https://www.infoq.com/presentations/soundcloud-cassandra
[11]Spotify: How to Use Apache Cassandra. https://www.youtube.com/watch?v=JWaECFyhvxI
[12]Netflix: A State of Xen Chaos Monkey & Cassandra. https://www.youtube.com/watch?v=Mu01DmxQjWA

CHAPTER 6

The Engine: Apache Spark

If our stack were a vehicle, now we have reached the engine. As an engine, we will disarm it, analyze it, master it, improve it, and run it to the limit.

In this chapter, we walk hand in hand with you. First, we look at the Spark download and installation, and then we test it in Standalone mode. Next, we discuss the theory around Apache Spark to understand the fundamental concepts. Then, we go over selected topics, such as running in high availability (cluster). Finally, we discuss Spark Streaming as the entrance to the data science pipeline.

This chapter is written for people who have never touched Apache Spark before. But as you can imagine, due to space, we will not delve into many specific issues.

The following topics are covered in this chapter:

- Introducing Spark

- Spark concepts

- Working with RDD

- Running in cluster

- Spark Streaming

Introducing Spark

Perhaps Apache Spark is the most important technology in the stack. It is divided into five modules: Core, SQL, MLIB, Streaming, and GraphX. Simply put, each module deserves a book the same size of the book that you are now reading. Spark has captured the imagination of developers and analysts, simply because it takes data manipulation from large laboratories to laptops, from large interdisciplinary teams to lone enthusiasts who want to make data analysis, and from large corporate clusters to a cheap infrastructure accessible to all.

Spark is both infrastructure software and data science laboratory. Spark as an infrastructure engine can be attached to powerful tools like Apache Kafka to produce *data science pipelines*. Simultaneously, it is a data science laboratory because it represents an engine for machine learning in both a laptop and a productive cluster, from a few data kilobytes up to what the hardware capacity allows. Likewise, you can build models based on sample data and then apply them in larger datasets.

In times not so distant, installing the infrastructure for data analysis was an interdisciplinary task among database specialists, operating system and network analysts, and application engineers and architects.

What makes Apache Spark so attractive is its ability to download and run it on a small and inexpensive laptop.

Apache Spark (like all the technologies covered in this book) is an open source tool. It only requires Java version 6 or higher. All the Scala and Akka dependencies are packaged within the distribution.

© Raul Estrada and Isaac Ruiz 2016
R. Estrada and I. Ruiz, *Big Data SMACK*, DOI 10.1007/978-1-4842-2175-4_6

Apache Spark Download

Regardless of whether you use the development or production version, you must download the latest build from https://spark.apache.org/downloads.html (version 1.6.1 as of this writing).

As shown in Figure 6-1, select **Pre-built for Hadoop and later**.

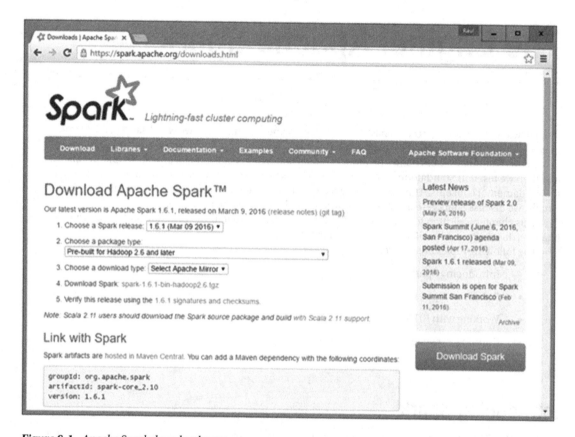

***Figure 6-1.** Apache Spark download page*

Spark has a new release every 90 days. For hard-core coders who like to work with the latest builds, try to clone the repository at https://github.com/apache/spark. The instructions for generating the build are available at https://spark.apache.org/docs/latest/building-spark.html. Both the source code and the binary prebuilds are available at this link.

To compile the Spark sources, we need the appropriate versions of Scala and the corresponding SDK. Spark source tar includes the Scala components required.

The Spark development group has done a good job keeping the dependencies. On https://spark.apache.org/docs/latest/building-spark.html, you can see the latest information about it. According to the site, to build Spark with Maven, Java version 6 or higher and Maven 3.0.4 are required.

To uncompress the package, execute the following command:

```
tar xvf spark-1.6.1-bin-hadoop2.4.tgz
```

Let's Kick the Tires

To test the installation, run the following command:

```
/opt/spark-1.6.1-bin-hadoop2.6/bin/run-example SparkPi 10
```

You should see an output like the one shown in Figure 6-2, with the line `Pi is roughly`.

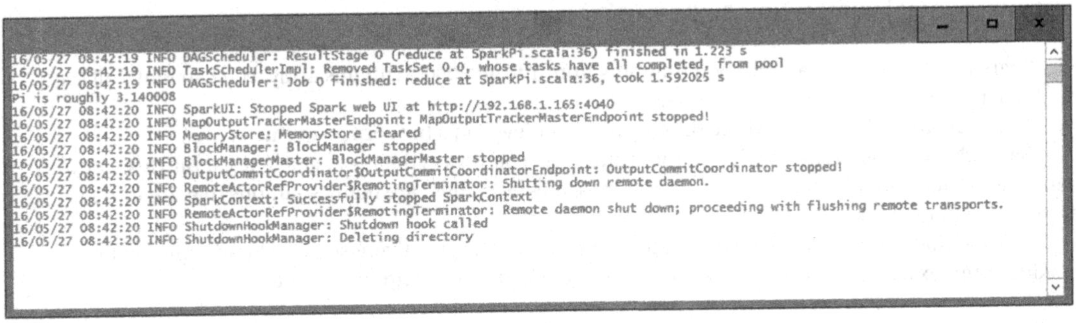

Figure 6-2. *Testing Apache Spark*

To open a Spark interactive shell, go to the bin directory and run the spark-shell:

```
$> /bin/spark-shell
```

You should see output similar to Figure 6-3 (which shows Windows 64-bit so that no one feels left out of this party):

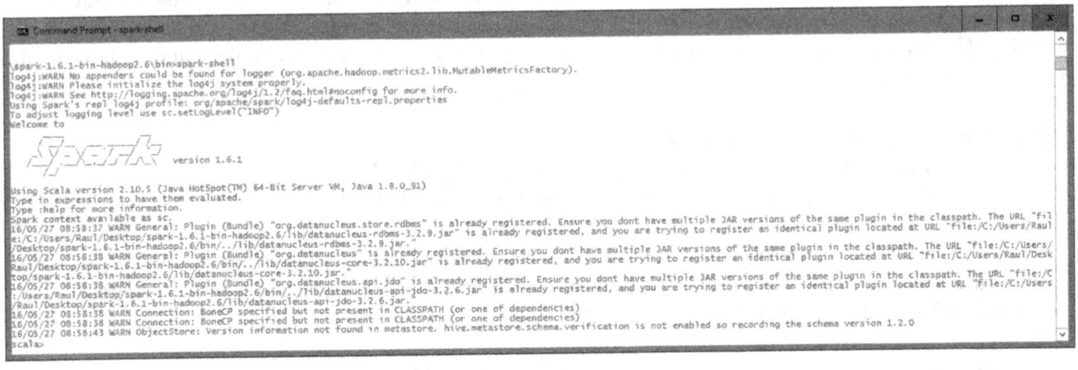

Figure 6-3. *The Apache Spark shell*

Like all modern shells, the Spark shell includes history. You can access it with the up and down arrows. There are also autocomplete options that you can access by pressing the Tab key.

As you can see, Spark runs in Scala; the Spark shell is a Scala terminal with more features. This chapter's Scala examples run without problems. You can test, as follows:

```
scala> val num = 1 to 400000
num: scala.collection.immutable.Range.Inclusive = Range (...
```

To convert our Range to a RDD (now we see it is that), do the following:

```
scala> val myRDD = sc.parallelize(num)
myRDD: org.apache.spark.rdd.RDD [Int] = ParallelCollectionRDD [0] at parallelize at <console>
```

In this case, there is a numeric RDD. Then, as you may guess, you can do all the math operations with Scala data types. Let's use only the odd numbers:

```
scala> myRDD.filter (_% 2 != 0) .collect ()
res1: Array [Int] = Array (1, 3, 5, 7, 9 ...)
```

Spark returns an int array with odd numbers from 1 to 400,000. With this array, you can make all the math operations used with Scala int arrays.

Now, you are inside Spark, where things can be achieved in a big corporate cluster.

Basically, Spark is a framework for processing large volumes of data— in gigabytes, terabytes, or even petabytes. When you work with small data volumes, however, there are many solutions that are more appropriate than Spark.

The two main concepts are the calculations and scale. The effectiveness of the Spark solution lies in making complex calculations over large amounts of data, in an expeditious manner.

Loading a Data File

Upload a text file in Spark within the Spark shell:

```
scala> val bigfile = sc.textFile ("./big/tooBigFile.txt")
```

This magically loads the tooBigFile.txt file to Spark, with each line a different entry of the RDD (explained shortly). The RDDs are very versatile in terms of scaling.

If you connect to the Spark master node, you may try to load the file in any of the different machines in the cluster, so you have to ensure that it can be accessed from all worker nodes in the cluster. In general, you always put your files in file systems like HDFS or S3. In local mode, you can add the file directly (e.g., sc. textFile ([path_to_file)). You can use the addFile()SparkContext function to make a file available to all machines in this way:

```
scala> import org.apache.spark.SparkFiles
scala> val myFile = sc.addFile( "/opt/big/data/path/bigFile.dat" )
scala> val txtFile = sc.textFile (SparkFiles.get("bigFile.txt"))
```

For example, if you load a (big) input file where each line has a lot of numbers, the first RDD file whose elements are strings (text lines) is not very helpful. To transform the string elements to an array of doubles, use your knowledge of the Scala language:

```
scala> val myArrays = textFile.map (line => line.split('').map(_. toDouble))
```

To verify that this is what you wanted, you can use the first() operator on both txtFile and myArrays to see that the first element in the txtFile is a string and in myArrays is an Array[Double].

Loading Data from S3

As part of Amazon support, you have access to a file system called Amazon S3. To access it, you need the AWS_ACCESS_KEY_ID and AWS_SECRET_ACCESS_KEY variables (to configure them, see the "Running Spark on EC2" section in this chapter).

For instance, you can use the Amazon examples on a data file from Wikipedia:

```
scala> val myWiki = sc.textFile ("S3N://bigdatademo/sample/wiki/")
```

We don't need to set our AWS credentials as parameters for the Spark shell; this is the general path form for access the S3 file system:

```
S3N://<AWS ACCESS ID>:<AWS SECRET>@bucket/path
```

As another example, you can get Wikipedia's traffic statistics from over the last 16 months at `https://aws.amazon.com/datasets/wikipedia-traffic-statistics-v2/`.

Spark Architecture

Now is a good time to discuss the Spark mechanism. Let's first talk about the architecture and then about the programming.

Parallelism is computational term used when we talk about performing operations in parallel; that is, if we have a process that works on a portion of data, we can "make copies" of that process to act simultaneously on the same portion of data. Not all processes are parallelizable. Spark's power is in its ability to do parallel computing in a simple way; this is just one of its main advantages.

When you program on your machines or laptops, the Spark shell is run locally. The work is performed in a single node. When you are working on a cluster, all you have to do is connect the same shell to the cluster to run it in parallel. Figure 6-4 explains how Spark runs on a cluster.

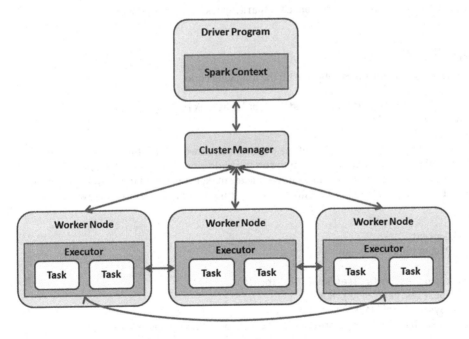

Figure 6-4. *Spark cluster with three executor nodes*

The two main concepts of Spark are the *resilient distributed dataset* (RDD) and the cluster manager. In a nutshell, the RDD is a parallelized computational abstraction of a collection. The cluster manager distributes the code and manages the data represented in the RDDs. The cluster manager has three responsibilities: controls the distribution and interaction with RDDs, distributes code, and manages the fault-tolerant execution.

Spark can work over several types of cluster managers; in this chapter, we talk about the standalone manager, and in a subsequent chapter, we talk about Apache Mesos. Hadoop Yarn is not covered in this book because we focus only on pipeline architectures, not Hadoop.

If you have Hadoop 2.0 installed, we recommend that you install Spark on Hadoop Yarn. If you have Hadoop 1.0 installed, we recommend that you use Spark Standalone. It is not suitable to install Apache Mesos and Hadoop Yarn at the same time.

The Spark driver program distributes the program classes in the cluster. The cluster manager starts the executors, one on each node, and assigns them a tasks set. When you run a program, all of this enginery runs transparently in your machines. For example, when you run on a cluster, the entire administration is transparent to you. That is Spark's power.

SparkContext

Now that you have Spark running on your laptop, let's start programming in more detail. The driver programs access the Spark core through the SparkContext object, which represents the connection between the cluster and the nodes. In the shell, Spark is always accessed through the sc variable; if you want to learn more about the sc variable, type this:

```
scala> sc
res0: org.apache.spark.SparkContext = org.apache.spark.SparkContext@4152bd0f
```

Creating a SparkContext

In a program, you can create a SparkContext object with the following code:

```
val sparkContext = new SparkContext( masterPath, "applicationName", ["SparkPath
(optional)"],["JarsList (optional)"])
```

It is always possible to hard-code the value of the parameters; however, it is best read from the environment with suitable defaults. This allows you to run the code when you change the host without recompiling it. Using local as the default for the master makes it easy to launch the application in a local testing environment. You must be careful when selecting the defaults. Here's an example snippet:

```
import spark.sparkContext._
import scala.util.Properties

val masterPath = Properties.envOrElse("MASTER","local")
val sparkHome = Properties.get("SPARK_HOME")
val jarFiles = Seq(System.get("JARS"))
val sparkContext = new SparkContext(masterPath, "MyAppName", sparkHome, jarFiles)
```

SparkContext Metadata

The SparkContext object has useful metadata (see Table 6-1); for example, the version number, the application name, and the available memory. If you recall, information about the version is displayed when you start the Spark shell.

Table 6-1. *Some Useful SparkContext Metadata*

Value	Type	Use
appName	String	The application name. If you followed the convention, this value is useful at runtime.
getConf	SparkConf	Return a copy of this SparkContext's configuration.
getExecutorMemoryStatus	Map[String, (Long, Long)]	Return a map from the slave to the maximum memory available for caching and the remaining memory available for caching. As it is distributed, it does not prevent OOM exceptions.
isLocal	Boolean	Are we running in local?
isStopped	Boolean	Are we running?
master	String	Master node name.
sparkUser	String	Spark OS username.
startTime	Long	Node start time.
version	String	Useful when testing several Spark versions.

Here are some examples of SparkContext metadata to print the Spark version, the application name, the master node's name and the memory:

```
$ bin/spark-shell

scala> sc.version
res0: String = 1.6.1

scala> sc.appName
res1: String = Spark shell

scala> sc.master
res2: String = local[*]

scala> sc.getExecutorMemoryStatus
res3: scala.collection.Map[String,(Long, Long)] = Map(localhost:52962 ->
(535953408,535953408))
```

SparkContext Methods

The SparkContext object is the main entry point for your application and your cluster. It is also used for loading and saving data. You can use it to launch additional Spark jobs and remove dependencies.
Table 6-2 shows some SparkContext methods, but you can see all the SparkContext attributes and methods at https://spark.apache.org/docs/latest/api/scala/#org.apache.spark.SparkContext$.

Table 6-2. *Some Useful SparkContext Methods*

Method	Parameter	Return	Use
addJar()	path:String	Unit	Adds jar files for all tasks to be executed on the SparkContext in the future.
addFile()	path:String	Unit	Distribute a file to all nodes on a cluster.
accumulator()	value: T name: String	Accumulator	Creates an accumulator (a distributed variable among the cluster).
cancelAllJobs()	---	Unit	Cancel all jobs (scheduled and running).
clearJobGroup()	---	Unit	Clear the current thread's job.
killExecutor()	id:String	Boolean	Request to cluster manager to kill the specified executors.
setJobDescription()	value:String	Unit	Set a human-readable description of the current job.
textFile()	path:String minPartitions: int	String	Read a text file and return it as an RDD of strings.
stop()	---	Unit	Shut down the SparkContext.

Working with RDDs

The resilient distributed dataset is Apache Spark's core concept. Spark has four design goals:

- **In-memory data storage**. This is where Apache Hadoop is defeated, because Hadoop is primarily disk storage.

- **Fault tolerant**. Achieved with two features: cluster operations and the application of linear operations on small data chucks.

- **Efficiency**. Achieved with operation parallelization between cluster parts.

- **Fast**. Achieved by minimizing data replication between cluster members.

The main idea is that with RDD, you only can perform two types of operations:

- **Transformations**. When a transformation is applied on an RDD, a new RDD is created. For example, the set operations (union, intersection, and join) or as you learned in Chapter 3, mapping, filtering, sort, and coalesce.

- **Actions**. When we apply an action over an RDD, the original RDD does not change. For example: count, collect, and first.

Computer science has a solid foundation in mathematics; all computer models have a solid mathematical model behind them. In functional programming, functions are first-class citizens; that is, functions are not modeled as objects, but are simply functions. When you apply a function to another function, the result is another function. In algebra this is known as *function composition*. If function f is applied to the function g, the operation is denoted as $f \circ g$, which is equivalent to $f(g())$.

In linear algebra, there are operations between vectors. There are vector operations whose input is various vectors and the result is a new vector (for example, vector addition). In Spark, vectors would be RDDs and operations whose return value is an RDD are equivalent to transformations.

On the other hand, there are functions whose input is several vectors and the output is a scalar value; for example, the inner product. In Spark, actions are the equivalent of these operations.

As with functional programming, there are also rules for RDDs:

- **Immutability**. In both actions and transformations, the original RDD is not modified. Yes, the concept of a "variable" value in functional programming is an aberration: it does not exist; all the things (functions, values, objects) must be immutable.

- **Resilient**. In Spark, the chain of transformations from the first RDD to the last RDD is always logged; that is, if a failure occurs (the power goes out or someone trips over the power cord), the process can be reproduced again from the beginning or from the point of failure.

- **Lazy evaluation**. Since we live in a functional context, the transformations on RDDs are always lazy. They are not executed until (and only until) the end result is required. As you saw in Chapter 3, this exists to improve performance, because it avoids unnecessary data processing and the waste of resources (usually caused by the developer).

- **Process aware**. As you saw in Chapter 4, lazy evaluation prevents deadlocks and bottlenecks, because it prevents the indefinite process of waiting for other processes' output. Recall that the lazy evaluation emulates all the operations already made and uses a "result avatar" to estimate the final result.

- **Memory storage**. By default, RDDs are born, and live and die in memory. The RDDs are stored on disk only if explicitly requested. This increases the performance terrifically, because you don't fetch them from the file system or database.

In addition, we now have the DataFrames API (since 2015). This API offers the following:

- **Scalability**. You can test kilobyte-sized data samples on your laptop, and then run the same programs on a production cluster with several terabytes of data.

- **Optimization**. The powerful Spark SQL Catalyst optimizer offers two advantages: SQL beautification and SQL optimization. It also provides source code generation from actual SQL.

- **Integration**. Smooth integration with the other members of the Spark family (Core, SQL, Streaming, MLlib, GraphX).

- **Multiformat**. Supports several data formats and storage systems.

Before continuing, we must take the time to learn about what RDDs are and what they are not. It is crucial to understand that when an RDD is defined, it actually contains no data. You only create a container for it. RDDs follow the lazy evaluation principle; an expression is not evaluated until it is necessary (i.e., when an action is requested). This means that when you try to access the data in an RDD, you could fail. The data operation to create an RDD is only performed when the data is referenced to store or catch the RDD.

This also means that when you concatenate a large number of operations, you don't have to worry about the excessive operations locking a thread. It is important to keep this in mind during application development—when you write and compile code, and even when you run the job.

Standalone Apps

You can run Spark applications in two ways: from the pretty Spark shell or from a program written in Java, Scala, Python, or R. The difference between the two modes is that when you run standalone applications, you must initialize the SparkContext, as you saw in previous sections.

To run a program in Scala or Java, it is best to use Maven (or Gradle or SBT, whichever you want). You must import the dependency to your project. At the time of this writing, the Spark version is 1.6.1 (version 2 exists, but it's very new).

The following are the Maven coordinates for version 1.6.1:

```
groupId = org.apache.spark
artifactId = spark-core_2.10
version = 1.6.1
```

Initializing the SparkContext

Once you have Spark dependencies installed in your project, the first thing that you have to do is create a SparkContext.

As you saw earlier, you must first create an object of type SparkConf to configure your application, and then build a SparkContext object from it.

```
// All the necessary imports
import org.apache.spark.SparkConf
import org.apache.spark.SparkContext
import org.apache.spark.SparkContext._
// Create the SparkConf object
val conf = new SparkConf().setMaster("local").setAppName("mySparkApp")

// Create the SparkContext from SparkConf
val sc = new SparkContext(conf)
```

The SparkConf constructor receives two parameters:

- **Cluster URL**. This is "local" when you want to run the program on one thread on the local machine, (i.e., without a cluster).

- **Application name**. This name is used to identify your application in the cluster manager UI (running in cluster mode). Here we called it mySparkApp.

Standalone Programs

We already have the necessary imports: the SparkConf object and the SparkContext object. Now let's give our program a body. It is important to note that all the stuff that runs on the Spark shell should run on Spark Standalone programs.

In all the "big data" books there is a word-count example; this book could not be the exception. Our program input is a file (yes, we already know how to load files) of the Franz Kafka novel *The Process*, in English.

The exercise objective is to see the number of times a word occurs and to see the most repeated words.

```
// We create a RDD with the the-process.txt file contents
val myfile = sc.textFile("the-process.txt")
```

```
// Then, we convert the each line text to lowercase
val lowerCase = myFile.map( line => line.toLowerCase)
// We split every line in words (strings separated by spaces)
// As we already know, the split command flattens arrays
val words = lowerCase.flatMap(line => line.split("\\s+"))
// Create the tuple (word, frequency), initial frequency is 1
val counts = words.map(word => (word, 1))
// Let's group the sum of frequencies by word, (easy isn't?)
val frequency = counts.reduceByKey(_ + _)
// Reverse the tuple to (frequency, word)
val invFrequency = frequency.map(_.swap)
// Take the 20 more frequent and prints it
invFrequency.top(20).foreach(println)
```

It is fundamental to note that everything doesn't run until the last `println` invocation. Yes, all the previous words are transformations, and the last line is the action. We will clear this up later.

Hold on, the most frequent types of words (in all human languages) are conjunctions and prepositions, so before separating each sentence into words in the third step, we filter the "stop words" in English (obviously there are better lists on Internet, this is just an example).

```
val tinytStopWords = Set("what", "of", "and", "the", "to", "it", "in", "or", "no", "that",
"is", "with", "by", "those", "which", "its", "his", "her", "me", "him", "on", "an", "if",
"more", "I", "you", "my", "your", "for" )

val words = lowerCase
.flatMap(line => line.split("\\s+"))
.filter(! tinyStopWords.contains(_))
```

Run the Program

When your program is complete, use the script located on `/bin/spark-submit` to run it. Modern Java/Scala IDEs have embedded the Spark integration to run it smoothly.

But this book is mostly read by command-line fellas and old-school soldiers. Here we show how to run it from a command line with SBT and with Maven:

```
// To run it with sbt
sbt clean package
$SPARK_HOME/bin/spark-submit \
--class com.apress.smack.WordFreq \
./target/...(as above) \
./README.md ./wordfreq

// To run it with Maven
mvn clean && mvn compile && mvn package
$SPARK_HOME/bin/spark-submit \
--class com.apress.smack.WordFreq \
./target/WordFreq-0.0.1.jar \
./README.md ./wordfreq
```

If nothing works, you can always refer to the official Spark guide at `http://spark.apache.org/docs/latest/quick-start.html`.

RDD Operations

RDDs have two types of operations: transformations and actions. Transformations are operations that receive one or more RDD as input and return a new RDD. Actions return a result to the driver program and/or store it, and/or trigger a new operation.

If you still get confused and don't know how to distinguish them, this is the rule: *transformations return RDDs; actions don't.*

Transformations

Transformations are operations with these characteristics:

- **Lazy evaluation**. Transformations are lazy operations; they aren't calculated until you perform an action or explicitly invoke the collect method. This behavior is inherited from the actor model and functional programming.

- **Element-wise**. Transformations work on each individual element of a collection; one at a time.

- **Immutable**. RDDs are immutable, thus transformations are immutable too (i.e., they can't modify the value of the RDD received as a parameter. There are no global variables).

- **Lineage graph**. Let's suppose you have a transformations sequence. We have RDDs as result of transformations in other RDDs. Spark keeps a track of each operation and of the dependencies among all the RDDs. This record, known as a *lineage graph*, is kept to recover the system from a failure. Spark always builds a lineage graph when running distributed applications on a cluster.

Table 6-3 enumerates the main transformations.

Table 6-3. Spark Main Transformations

Transformation	Purpose	Example
filter(function)	Builds a new RDD by selecting the elements on which the function returns true.	> val rdd = sc.parallelize(List("Spark", "Mesos", "Akka", "Cassandra", "Kafka")) > val k = rdd.filter(_.contains("k")) > k.collect() Result: Array[String] = Array(Spark, Akka, Kafka)
map(function)	Builds a new RDD by applying the function on each element.	> val rdd = sc.parallelize(List(1, 2, 3, 4)) > val t = rdd.map(_*5) > t.collect() Result: Array[Int] = Array(5, 10, 15, 20)
flatMap(function)	The same as map() but it returns a sequence instead of a value.	> val rdd = sc.parallelize(List("Big Data are Buzzwords", "Make Fast Data")) > val fm = rdd.flatMap(s => s.split(" ")) > fm.collect() Result: Array[String] = Array(Big, Data, are, Buzzwords, Make, Fast, Data)

(continued)

Table 6-3. (*continued*)

Transformation	Purpose	Example
reduceByKey(function, [number])	Aggregates the values of a key using the function.	> val words = fm.map(w => (w, 1)) > val wordCount = words.reduceByKey(_+_) > wordCount.collect() Result: Array[(String, Int)] = Array((are,1), (Big,1), (Fast,1), (Make,1), (Buzzwords,1), (Data,2))
groupByKey([numTasks])	Converts (K, V) to (K, Iterable<V>).	> val wc = wordCount.map{case(w,c) => (c,w)} > wc.groupByKey().collect() Result: Array[(Int, Iterable[String])] = Array((1,CompactBuffer(are, Big, Fast, Make, Buzzwords)), (2,CompactBuffer(Data)))
distinct([numTasks])	Eliminates duplicates.	> fm.distinct().collect() Result: Array[String] = Array(are, Big, Fast, Make, Buzzwords, Data)

Table 6-4 lists the main transformations on sets.

Table 6-4. *Main Transformations on Sets*

Transformation	Purpose	Example
union()	Builds a new RDD containing all elements from the source and the argument.	> val foo = sc.parallelize(List("Big", "Data")) > val bar = sc.parallelize(List("Fast", "Data")) > foo.union(bar).collect() Result: Array[String] = Array(Big, Data, Fast, Data)
intersection()	Builds a new RDD containing only common elements between the source and argument.	> foo.intersection(bar).collect() Result: Array[String] = Array(Data)
cartesian()	Builds an RDD with cross product of all elements from the source and the argument.	> foo.cartesian(bar).collect() Result: Array[(String, String)] = Array((Big,Fast), (Big,Data), (Data,Fast), (Data,Data))
subtract()	Builds a new RDD by removing common data elements between source and argument.	> foo.subtract(bar).collect() Result: Array[String] = Array(Big)

(*continued*)

Table 6-4. (*continued*)

Transformation	Purpose	Example
join(RDD, [number])	When invoked on (K,V) and (K,W), creates a new RDD with (K, (V,W))	> val foo = sc.parallelize(Seq((1, "S"), (2, "M"), (3, "A"), (1, "C"), (4, "K"))) > val bar = sc.parallelize(Seq((1, "W"), (2, "X"), (3, "Y"), (2, "Z"))) > foo.join(bar).collect() Result: Array[(Int, (String, String))] = Array((1,(S,W)), (1,(C,W)), (2,(M,X)), (2,(M,Z)), (3,(A,Y)))
cogroup(RDD, [number])	Converts (K, V) to (K, Iterable<V>).	> foo.cogroup(bar).collect() Result: Array[(Int, (Iterable[String], Iterable[String]))] = Array((4,(CompactBuffer(K),CompactBuffer())), (1,(CompactBuffer(S, C),CompactBuffer(W))), (2,(CompactBuffer(M),CompactBuffer(X, Z))), (3,(CompactBuffer(A),CompactBuffer(Y))))

Actions

Although actions return scalar (simple) values, you must never underestimate them, since the internal process can become really complex. Actions return the result to the driver program and/or write in and store the result.

Pipeline of operations are advanced sequentially, operation by operation; however, remember that everything is lazy evaluation. Flow can advance, and when it finds an action, everything is evaluated to that point. Actions trigger the evaluation of all previous transformations.

Actions always trigger an evaluation because they must always return a value; if they don't return a value or store something, they can't continue. Table 6-5 enumerates the main Spark actions.

Table 6-5. *Main Spark Actions*

Action	Purpose	Example
count()	Obtains the number of RDD elements.	> val smack = sc.parallelize(List('s', 'M', 'A', 'C', 'K')) > smack.count() Result: long = 5
collect()	Returns all the RDD elements as an array.	> val smack = sc.parallelize(List("S", "M", "A", "C", "K")) > smack.collect() Result: Array[String] = Array(S, M, A, C, K)
reduce(function)	Aggregates the RDD elements using the function.	> val smack = sc.parallelize(List(1, 5, 2, 4, 3)) > smack.reduce(_+_) // the sum of all Result: Int = 15

(*continued*)

Table 6-5. (*continued*)

Action	Purpose	Example
take(n)	Fetches the first n elements of the RDD.	> val smack = sc.parallelize(List('s', 'M', 'A', 'C', 'K')) > smack.take(4) Result: Array[Char] = Array(S, M, A, C)
foreach(function)	Executes the function in each RDD element.	> val s = sc.parallelize(List(1, 4, 2, 3)) > s.foreach(n => print("%s*7=%s ".format(n, n*7))) Result: 1*7=7 4*7=28 2*7=14 3*7=21
first()	Fetches the RDD first element, the same as take(1).	> val rdd = sc.parallelize(List(4, 3, 2, 1)) > rdd.first() Result: Int = 4
saveAsTextFile(path)	Writes the RDD content to the text file on local file system/HDFS.	> val myLogs = sc.textFile("/users/smack/evidence.log") > myLogs.filter(_.contains("Fatal")). myLogs.saveAsTextFile("/users/smack/fact.txt") Result: smack@localhost~/smack$ ls _SUCCESS part-00000 part-00001

RDD Persistence (Caching)

Now you know that RDDs support lazy evaluation. But what if you want to use the same RDD several times? If you don't do this work conscientiously, by default, Spark will recalculate the RDD and all of its dependencies each time that you apply an action on it. If not done carefully, this can be very expensive.

You can tell Spark to persist the RDD to avoid recalculating them all the time. When you persist an RDD, the nodes working with it store the RDD partitions assigned to them. If a node fails, Spark recalculates lost partitions as needed (yes, it's powerful).

You can also replicate your RDD among several nodes if you want to handle a node failure without performance implications. As shown in Table 6-6, Spark offers several levels of persistence to suit all of our scenarios and needs. Note that when writing data to disk the data is always serialized.

Table 6-6. *RDD Persistence Levels*

Persistence Level	CPU Used	Space Used	On Disk	In Memory
MEMORY_ONLY	Low	High	No	Yes
MEMORY_AND_DISK(*)	Medium	High	Some	Some
MEMORY_ONLY_SER	High	Low	No	Yes
MEMORY_AND_DISK_SER(*)	High	Low	Some	Some
DISK_ONLY	High	Low	Yes	No
OFF_HEAP (experimental)	Low	Low	Some	Some

Write to disk if there is much data stored in memory. (Note that SER means serializable)

An important caching scheme is off-heap, a mixed scheme. It was previously called Tachyon, but now it's called Alluxio (http://alluxio.org/). Note that the off-heap catching doesn't guarantee recovery after failure.

This is a code example:

```
import org.apache.spark.storage.StorageLevel
val rdd = input.map( foo )
rdd.persist( StorageLevel.DISK_ONLY )
rdd.reduce( bar )
rdd.collect()
```

Here are some points to consider:

- You must call the persist() method in the code before the first action.

- The persist() function doesn't force the evaluation.

- Spark automatically evicts old partitions using an LRU (least recently used) cache policy.

- The persist() method counterpart is the unpersist() method to manually remove RDDs from the cache.

Spark in Cluster Mode

In this chapter, we have focused on running Spark in local mode. As we mentioned, horizontal scaling is what makes Spark so powerful. To run Apache Spark on a cluster, you do not need specialized software-hardware integration engineers. To escalate, you don't need to make great efforts and stop the entire production to add more machines to your cluster.

The good news is that the same scripts that you are building on your laptop with examples that are only a few kilobytes can run on business clusters running terabytes of data. There is no need to change your code, nor invoke another API. All you have to do is test your model several times to know if it runs correctly, and then you can deploy it.

In this section, you analyze the runtime architecture of a distributed Spark application. Then you see the options to run Spark on a cluster.

Apache Spark has its own built-in standalone cluster manager. But you can run it on multiple cluster managers, including Hadoop YARN, Amazon EC2, and Apache Mesos. This topic is so large that it has its own chapter in this book.

Runtime Architecture

Before running Spark on a cluster, it's important to understand the distributed Spark architecture.

As shown in Figure 6-5, Spark uses a master/slave architecture. The master is called the *driver* and the slaves are called *executors*. When running on a single machine, there is a distributed architecture: a driver with several executors. The driver runs in its own Java process, and each executor runs in a separate Java process. This architecture is made on the actor model.

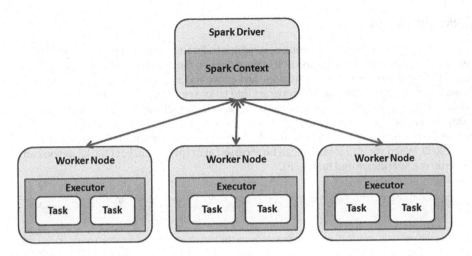

Figure 6-5. *Distributed Spark application*

The driver and executors set is known as a Spark application. If you have more than one machine, the Spark application must be launched using the cluster manager service. The Spark application architecture is always the same; it does not matter if it's clustered or not.

In a typical Spark clustered application architecture, each physical machine has its own executor. You will see several strategies to know when an executor dies or goes offline.

Driver

The driver is the process where the SparkContext runs. It is in charge of creating and executing transformations and actions on RDDs. When you run the Spark shell command on your laptop, you are actually creating a driver program. Its first task is to create the SparkContext, called sc. When the driver program dies, the entire application dies.

The following sections explain the two responsibilities in the life of a driver program: dividing a program into tasks and scheduling tasks on executors.

Divide a Program into Tasks

The Spark driver is responsible for splitting the *user program*, which could be programmed in an inefficient way in execution units called *tasks*.

A user program basically applies transformations and actions into one or more RDDs to generate new RDDs and calculate and/or store data.

Another task of the Spark driver is to generate an operation's *directed acyclic graph* (DAG). With this graph, the driver knows which tasks are assigned to which node; so if you lost a node, the driver knows at which point it was at and how to assign the lost node's tasks to the remaining nodes.

The driver also does pipeline optimizations; it splits the DAG into stages. Each stage has multiple tasks. In Spark, the task is the smallest work unit; a normal program can launch thousands of tasks.

Scheduling Tasks on Executors

Given a physical execution plan, the Spark driver coordinates which tasks are performed by each executor node. When an executor starts operating, it registers itself in the driver, so the driver always has an entire view of all the executor nodes. Each executor is a standalone Java process that can run tasks and store RDDs.

When a program runs, the driver subdivides the program into tasks, sees all the available executor nodes, and tries to balance the workload among them. The driver also knows which part of the data that each node has, in order to rebuild everything at the end.

The driver displays its information on the Web, so that the user can always see what is happening; by default, it runs on port 4040. When you run locally, it can be accessed at http://localhost:4040, as you can see in Figure 6-6 (let's run the Spark shell and browse it).

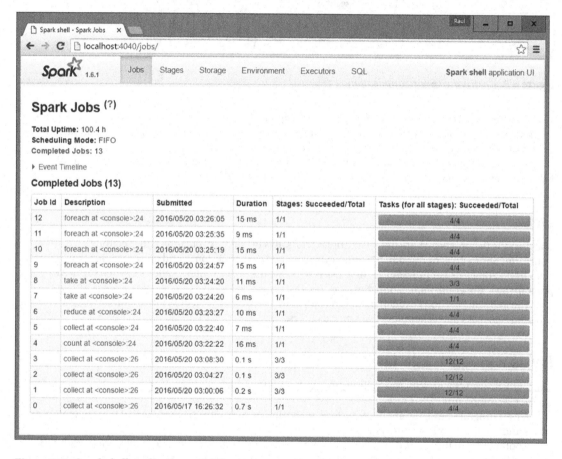

Figure 6-6. Spark shell application web UI

Executor

Executors are responsible for running the individual tasks of a given Spark job. Executors are launched when you start the Spark application; they live while the Spark application lives.

Executors have two roles:

- Run the assigned tasks and deliver results to the driver.

- Provide in-memory storage for RDDs. A program called Block Manager runs on each executor and manages memory and RDDs.

When running Spark in local mode, the driver and executors run in the same process. This is for development purposes; it is not recommended in a production environment.

Cluster Manager

Spark depends on a cluster manager to coordinate and launch the executors. The cluster manager that ships with the Spark distribution is called the *standalone manager*, but it is a pluggable component. You can change it and use a custom cluster manager like Hadoop Yarn, Amazon EC2, or Apache Mesos.

It is important to note that the terms *driver* and *executor* are used when talking about the Spark application. When we talk about the cluster manager, we use the terms *master* and *worker*. It is important not confuse the terms or to exchange them, because they are different concepts.

Regardless of the cluster manager that you use, Spark provides a single script, called spark-submit, to launch the program. The spark-submit script can connect to different managers through various options and manage the cluster resources that the application needs.

Program Execution

When you run a Spark application on a cluster, these are the steps followed by the program:

1. The user runs the spark-submit shell.

2. The spark-submit shell launches the driver program, and calls the user program's main() method.

3. The driver program establishes the connection to the cluster manager, which has the slave machines list. Then, the necessary resources are requested to launch the executors.

4. The cluster manager launches executors in each slave node.

5. The driver program analyzes, divides, and distributes the user application, sending each executor its tasks.

6. The tasks run in the executors, calculating and storing the results.

7. The user program ends when the exit() method in the main()method is invoked, or when the SparkContext stop() method is called.

8. The driver program ends the executors and frees the cluster manager's resources.

Application Deployment

Spark uses the spark-submit tool to send jobs to the cluster manager.

When you run a program in local mode, you only invoke spark-submit passing your script name or jar file as a parameter.

When you run a program in cluster mode, you have to pass additional parameters—for example, the size of each executor process.

The --master flag specifies the cluster URL to which you want to connect. In this case, spark:// means that we are using Spark in stand-alone mode.

For example:

```
bin/spark-submit --master spark://skynet:7077 --executor-memory 10g Terminator.jar
```

Here we indicate that we will run our Terminator program in stand-alone cluster mode in the master node called SkyNet and each executor node will have 10 gigabytes of memory.

In addition to the cluster URL, spark-submit has several options to specify how you want to run your application. These options are in of two categories:

- **Scheduling data.** The amount of resources that each job will have.

- **Dependencies**. The files and libraries available in the slaves.

Table 6-7 lists and describes some of the spark-submit flags.

Table 6-7. *spark-submit Flags*

Flag	Purpose
--master	The cluster manager to connect to (sample values explained in Table 6-8).
--deploy-mode	Indicates if the program is launched in local mode (client) or cluster mode. In local mode, the driver is launched where spark-submit is launched. The default value is client mode.
--class	The main application class is Java/Scala.
--name	Human-readable name for your application, as displayed in Spark web UI.
--jars	List of jar files to upload on application classpath.
--files	List of files uploaded on the application's working directory on each node.
--executor-memory	Memory for executors: k for kilobytes, m for megabytes, g for gigabytes.
--driver-memory	Memory for the driver process: k for kilobytes, m for megabytes, g for gigabytes.
--conf prop=value	A single configuration property value in key-value form.
--properties-file	A configuration file with properties in key-value form.

Table 6-8 lists a few example values that the --master flag could have.

Table 6-8. *Master Flag Sample Values*

Value	Meaning
spark://host:port	Connect to a cluster in stand-alone mode at specified host and port. 7077 is the default port for a stand-alone master.
mesos://host:port	Connect to a Mesos cluster at the specified host and port. 5050 is the default port for the Mesos master.
local	Local mode master with a single core.
local[N]	Local mode master with N cores.
local[*]	Local mode master using as many cores as the machine has.

Now you are able to read this:

```
$ ./bin/spark-submit \
--master spark://skynet:7077 \
--deploy-mode cluster \
--class com.cyberdyne.Terminator \
--name "T1000 model" \
--jars neuralNetwork.jar,geneticAlgorithm.jar \
--total-executor-cores 300 \
--executor-memory 10g \
terminator.jar
```

Here we indicate that we will run our terminator.jar program:

- In stand-alone cluster mode in the SkyNet master node on port 7077

- The driver program is launched in cluster mode

- The main class is com.cyberdyne.Terminator

- The application display name is T1000 model

- The neuralNetwork.jar and geneticAlgorithm.jar files are used

- Each executor node uses 300 cores and has 10 gigabytes of memory

Running in Cluster Mode

This section discusses some of the most common methods to install Spark in cluster mode. On a single laptop, Spark is excellent for developing and testing; but in practice, it is necessary to know how to install Spark with built-in scripts on a dedicated cluster via SSH (Secure Shell). This section covers how to deploy on a cluster in Spark Standalone and with Mesos. This section also covers how to deploy Spark in the cloud with Amazon EC2.

Spark Standalone Mode

When you run bin/start-master.sh, you start an individual master. When you run sbin/start-slaves.sh, you start a worker. The default port of the Spark master is always 8080. Because no one wants to go to each machine and run scripts by hand in each, there is a set of useful scripts in the /bin directory that can help you run your servers.

A prerequisite to use any of the scripts is to have passwordless SSH access from the master to all worker machines. It is always advisable to create a special user to run Spark on all machines. In this book, the examples use the name *sparkuser*. From the master, you can run the ssh-keygen command to generate the SSH keys. When an RSA key is generated, by default, it is stored in ~/.ssh/id_rsa.pub. You have to add it to each host in ~/.ssh/authorized_keys.

The Spark administration scripts require that user names match. If this is not the case, you can configure alternative user names in ~/.ssh/config.

Now that you have SSH access to the machines, it's time to configure Spark. There is a template in the conf/spark-env.sh.template directory, which should be copied to conf/spark-env.sh. Table 6-9 lists some of the environment variables.

Table 6-9. *Spark Environment Variables*

Name	Purpose	Default value
MESOS_NATIVE_LIBRARY	Points to Mesos installation directory.	---
SCALA_HOME	Points to Scala installation directory.	---
SPARK_MASTER_IP	The IP address where the Spark master listens and where the workers connect to; for example, a public one.	hostname command output
SPARK_MASTER_PORT	The port number where the Spark master listens.	7077
SPARK_MASTER_WEBUI_PORT	The port number for the master web user interface.	8080
SPARK_MASTER_OPTS	Configuration properties that apply only to the master in the form of "-Dx=y".	---
SPARK_WORKER_CORES	Number of cores to be used by the worker.	Total number of cores
SPARK_WORKER_MEMORY	Amount of memory to be used by the worker.	Total system memory minus 1GB; if you have less than 1GB, it's 512MB.
SPARK_WORKER_PORT	The port number on which the worker runs on.	Random
SPARK_WORKER_WEBUI_PORT	The port number of the worker web user interface.	8081
SPARK_WORKER_DIR	Directory on which files from the worker are stored.	SPARK_HOME/work
SPARK_WORKER_OPTS	Configuration properties that apply only to the worker in the form of "-Dx=y".	---
SPARK_DAEMON_MEMORY	Memory to allocate to the Spark master and worker daemons.	1GB
SPARK_DAEMON_JAVA_OPTS	JVM options for the Spark master and worker daemons in the form of "-Dx=y".	---

Once the configuration is made, you must start the cluster. We highly recommend that you install the pssh tool, which is a set of tools that includes pscp SSH. The pscp command makes it easy to secure copying between hosts (although it takes a little while); for example:

```
pscp -v -r -h conf/slaves -l sparkuser ../spark-1.6.1 ~/
```

When you have finished changing the settings, you need to distribute the configuration to workers, as shown here:

```
pscp -v -r -h conf/slaves -l sparkuser conf/spark-env.sh ~/spark-1.6.1/conf/spark-env.sh
```

After you have copied the files, you are ready to start the cluster. Use these scripts: sbin/start-all.sh, sbin/start-master.sh, and sbin/start-slaves.sh.

It is important to note that `start-all.sh` and `start-master.sh` are assumed to be running on the master node in the cluster. All scripts start demonizing, so there is no problem running them on the screen:

```
ssh master bin/start-all.sh
```

In the event that you get a java.lang.NoClassDefFoundError: scala/ScalaObject error, check that you have Scala installed on the host and that the SCALA_HOME environment variable is set properly.

Spark scripts assume that the master has Spark installed in the same directory as your workers. If this is not the case, you must edit `bin/spark-config.sh` to point to the correct directories.

Table 6-10 shows the commands provided by Spark to manage the cluster. If you want more information, go to `http://spark.apache.org/docs/latest/spark-standalone.html#cluster-launch-scripts`.

Table 6-10. *Spark Cluster Administration Commands*

Command	Purpose
`bin/slaves.sh <command>`	Runs the provided command on all of the worker hosts. For example, to show how long each hosts worker has been up: `bin/slave.sh uptime`
`bin/start-all.sh`	Starts the master and all the worker hosts. Must be run on the master.
`bin/start-master.sh`	Starts the master host. Must be run on the master.
`bin/start-slaves.sh`	Starts all the worker hosts.
`bin/start-slave.sh`	Starts a specific worker host.
`bin/stop-all.sh`	Stops all master and workers hosts.
`bin/stop-master.sh`	Stops the master host.
`bin/stop-slaves.sh`	Stops all the worker hosts.

Now the Spark cluster is running. As shown in Figure 6-7, there is a useful web UI running in the master on port 8080, and in workers running on port 8081. The web UI contains important information about the workers' current and past jobs.

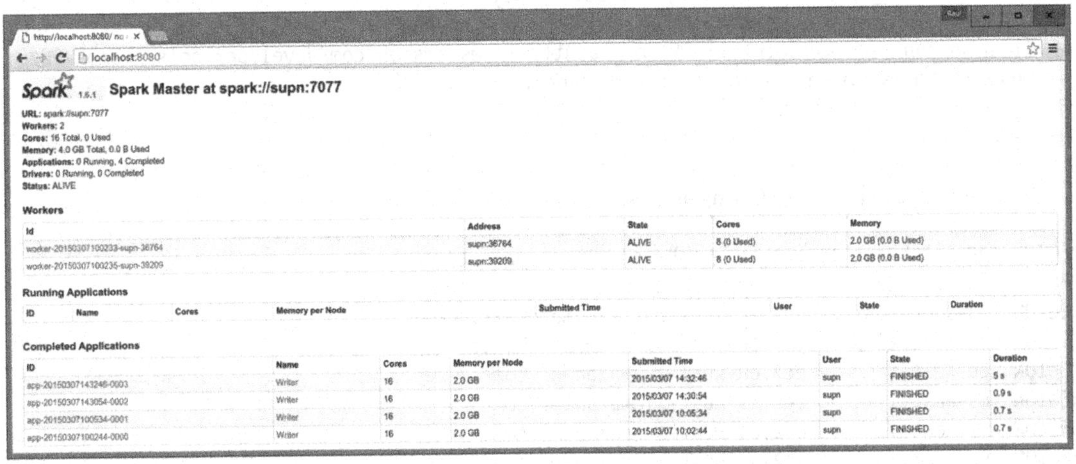

Figure 6-7. *Spark Master UI*

Now that you have a cluster up and running, you can do several things with it. As with single host examples, you have the same scripts to run Spark examples on a cluster.

All the example programs are in the examples/src/main/scala/spark/examples/ directory and take the master parameter, which points them to the master IP host. If you are running on the master host, you can run the example:

```
./run spark.examples.GroupByTest spark://'hostname':7077
```

If you get a java.lang.UnsupportedClassVersionError error, it is because you need to update the JDK. Always use the supported versions. To check which version compiled your Spark distribution, use the command:

```
java -verbose -classpath ./core/target/scala-2.11.8/classes/ spark.SparkFiles | head -n 20
```

Version 49 is JDK 1.5, version 50 is JDK 1.6, and version 60 is JDK 1.7

If you cannot connect to the host, make sure that you have configured your master to listen to all IP addresses.

Running Spark on EC2

The ec2 directory contains the scripts to run a Spark cluster in Amazon EC2. These scripts can be used to run Spark in single or cluster mode. Spark can also run on Elastic MapReduce, which is the Amazon solution for MapReduce cluster management.

The final configuration to run Spark in EC2 is at http://spark.apache.org/docs/latest/ec2-scripts.html.

To begin, you must have EC2 enabled in your Amazon account. It should generate a key pair for the Spark cluster. This can be done at https://portal.aws.amazon.com/gp/aws/securityCredentials. Remember that the key pairs are generated by region. You must make sure to generate them in the same region where you run your hosts. You can also choose to upload a SSH public key instead of generating a new one. They are sensible, so you have to be sure to keep them in a safe place. In our environments, we need two environment variables, AWS_ACCESS_KEY_ID and AWS_SECRET_ACCESS_KEY, which are available from our EC2 scripts:

```
export AWS_ACCESS_KEY_ID = {our} AWS access key
export AWS_SECRET_ACCESS_KEY = {our} AWS secret key
```

There are some scripts provided by Amazon at http://aws.amazon.com/developertools/Amazon-EC2. To check that everything is running correctly, type this command:

```
$ Ec2-describe-regions
```

That should result in the following output:

```
REGION   ap-northeast-1   ec2.ap-northeast-1.amazonaws.com
REGION   ap-southeast-1   ec2.ap-southeast-1.amazonaws.com
REGION   ap-southeast-2   ec2.ap-southeast-2.amazonaws.com
REGION   eu-central-1     ec2.eu-central-1.amazonaws.com
REGION   eu-west-1        ec2.eu-west-1.amazonaws.com
REGION   us-east-1        ec2.us-east-1.amazonaws.com
REGION   us-west-1        ec2.us-west-1.amazonaws.com
REGION   us-west-2        ec2.us-west-2.amazonaws.com
REGION   sa-east-1        ec2.sa-east-1.amazonaws.com
```

The Spark EC2 script automatically generates a group of different security and firewall rules to run the Spark cluster. By default, our Spark cluster is accessible on port 8080. For security, we strongly recommend changing the 0.0.0.0/0 address in the spark_ec2.py script with our public IP address.

To start the cluster, use this command:

```
./ec2/spark-ec2 -k spark-keypair -i pk-{....}.pem -s 1 launch lePetitCluster
```

Where {....}.pem indicates the path to our private key.

If you get a "not being reliable to SSH to the master" error, it is because the key can be accessed by others users. Try changing the access permissions to the key so that only one user can read it. If more users can read it, the SSH will refuse it.

If you get the "cannot yet SSH script to the master" error, it is because we are having a race condition; the hosts are reporting them as alive. Try changing the -w in setup_cluster by using a sleep of 120 seconds.

If you get a "transient error while launching a cluster" error, try to run the script with the --resume option.

This makes the scaffolding to make a cluster with a master and a worker node with all default values. The next task is to verify that the firewall rules work. Access the master on port 8080.

The JPS command gives the following information about our cluster:

```
root @ ip-172-31-45-56 ~] $ jps
1904 NameNode
2856 Jps
2426 MasterNameNode
2078 SecondaryNodeName
```

This information is about the name of Spark master, the Hadoop node, and slave nodes.

You can take the example of Pi that you ran on your machine at the beginning of this chapter:

```
cd spark
bin/run-example SparkPi 10
```

To terminate the instances, use this command:

```
ec2/spark-ec2 destroy <cluster name>
```

To learn all the options that the spark-ec2 command has, run this:

```
ec2/spark-ec2 -help
```

There are many types of EC2 instances available; the type has an important impact on the cluster performance. The type can be specified with --instance-type = [typeName]. If you need a lot of memory, you can specify it here.

By default, the same instance type is used for masters and workers. To specify a different type of master you use --master-instance-type = [typeName].

EC2 has also instances of the type GPU, which are very powerful if you run on Envidia graphic cards because they usually have hundreds of GPUs at a very low cost. The GPU instance type is useful when you run a worker, if the master is not used. It is important to note that EC2 performance on the GPU may be lower than when testing locally, because you have more I/O imposed by the hypervisor.

EC2 scripts use the Amazon Machine Images (AMI) provided by the Spark development team; they are enough for most applications.

Running Spark on Mesos

This book devotes an entire chapter on Mesos (Chapter 7), but we must include a special mention in this Spark chapter.

Mesos is a cluster management platform to run multiple distributed applications (or frameworks) on a cluster. Mesos intelligently manages and runs clusters of Spark, Hadoop, Cassandra, Akka, and Kafka. Mesos can run Spark as separate Mesos tasks or run all in a single Mesos task. Mesos quickly scales horizontally to manage clusters beyond the size that individual Python scripts allow.

Mesos has a large number of configuration scripts that you can use. For Ubuntu installations, use configure.ubuntu-lucid-64. In addition to the Spark requirements, you need to ensure that you have the Python C header files installed. Since Mesos must be installed on all of your machines, you can use Mesos to configure other machines:

```
./configure --prefix=/home/sparkuser/mesos && make && make check && make install
```

As with the Spark Standalone mode configuration, you must ensure that Mesos nodes can find each other.

Let's begin by adding the master hostname to mesosprefix/var/mesos/deploy/masters and all the worker hostnames to mesosprefix/var/mesos/deploy/slaves. Then point the workers to the master in mesosprefix/var/mesos/conf/mesos.conf.

Once Mesos is configured on your machines, you need to configure Spark to run on Mesos. This is as simple as copying the conf/spark-env.sh.template file to conf/spark-env.sh and updating the MESOS_NATIVE_LIBRARY variable to point to the path where Mesos is installed.

Then copy the build to all machines using this secure shell copy command:

```
pscp -v -r -h  -l sparkuser ./mesos /home/sparkuser/mesos
```

To start Mesos clusters, use mesosprefix/sbin/mesos-start-cluster.sh. Use mesos://[host]:5050 as the master.

Well, that's roughly what you have to do to run an Apache Spark cluster on Apache Mesos.

Submitting Our Application

To submit our application to a standalone cluster manager, type this:

```
spark-submit --master spark://masterNodeHost:masterNodePort appName
```

Previously, you saw the spark-submit command syntax. Now just change the master node address, and that's it.

The cluster URL is also displayed in the cluster administrator web UI at http://[masternode]:8080. The host name and port should exactly match the URL present in the web UI. As administrators, we can configure ports other than 7077.

The standalone cluster manager has a --deploy-mode option:

- **Client mode** (local, default). The driver runs in the same process as spark-submit. If you shut down the spark-submit, your cluster goes down.

- **Cluster mode**. The driver is launched as a different process on a worker node. You can shut down the machine on which spark-submit is running and everything will continue running.

For each executor node, the `--total-executor-cores` and `--executor-memory` parameters specify the number of cores and the available memory. A common error is to ask for more resources than can be assigned. In this case, the cluster manager can't start the executor nodes. Always check that your cluster has the resources that you state in the parameters.

Configuring Resources

In the standalone cluster manager, the resources are controlled by two variables:

- `--executor-memory` argument of the spark-submit command

- The total memory on each executor. By default, this value is set to 1GB; unfortunately, in production environments, one gigabyte of memory assigned to each executor won't be enough.

- `--total-executor-cores` argument of the spark-submit command

- The total number of cores used on each executor. The default value is unlimited (i.e., the application starts an executor on each available node in the cluster).

To check your current parameters, you can browse the standalone cluster manager's web UI at `http://[masterNode]:8080`.

By default, the standalone cluster manager disperses the executors onto the largest number of machines available. For example, suppose you have an eight-node cluster and each machine has four cores. You launch the application with `--total-executor-cores 6`. Spark will raise only six executors, and tends to use the largest number of machines possible (i.e., an executor on each machine, leaves two nodes without an executor).

If you want to use the fewest number of nodes possible, change the spark.deploy.spreadOut configuration property to false in the `conf/spark-defaults.conf` configuration file. If we turn off this flag in our example, we will use only two machines: one with four executors and the other with two executors. The other six machines won't run executors.

These settings affect all the applications on the cluster, so use it with caution.

High Availability

You saw how to specify the cluster mode in the Standalone cluster manager deploy mode, so if the spark-submit process dies, the manager doesn't also die. This is because the driver runs on one member of the cluster.

You want to keep your manager running while the last node is still standing. To increase manager life, there is a top-notch tool called Apache ZooKeeper, which is discussed in Chapter 7.

Spark Streaming

Life is a continuous process, it is not discrete. Life is a continuous flow.

As we mentioned in earlier chapters, the benefits of the data are greater when the information is fresher. Many machine learning computations should be calculated in real time from streaming data.

Spark Streaming is the Apache Spark module for managing data flows. Most of Spark is built over the RDD concept. Spark Streaming introduces a new concept: discretized streams, known as DStreams. A DStream is an information sequence related to time. Note that a DStream is internally a sequence of RDDs, thus the name *discretized*.

Just as RDDs has two operations, DStreams also have two types of operations: *transformations* (results in another DStream) and *output operations*, which are designed to store information on external systems. DStreams have many of same the operations available to RDDs, plus time-related operations, such as sliding windows.

Unlike batch operations, Spark Streaming applications require additional configurations to provide 24/7 services. Let's talk about resetting applications in the event of a failure and discuss how to configure automatic restarts.

Spark Streaming Architecture

Spark Streaming uses the microbatch architecture, in which streaming is considered a continuous series of small batches of data (see Figure 6-8). The magic of Spark Streaming is receiving a continuous flow and splitting it into small data chunks.

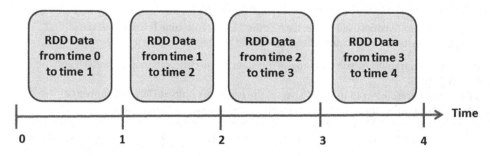

Figure 6-8. *A DStream is an RDD sequence*

Batches are generated at regular time intervals; if two data chunks come in the same time window, they are included in the same data batch. The batch size is determined by the parameter *batch interval*, which usually has a value between 500 milliseconds and several seconds. The developer specifies this value.

As you can see in Figure 6-9, the primary Spark Streaming task is to receive a data stream from multiple sources, and then build a DStream, which is a sequence of RDDs. Each RDD corresponds to a time slice of the original flow.

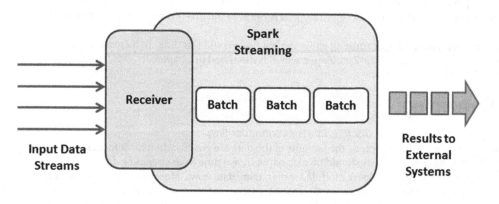

Figure 6-9. *Spark Streaming operation*

We can create DStreams from input sources or through applying transformations to other DStreams. The DStreams support most of the operations that RDDs support. Additionally, DStreams have "stateful" operations to aggregate data across time.

In addition to transformations, DStreams support output operations, which are similar to actions in the aspect that RDDs write to external systems; but Spark Streaming batches run periodically, producing the output batch.

For each input source, Spark launches streaming receivers, which are tasks that run on executors, gather data from information sources, and store it in RDDs. The receivers are also responsible for replicating data among other executors to support fault tolerance. This data is stored in the memory of executors in the same way as the RDDs. As shown in Figure 6-10, the StreamingContext in the driver program periodically runs Spark jobs to process this data and combine them with the new RDDs.

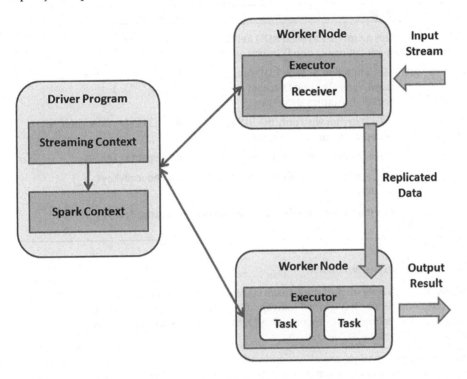

Figure 6-10. *Spark Streaming execution with Spark components*

The same fault tolerance properties offered by RDDs are also offered with DStreams. In the event of a failure, Spark can recalculate the DStreams at any point in time. However, the recalculation can take time, especially if the rebuild goes back to the beginning of the execution.

Spark Streaming provides a mechanism called *checkpointing* that periodically saves the state to a reliable file system. Typically, a checkpoint occurs every five to ten data batches. When a failure occurs, Spark restores from the last checkpoint.

Transformations

Transformations on DStreams can be grouped into stateless or stateful.

- **Stateless**. The data of each processing batch doesn't depend on the data from previous batches. These include the RDD transformations such as map(), reduce(), and filter().

- **Stateful.** The data or intermediate results from previous batches are used to calculate the current batch's results. These include transformations based on sliding windows and tracking status over time.

Stateless Transformations

Stateless transformations are common RDD transformations applied to each RDD on the DStream. Table 6-11 enumerates the main stateless transformations:

Table 6-11. *Main Stateless Transformations*

Transformation	Purpose	Example
map(function)	Applies a function to each RDD in the DStream, returning one DStream as a result.	ds.map(_*3)
flatMap(function)	Applies a function to each RDD in the DStream, returning one DStream with the content of the returned iterators.	ds.flatMap(str => str. split(" "))
filter(function)	Builds a DStream with only the RDDs evaluated with true on the function.	ds.filter(_.contains("k"))
repartition(number)	Changes the number of DStream partitions.	ds.repartition(9)
reduceByKey(function, [number])	Combines the values with the same key in each batch.	ds.reduceByKey(_+_)
groupByKey()	Groups the values with the same key in each batch.	ds.groupByKey()

Bullet points about stateless transformations:

- **Individual.** Although it seems as if the transformation is applied to the whole DStream, it is not. Actually, it is applied individually to each batch element (RDD) of the DStream. For example, with reduceByKey(), the function is applied on each individual RDD, not on the whole DStream.

- **Join.** Stateless transformations can also combine data from multiple DStreams. For example, DStreams have the same join transformations than RDDs, these are cogroup(), join(), and leftOuterJoin(). You can use these operations to perform a join in each DStream batch.

- **Merge.** You can merge the contents of two different DStreams by using the union() operation, or by using StreamingContext.union() to merge several DStreams.

- **Reuse.** DStreams provide the powerful operator called transform() and can operate directly on the RDDs within a DStream. This operation is called on each element of the DStream, producing a new DStream. If you have written code for some RDDs and you want to reuse in Spark Streaming, the transform() method is a good option.

- **Transform.** In addition to StreamingContext.transform(), you can combine several DStreams using DStream.transformWith (anotherDStream, function).

Stateful Transformations

Stateful transformations are DStream operations that track data across time; data from old batches are used to generate new batches.

There are two types of stateful transformations:

- **Windowed transformations**: Operates on data over a window duration.

- **Update state by key**: Tracks the status between the same key events; for example, a user session.

Stateful transformations require checkpointing to enable fault tolerance.

Windowed Operations

Windowed operations calculate results in a period longer than the StreamingContext batch interval time, which allows it to combine the results of several batches.

Windowed operations require two parameters: the window duration and the slide duration. Both must be multiples of the StreamingContext batch interval.

- The window duration states the number of previous batches that will be considered; this is the formula:

- *Batches considered = Window duration/Batch interval*

- Using Figure 6-11 as an example, a DStream with an interval of 2 seconds and a window duration of 6 seconds considers only the last six batches.

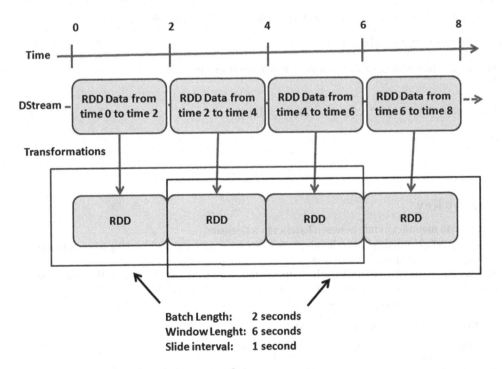

Figure 6-11. Windowed operations example

- The slide duration indicates how often you want to calculate the results; the default value is the duration of batch interval.

- For example, if you have a batch interval of 10 seconds and you calculate our window every 2 seconds, you must change your slide duration to 20 seconds.

The simplest operation that can be performed on a DStream is window(); it returns information about the current window to the DStream.

```
window(windowLength, slideInterval)
```

Purpose: Returns a new DStream computed from windowed batches of the source DStream. Example:

```
val wind = lines.window(Seconds(30),Seconds(10));
wind.foreachRDD( rdd => { rdd.foreach( x => println(x+ " ")) })
```

Output:

```
10 10 20 20 10 30 20 30 40 // drops 10
```

Spark Streaming provides other windowed operations to improve efficiency. For example, reduceByWindow() and reduceByKeyAndWindow() allow you to make reductions to each window in a very efficient way. They have a special form that calculates the reduction incrementally and considers only the input and output data.

Finally, to count data, DStream offers the following:

- countByWindow() returns a DStream with the number of elements in each window.

- countByValueAndWindow() returns a DStream with the counts of each value.

```
countByWindow( windowLength, slideInterval )
```

Purpose: Returns a new sliding window count of the elements in a stream. Example:

```
lines.countByWindow( Seconds(30), Seconds(10) ).print()
```

Output:

```
1 2 3 3
```

Update State by Key

Sometimes you need to maintain a state between batches in a DStream.

The updateStateByKey()method provides access to DStream state variables by taking a function that specifies how to update each key status given new events.

Using the updateStateByKey() method with an update function(event, oldState) takes the past event (with some key) and its previous state, and returns a new state to make the update.

The following are the parameters of this function:

- **events**. Lists events in the current batch (can be empty)

- **newState**. (Optional) If you want to delete the previous state.

The result of updateStateByKey() is a new DStream with RDD in pairs (key, state) at each time frame.

Output Operations

Output operations specify what to do with the data transformed into a stream. It could be printed on the screen or stored in a database, for example.

As with the RDD lazy operations, if there is no output operation applied to a DStream or any of its dependents, the DStream won't be evaluated. In the same way, if there is no output operations on a StreamingContext, it won't start.

Usually, an output operation used for debugging is a simple print() method. Printing the results on screen counts as an output operation. When going into production, it is vital to consider this. If you remove all the print(), you may be leaving your program without output operations, and it won't run.

Once our program is debugged, we can use output operations to store our results. Spark Streaming has the RDD save() operation for DStreams. Like the RDD operation, it takes the directory on the file system where you want to store results. Each batch's results are stored in subdirectories of the specified directory, with the time and the specified suffix as the file name.

Finally, foreachRDD() is a generic output operation used to make computations on each RDD of the DStream. It is similar to transform(). It gives also the time of each batch, which saves each time period in a different location.

24/7 Spark Streaming

Spark Streaming provides a mechanism to ensure fault tolerance. If the input data is stored reliably, Spark Streaming always calculates the result from it, providing the correct semantics (i.e., as if the data had been processed without failing nodes).

Spark Streaming applications that run 24/7 need special installation. The first step is to enable checkpointing on a reliable storage system: HDFS or Amazon S3. Also, note that you must deal with the driver program fault tolerance, changing some portion of the code.

Checkpointing

Checkpointing is the primary mechanism to enable fault tolerance in Spark Streaming. Spark Streaming allows you to periodically save the application data in a reliable file system, such as HDFS, or Amazon S3. Checkpointing has two purposes:

- **Limits** the state to be recomputed when a fault occurs. Spark Streaming recalculates the state using a lineage graph of transformations; checkpointing tells you how far back you should go.

- **Driver program** fault tolerance. If the driver program of a streaming application crashes, you can start it again and recover from the last checkpoint. Spark Streaming reads how much had processed and will resume from that point.

For these reasons checkpointing is important when you run production Spark Streaming applications.

Note that when running in local mode, Spark Streaming won't run a stateful operation if you don't have checkpointing enabled. In this case, you can use a local file system. In a production environment, you should use a replicated file system, such as HDFS, Amazon S3, or NFS.

Spark Streaming Performance

Spark Streaming has specific considerations in addition to Spark performance considerations.

Parallelism Techniques

A common way to reduce batch processing time is by increasing the parallelism. There are three ways to increase it.

- **Increasing parallelism**. For operations such as reduceByKey(), you can specify parallelism as an operation parameter.

- **Adding receptors**. Receptors can be a bottleneck if there are many records to read and distribute for a single machine. You can add more recipients by creating multiple input DStreams, which creates multiple receivers, and then apply a union() operation to merge into a single stream.

- **Repartitioning data**. If you can't increase the receivers number, you can redistribute the input data by explicitly repartitioning it using the repartition() method.

Window Size and Batch Size

A perfect batch size is a common quest. For most applications, 500 milliseconds is a good number for the minimum batch size. The best method is to start the minimum size batch at a large number, about 10 seconds, and decrease it until reaching the optimal size. If the processing times remain consistent, you can continue decreasing the batch size, but if the time increases, you have found your number.

Similarly, with windowed operations, the interval to calculate a result has great performance impact. If it's a bottleneck, consider increasing this interval for expensive calculations.

Garbage Collector

Garbage collection is problem associated with JVM. You can minimize garbage collection pauses by enabling the concurrent Mark-and-Sweep garbage collector. Generally, this consumes more resources but has fewer pauses.

If you do not know how to enable it, use -XX: +UseConcMarkSweepGC in spark.executor. extraJavaOptions when launching spark-submit. To use the garbage collector less, you can decrease the GC pressure; for example, by caching RDDs in serialized form.

Summary

This chapter took a very quick look at the engine. You learned how to download, install, and test Apache Spark. You learned about Spark's main concepts: RDD, run applications, and the RDD operations: transformations and actions. You also saw how to run Apache Spark in cluster mode, how to run the driver program, and how to achieve high availability. Finally, you took a look at Spark Streaming, stateless and stateful transformations, output operations, how to enable 24/7, and how to improve Spark Streaming performance.

In the following chapters, you will see how Apache Spark is the engine of the stack. All the other SMACK technologies are related to Spark.

CHAPTER 7

The Manager: Apache Mesos

We are reaching the end of this trip. In this chapter, you will learn how to create your own cluster in a simple way.

The M in SMACK gives us the guidelines to reuse physical or virtual resources, so that you have nothing to envy to a big data center.

Divide et Impera (Divide and Rule)

While writing this chapter, we participated in several meetups related to topics discussed here, to don't miss anything current.

These topics have generated much expectation and interest and it is becoming common to reach newbies more than those who already know about the subject.

During these talks, several participants asked about *distributed systems* and *distributed processes*. These dynamics[1] were a quick way to understand *distributed computing*. The group activity seemed simple: Find the rock-paper-scissors champion among the nearly 40 attendees.

The initial rule: choose someone near, play one match, and the winner finds another winning contender. The losers serve as "spokespersons" repeating the name of winner; if a new champion beats your leader, the entire group becomes followers of the new champion.

Simple, right? Well, not so much.

As the time passed and the first winners emerged, the shouting and disorder increased, because it was not easy to locate new challengers. The dynamics took a few minutes until finally emerged the "furious" champion (there was a lot of testosterone in the event).

In Figure 7-1, the circles represent each person and the diamond symbolizes a match. The line coming out of each diamond represents the winner of the match, and so on, until it reaches the winner.

---

[1] https://twitter.com/isragaytan/status/736376936562233344

© Raul Estrada and Isaac Ruiz 2016

R. Estrada and I. Ruiz, *Big Data SMACK*, DOI 10.1007/978-1-4842-2175-4_7

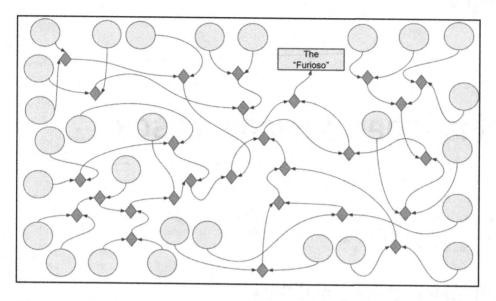

Figure 7-1. *Sequence to find the rock-paper-scissors champion*

After the activity, the question was if it is possible to find the champion in less time. It was definitely possible, but the question was designed to define a strategy. The discussed proposal to remove noise and disorder concluded that there should be people whose function was locate and "match" winners, which should expedite the activity.

To give order, these people should also be organized between them to perform their task more efficiently. These people could also be called *coordinators*.

Each match requires two participants and generates a winner. You can see that to reach the final match, the finalists had to win more games than others.

In Figure 7-2, you can see the first variant to the solution to make our championship more agile. You might call this dynamic a *process*.

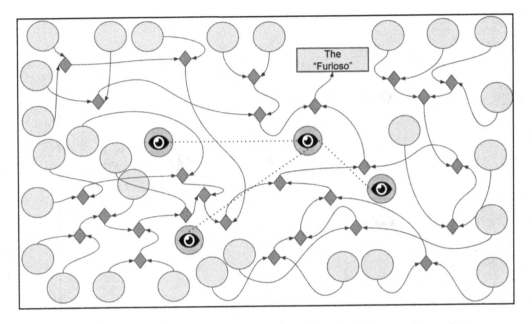

Figure 7-2. *Sequence to find the rock-paper-scissors champion using just one main coordinator*

Our process has something different in this first variant: it uses coordinators.

Now, what happens if you want to more strictly validate each match?

While the coordinators are in communication, the participants may not properly perform a match, so you must rely on coordinators not for only gain speed but also to ensure that the process is successfully completed.

A second approach is to generate two large groups (with few coordinators), and in each of these groups, the coordinator is responsible for validating each match. The winner is sent to a pool of partial winners (that have won at least one time, but they are not still champions). Two participants are taken from this pool and the match is made (with supervision of a third coordinator), the winner returns to the pool and the loser is eliminated from the game.

This pool coordinator is in constant communication with the other two to speed up (or pause) the participants' flow. At the end, there is only one winner.

Figure 7-3 shows the implementation of the second variant.

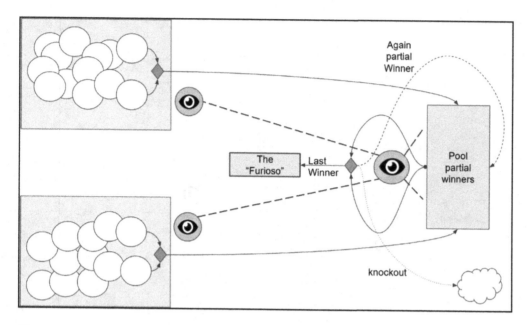

Figure 7-3. Sequence to find the rock-paper-scissors champion using a main coordinator and ordering the execution

At this point, you are probably already considering a better strategy to achieve the successful completion of these tasks. And if theory is correct, the solution should have something to help coordinate and something to help distribute, so *distributes et impera* is the modern "divide and conquer."

Surely, you're thinking that this exercise is used to illustrate only the concurrency, and that is true. It is also true that distributed systems make use of concurrency to achieve their goals. If you are particularly interested in the concurrency topics, you can see another example that clearly and in a fun way shows the importance of having a coordinator agent in problem resolution.

In the presentation "Concurrency Is Not Parallelism,"[2] Rob Pike, the GO language creator, shows an interesting example where communication works as "coordinator." In any case, we decided to tackle the example from the audience perspective, as we experienced on the meetup.

With this little anecdote, you begin to see what the distribution task involves.

Distributed Systems

To talk about distributed systems today is to talk about how the Internet works.

The Internet is a huge system that shares hardware and software for different purposes; one of them is to enjoy the Web (http). Today, saying that a system shares hardware and software seems very simple, but it is still complex.

Distributed systems are not new; they have emerged as computing capacity has increased and data manipulation has grown. Over the years, research focused on how to share resources in order to optimize tasks.

These resources could be a data repository, RAM, or a printer if you are looking at sharing both physical and logical resources. But what happens if two people try to access the same resource at the same time?

---

[2]https://blog.golang.org/concurrency-is-not-parallelism

In earlier days, new requirements encouraged the creation of models that allowed concurrency. Once concurrency and resource sharing were satisfied, new needs appeared. How to add a new resource to the system? How to make the entire system scalable?

In these past few paragraphs, we touched on the key points that evolved so that we could have today's distributed systems.

It is still difficult to implement a distributed system and thus new tools emerge; one of them is Apache Mesos, which is what this chapter is about.

Figure 7-4 shows the importance of a distributed systems coordinator.

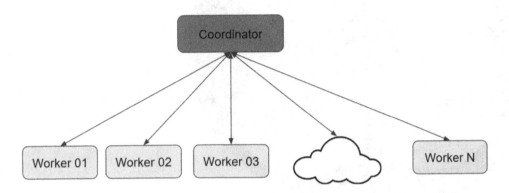

Figure 7-4. *Distributed system anatomy*

Why Are They Important?

Reliability and availability (also called *high availability*) are the two basic characteristics in today's systems. Having information always available and having access to a vital process in economic, healthcare, and government scopes are requirements that we assume already done. If you also add the growth of users to a critical system (or a popular system, in the case of the Internet) is almost geometric in some cases, which requires these systems to be scalable and flexible.

All of these features were achieved years ago, but now they can be achieved at low cost. With few resources carrying the ease-of-use to other systems, we can take the distributed systems benefits available at new levels.

It Is Difficult to Have a Distributed System

There are several tasks that must be inherently performed when having a distributed system. This includes not only monitoring what is happening, but also making a deployment in a whole cluster. It is a task that must not jeopardize the current version but must reach all the nodes. Each deploy implies a process to ensure that all nodes are ready to accept it.

And finally, we need to know which resources are available within the entire cluster, which are down (a node could go down for any reason), and which were recently added (when a new node is added to the cluster).

All of this results in high-cost data centers, where every hour of wasted time can lead to unnecessary but costly businesses expenses.

In summary, it's not easy to implement and maintain a distributed system. Figure 7-5 shows some of the main problems of working with distributed environments when increasing the number of nodes.

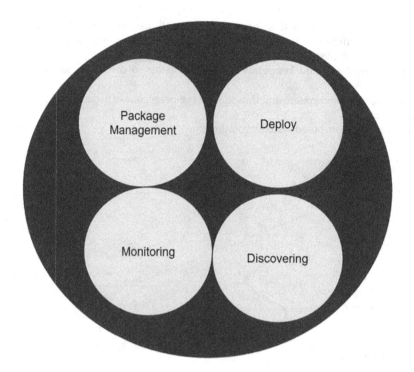

Figure 7-5. *Typical distributed system tasks that increase the complexity regardless the number of nodes*

Part of the complexity of a distributed system is due to its foundation and the way it is implemented, In the presentation "What You Talk About When You Talk About Distributed Systems,"[3] is discussed the importance of the fundamentals of distributed systems and reminds us of some of the models that are currently used to implement them.

Figure 7-6 summarizes some of these models.

Timing Model
Semi-synchronous model
Asynchronous model
Synchronous model

IPC. Inter Process Communication
Shared Memory
Message passing

Failure Models
Arbitrary Failures Mode (Byzantine)
Omission faults
Crash-recovery
Crash-stop

Figure 7-6. *The main distributed models and their implementations*

---

[3]https://www.infoq.com/presentations/topics-distributed-systems

Each of these models has its own implications, so it is possible that a feasible model for one scenario is not feasible for another scenario. Delving into the world of distributed systems requires a lot of theory. There is so much material on the subject that there is a post to complement this presentation. If you find this particular topic interesting, you can find more about it here.[4]

In short, it is not easy to implement and maintain a distributed system.

Ta-dah!! Apache Mesos

And it is in this context that Apache Mesos appeared on the scene in 2010.[5] Discussion of distributed systems a few years ago was about data centers. Having different machines (physical or virtual) connected together, and making them "seen" as a single large machine is something that data centers already do well, or at least somewhat good. The objective is to abstract Mesos as many layers that make up a distributed system; in this case, a data center system.

A Mesos goal is to program and deploy an application in a data center in the same way that it is done on a PC or a mobile device. Achieving this goal and having it supported on different frameworks is discussed later.

Although tools such as Ansible or Puppet can handle a certain number of nodes, performing the packaging and deployment tasks usually generate some interesting challenges. The use of resources of a large machine represents another challenge for data centers, it is common to run into some scenarios where once added more nodes to the cluster, the CPU usage is uneven, thus wasting much of that large machine computation power. Usually, this large machine is actually a cluster with several nodes.

The tricky part comes when we have several clusters.

And it is here that Mesos comes in. Mesos is essentially a "general purpose cluster manager," or a mechanism to administer several large machines used to drive a data center. This "general purpose" administration means that Mesos not only manages and schedules batch processes but also other processes.

Figure 7-7 shows the different types of processes that can be scheduled in Apache Mesos.

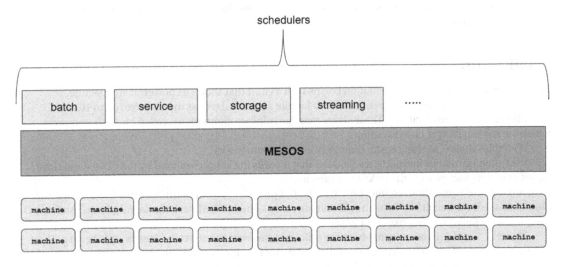

Figure 7-7. Mesos is a general-purpose cluster manager, not only focused on batch scheduling

---

[4]http://videlalvaro.github.io/2015/12/learning-about-distributed-systems.html
[5]"Mesos: A Platform for Fine-Grained Resource Sharing in the Data Center" by Benjamin Hindman, Andy Konwinski, Matei Zaharia, Ali Ghodsi, Anthony D. Joseph, Randy Katz, Scott Shenker, Ion Stoica, http://people.csail.mit.edu/matei/papers/2011/nsdi_mesos.pdf

Apache Mesos tries to solve problems inherent to distributed systems. It tries not only to be a manager but a whole cluster execution platform powered by the (Mesos) frameworks.

Mesos Framework

One way to better understand the Mesos architecture is with Figure 7-8. Mesos requires a layer on which provisioning functions, and then a top layer to expose applications.

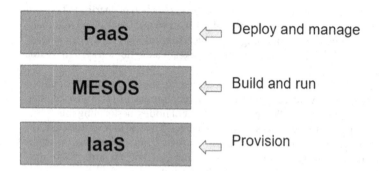

Figure 7-8. *Level of abstraction in Mesos*

In each of these layers, Mesos requires components that allow the service deployment, service finding, and keep running those services. The frameworks we discuss in this chapter cover some of these tasks.

ZooKeeper discovers services. Chronos is responsible for scheduling the services. Marathon and Aurora are responsible for executing the services. These are not the only frameworks to perform the tasks, but they are the most commonly used.

Architecture

The Apache Mesos official documentation begins with a chart that shows its powerful architecture.[6]

Mesos consists of master servers, which can handle as many slaves as they receive (up to 10,000 according to the documentation). These slaves manage software components called Mesos frameworks, which are responsible for task execution.

With this scheme, we can see the importance of the frameworks.

Every framework has two parts: a scheduler that records the services offered by the master and slave nodes or servers that process the tasks to be executed.

You can read more about architecture in an MIT paper "Mesos: A Platform for Fine-Grained Resource Sharing in the Data Center" by Benjamin Hindman, Andy Konwinski, Matei Zaharia, Ali Ghodsi, Anthony D. Joseph, Randy Katz, Scott Shenker, and Ion Stoica.[7]

Figures 7-9 and 7-10 are adapted from the official Mesos web site at http://mesos.apache.org. They show an overview of the Mesos architecture and the major frameworks with which it interacts.

---

[6]http://mesos.apache.org/documentation/latest/architecture/
[7]http://people.csail.mit.edu/matei/papers/2011/nsdi_mesos.pdf

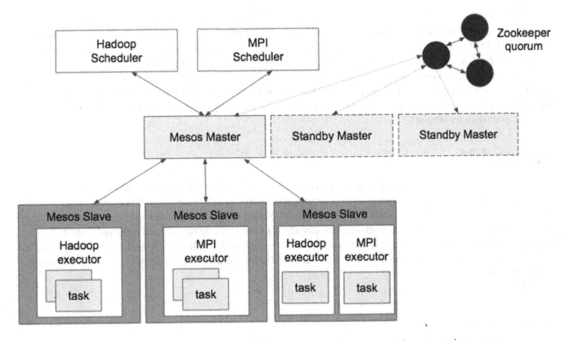

Figure 7-9. *Mesos architecture: master servers (only one at a time) interact with various slave servers*

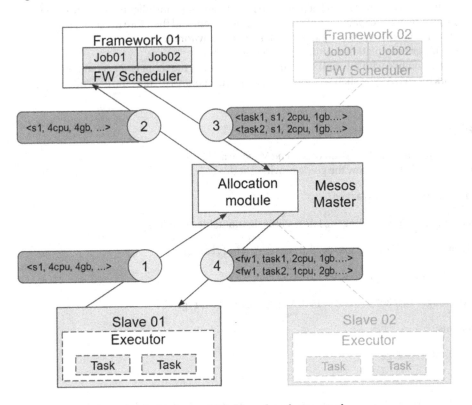

Figure 7-10. *A framework obtains a scheduler and performs a task*

In the first figure we can see that the center of all is the Mesos master, basically a daemon process that coordinates certain number of agents (Mesos prefers to call them *agents* rather than servers that are part of the cluster). These agents live in each node in a cluster. You also see an important component in the Mesos ecosystem: ZooKeeper. Later you will learn about the importance of this component.

The second figure describes the two components that all the frameworks need to run a task: a scheduler and an executor. While there are already a lot of Mesos frameworks ready to run, knowing the parts of a framework is attractive not only to better understand their execution, but also to know what involves creating your own framework.[8]

Mesos 101

Now that you have an overview of the Mesos ecosystem, let's look at Apache Mesos in action.

The Mesos ecosystem tries to work as an operating system in the data centers world; therefore, most documentation mentions that Mesos is the kernel of the operating system. In the following pages, you will learn the steps to install this kernel. Then you will learn how to install ZooKeeper, which is the responsible for maintaining information synchronized across all nodes. We continue with Chronos, who keeps running all the defined services. Finally, Marathon and Aurora are responsible for maintaining the services running, each one in their own way.

Here we go.

Installation

You are now ready to install Mesos. The installation has three steps: get the binary, get the dependencies, and start Mesos. Something very important to keep in mind is that there is no installer to perform all the steps. Mesos takes advantage of the capabilities of each operating system and therefore must make a compilation of components to leverage the capabilities of the native environment.

Generating native libraries by platform optimizes the performance.

If you're not going to compile with the make command, do not worry, the script is very complete and does almost all the work for you. As you shall see, the installation only requires to meet the dependencies to compile correctly.

Get the Installer

When this book was written, the stable version of Apache Mesos was 0.28.1.

For a step-by-step installation, follow the guide provided at this web page:

```
http://mesos.apache.org/gettingstarted/
```

This guide recommends downloading the latest stable distributable, as follows:

```
wget http://www.apache.org/dist/mesos/0.28.1/mesos-0.28.1.tar.gz
```

The following is the downloaded file size:

```
-rw-r--r--. 1 rugi rugi 29108023 Apr 13 15:07 mesos-0.28.1.tar.gz
```

Unpack it with this:

```
%>tar -zxf mesos-0.28.1.tar.gz
```

---

[8]Developing Frameworks for Apache Mesos. https://www.youtube.com/watch?v=ZYoXodSlycA

A folder called `mesos-0.28-1` should be created with this content:

```
-rw-r--r--    1 isaacruiz   staff      414 Apr  5 20:25 mesos.pc.in
-rw-r--r--    1 isaacruiz   staff    60424 Apr  5 20:25 configure.ac
-rwxr-xr-x    1 isaacruiz   staff     3647 Apr  5 20:25 bootstrap
-rw-r--r--    1 isaacruiz   staff     1111 Apr  5 20:25 README.md
-rw-r--r--    1 isaacruiz   staff      162 Apr  5 20:25 NOTICE
-rw-r--r--    1 isaacruiz   staff     3612 Apr  5 20:25 Makefile.am
-rw-r--r--    1 isaacruiz   staff    28129 Apr  5 20:25 LICENSE
-rw-r--r--    1 isaacruiz   staff   324089 Apr  5 20:25 ltmain.sh
-rw-r--r--    1 isaacruiz   staff    46230 Apr  5 20:25 aclocal.m4
-rwxr-xr-x    1 isaacruiz   staff   860600 Apr  5 20:25 configure
-rwxr-xr-x    1 isaacruiz   staff     6872 Apr  5 20:25 missing
-rwxr-xr-x    1 isaacruiz   staff    14675 Apr  5 20:25 install-sh
-rwxr-xr-x    1 isaacruiz   staff    23566 Apr  5 20:25 depcomp
-rwxr-xr-x    1 isaacruiz   staff    35987 Apr  5 20:25 config.sub
-rwxr-xr-x    1 isaacruiz   staff    42938 Apr  5 20:25 config.guess
-rwxr-xr-x    1 isaacruiz   staff     7333 Apr  5 20:25 compile
-rwxr-xr-x    1 isaacruiz   staff     5826 Apr  5 20:25 ar-lib
-rw-r--r--    1 isaacruiz   staff    45159 Apr  5 20:25 Makefile.in
drwxr-xr-x    4 isaacruiz   staff      136 Apr  5 20:28 support
drwxr-xr-x    5 isaacruiz   staff      170 Apr  5 20:28 mpi
drwxr-xr-x    3 isaacruiz   staff      102 Apr  5 20:28 include
drwxr-xr-x   23 isaacruiz   staff      782 Apr  5 20:28 bin
drwxr-xr-x   13 isaacruiz   staff      442 Apr  5 20:28 3rdparty
drwxr-xr-x   43 isaacruiz   staff     1462 Apr  5 20:28 src
drwxr-xr-x   15 isaacruiz   staff      510 May  8 18:40 m4
```

Once unzipped, go to the `mesos-0.28-1` directory, as follows:

```
%>cd mesos-0.28-1
```

Make a directory called `build` and then go to this directory:

```
%>mkdir build
%>cd build
```

Inside this folder, start generating the binaries for your machine:

```
%>../configure
%>make
```

The make operation can take a lot of time because in addition to dependency compilation, your machine configuration may be responsible for downloading and configuring the scripts to run Mesos.

If you have a modern computer, you probably have more than one processor. You can speed up the process by using the make command to indicate the number of processors that you have and by suppressing the console outputs (without verbose mode), as shown in the following:

```
%>make -j 2 V=0
```

This command indicates that you have a machine with two processors and you don't want verbosity. In Unix/Linux operating systems, we can see the status with the `%>nproc` or `%>lscpu` commands.

141

Missing Dependencies

The installation process is still in improvement, particularly because the compilation relies heavily on the computer characteristics in which we want to install Apache Mesos.

The compilation process assumes that we have all the required libraries for compiling; therefore, at http://mesos.apache.org/gettingstarted/ are listed the required libraries for the following operating systems:

- Ubuntu 14.04

- Mac OS: Yosemite and El Capitan

- CentOS 6.6

- CentOS 7.2

We strongly suggest to investigate before making an installation; also, install the following libraries on your computer according to your operating system and version:

```
libcurl
libapr-1
```

These are typically two missing dependencies.

If you use yum or apt-get, lean on the search options offered by each tool. If you are trying to install on a Mac, before anything, run the following command to ensure that you have the developer tools updated in the command line.

```
xcode-select --install
```

■ **Note**   Ensure the libraries' compatibility. The make command execution is a task that could exceed the 20 minutes. Be patient; it is always difficult to use something earlier than version 1.0.

Start Mesos

Once past the dependencies and make construction stages, starting Mesos is very simple, just need to run two lines.

Master Server

The first line starts the master server. Since the working directory points to a system directory, be sure to run the command as a privileged user:

```
%>cd build
%>./bin/mesos-master.sh --ip=127.0.0.1 --work_dir=/var/lib/mesos
```

This is the typical console output:

```
%>./bin/mesos-master.sh --ip=127.0.0.1 --work_dir=/var/lib/mesos
I0508 16:48:54.315554 2016645120 main.cpp:237] Build: 2016-05-08 16:20:08 by isaacruiz
I0508 16:48:54.315907 2016645120 main.cpp:239] Version: 0.28.1
I0508 16:48:54.315989 2016645120 main.cpp:260] Using 'HierarchicalDRF' allocator
I0508 16:48:54.320935 2016645120 leveldb.cpp:174] Opened db in 4589us
I0508 16:48:54.323814 2016645120 leveldb.cpp:181] Compacted db in 2845us
I0508 16:48:54.323899 2016645120 leveldb.cpp:196] Created db iterator in 32us
I0508 16:48:54.323932 2016645120 leveldb.cpp:202] Seeked to beginning of db in 18us
I0508 16:48:54.323961 2016645120 leveldb.cpp:271] Iterated through 0 keys in the db in 20us
I0508 16:48:54.325166 2016645120 replica.cpp:779] Replica recovered with log positions 0 ->
0 with 1 holes and 0 unlearned
I0508 16:48:54.336277 528384 recover.cpp:447] Starting replica recovery
I0508 16:48:54.338512 2016645120 main.cpp:471] Starting Mesos master
I0508 16:48:54.357270 528384 recover.cpp:473] Replica is in EMPTY status
I0508 16:48:54.368338 2016645120 master.cpp:375] Master 7f7d9b4b-c5e4-48be-bbb7-78e6fac701ea
(localhost) started on 127.0.0.1:5050
I0508 16:48:54.368404 2016645120 master.cpp:377] Flags at startup: --allocation_
interval="1secs" --allocator="HierarchicalDRF" --authenticate="false" --authenticate_
http="false" --authenticate_slaves="false" --authenticators="crammd5" --authorizers="local"
--framework_sorter="drf" --help="false" --hostname_lookup="true" --http_
authenticators="basic" --initialize_driver_logging="true" --ip="127.0.0.1" --log_auto_
initialize="true" --logbufsecs="0" --logging_level="INFO" --max_completed_frameworks="50"
--max_completed_tasks_per_framework="1000" --max_slave_ping_timeouts="5" --port="5050"
--quiet="false" --recovery_slave_removal_limit="100%" --registry="replicated_log"
--registry_fetch_timeout="1mins" --registry_store_timeout="20secs" --registry_strict="false"
--root_submissions="true" --slave_ping_timeout="15secs" --slave_reregister_timeout="10mins"
--user_sorter="drf" --version="false" --webui_dir="/Users/isaacruiz/Downloads/mesos/
mesos-0.28.1/build/../src/webui" --work_dir="/var/lib/mesos" --zk_session_timeout="10secs"
W0508 16:48:54.378363 2016645120 master.cpp:380]
*************************************************
Master bound to loopback interface! Cannot communicate with remote schedulers or slaves. You
might want to set '--ip' flag to a routable IP address.
*************************************************
```

Slave Server

The second line is responsible for starting the first Mesos slave server:

```
%>cd build
%> ./bin/mesos-slave.sh --master=127.0.0.1:5050
```

This is the typical console output:

```
%>./bin/mesos-slave.sh --master=127.0.0.1:5050
I0508 16:49:09.586303 2016645120 main.cpp:223] Build: 2016-05-08 16:20:08 by isaacruiz
I0508 16:49:09.587652 2016645120 main.cpp:225] Version: 0.28.1
I0508 16:49:09.588884 2016645120 containerizer.cpp:149] Using isolation: posix/cpu,posix/
mem,filesystem/posix
```

```
I0508 16:49:09.627917 2016645120 main.cpp:328] Starting Mesos slave
I0508 16:49:09.630908 3747840 slave.cpp:193] Slave started on 1)@192.168.1.5:5051
I0508 16:49:09.630956 3747840 slave.cpp:194] Flags at startup: --appc_simple_discovery_
uri_prefix="http://" --appc_store_dir="/tmp/mesos/store/appc" --authenticatee="crammd5"
--container_disk_watch_interval="15secs" --containerizers="mesos" --default_role="*"
--disk_watch_interval="1mins" --docker="docker" --docker_kill_orphans="true" --docker_
registry="https://registry-1.docker.io" --docker_remove_delay="6hrs" --docker_socket="/
var/run/docker.sock" --docker_stop_timeout="0ns" --docker_store_dir="/tmp/mesos/store/
docker" --enforce_container_disk_quota="false" --executor_registration_timeout="1mins"
--executor_shutdown_grace_period="5secs" --fetcher_cache_dir="/tmp/mesos/fetch" --fetcher_
cache_size="2GB" --frameworks_home="" --gc_delay="1weeks" --gc_disk_headroom="0.1"
--hadoop_home="" --help="false" --hostname_lookup="true" --image_provisioner_backend="copy"
--initialize_driver_logging="true" --isolation="posix/cpu,posix/mem" --launcher_dir="/Users/
isaacruiz/Downloads/mesos/mesos-0.28.1/build/src" --logbufsecs="0" --logging_level="INFO"
--master="127.0.0.1:5050" --oversubscribed_resources_interval="15secs" --port="5051"
--qos_correction_interval_min="0ns" --quiet="false" --recover="reconnect" --recovery_
timeout="15mins" --registration_backoff_factor="1secs" --sandbox_directory="/mnt/mesos/
sandbox" --strict="true" --switch_user="true" --version="false" --work_dir="/tmp/mesos"
I0508 16:49:39.704506 3747840 slave.cpp:464] Slave resources: cpus(*):2; mem(*):7168;
disk(*):482446; ports(*):[31000-32000]
I0508 16:49:39.704661 3747840 slave.cpp:472] Slave attributes: [  ]
I0508 16:49:39.704684 3747840 slave.cpp:477] Slave hostname: 192.168.1.5
I0508 16:49:39.719388 1064960 state.cpp:58] Recovering state from '/tmp/mesos/meta'
I0508 16:49:39.720755 4284416 status_update_manager.cpp:200] Recovering status update
manager
I0508 16:49:39.721927 4284416 containerizer.cpp:407] Recovering containerizer
I0508 16:49:39.728039 2674688 provisioner.cpp:245] Provisioner recovery complete
I0508 16:49:39.728682 3211264 slave.cpp:4565] Finished recovery
I0508 16:49:39.732142 2138112 status_update_manager.cpp:174] Pausing sending status updates
I0508 16:49:39.732161 3211264 slave.cpp:796] New master detected at master@127.0.0.1:5050
I0508 16:49:39.733449 3211264 slave.cpp:821] No credentials provided. Attempting to register
without authentication
I0508 16:49:39.733577 3211264 slave.cpp:832] Detecting new master
I0508 16:49:40.588644 2138112 slave.cpp:971] Registered with master master@127.0.0.1:5050;
given slave ID 7f7d9b4b-c5e4-48be-bbb7-78e6fac701ea-S0
I0508 16:49:40.589226 528384 status_update_manager.cpp:181] Resuming sending status updates
I0508 16:49:40.589984 2138112 slave.cpp:1030] Forwarding total oversubscribed resources
```

Like the other frameworks covered in this book, keep running the both commands to run successfully; first the master server and then the slave server.

In Figure 7-11, we can see the both windows running simultaneously.

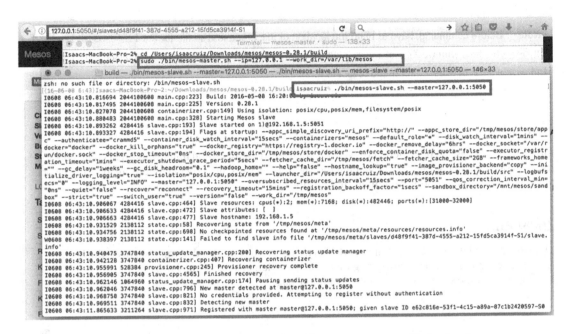

Figure 7-11. *Two consoles showing the execution, in front the master server, and in back a slave server*

At this point, with the master and slave started, it's already possible to access the Mesos web console. The console listens on port 5050. Thus, open your favorite browser and go to http://127.0.0.1:5050. See the Apache Mesos main screen running with one slave server. In Figure 7-12, you see the main screen of the Mesos console.

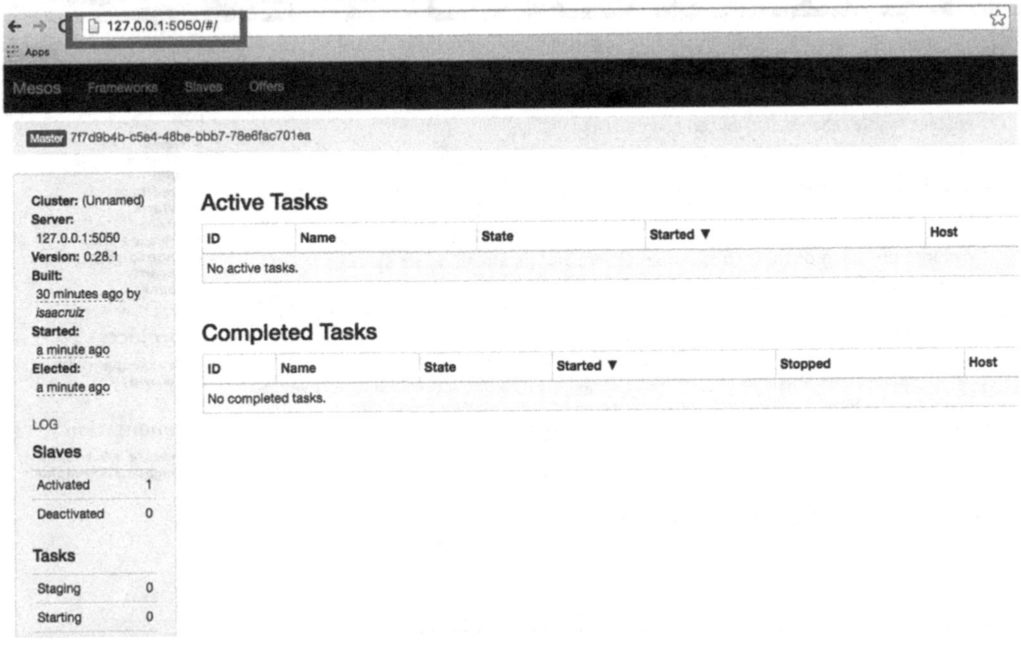

Figure 7-12. *Mesos server main screen running*

■ **Note**   Before continuing, have at hand the location of the `libmesos.so` file (or the `libmesos.dylib` file if compiling on a Mac with OS X). This file is required to integrate with frameworks, as discussed next. Use the `find -name * libmesos..` command to locate it.

Teaming

Although Mesos has still not reached version 1.0, there are already several frameworks that contribute to a robust ecosystem and perfectly complement the Mesos objectives. In particular, there are four frameworks to know: ZooKeeper, Chronos, Marathon, and Aurora.

ZooKeeper

The official site of the ZooKeeper framework tells us that it is a centralized naming service, which simultaneously allows to maintain configuration information in a distributed way.

Figure 7-13 shows the Apache ZooKeeper home page.

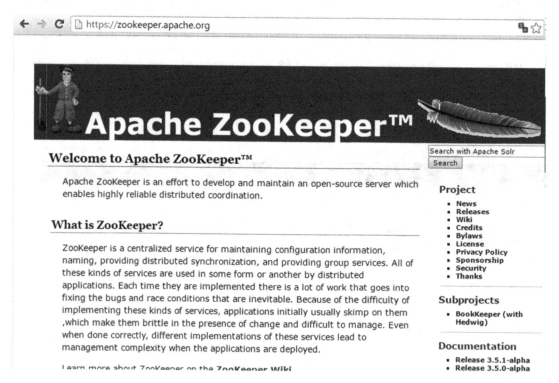

Figure 7-13. *The Apache ZooKeeper home page*

Do you remember the diagram showing the Mesos architecture? ZooKeeper's strength is to keep distributed processes through service replication; customers connect to multiple servers (there is one main server) and from there, they get the information they need.

To manage the information, ZooKeeper creates a distributed namespace (see Figure 7-14) across all nodes; this namespace is similar to a standard file system.

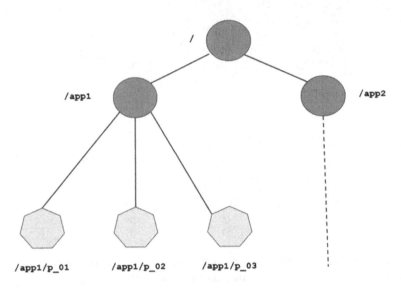

Figure 7-14. ZooKeeper namespace

ZooKeeper was designed to be simple to use. The API only has seven messages, as shown in Table 7-1.

Table 7-1. Messages in the ZooKeeper API

Message	Definition
create	Creates a node at a location in the three.
delete	Deletes a node.
exist	Tests if a node exists at a location.
get data	Reads the data from the node.
set data	Writes data to a node.
get children	Retrieves a list of a node's children.
sync	Waits for data to be propagated.

Figure 7-15 shows how ZooKeeper maintains high availability with the services scheduled. There is a main server (leader). All servers know each other and they all keep their status in memory. While more servers are active, the availability of services is assured.

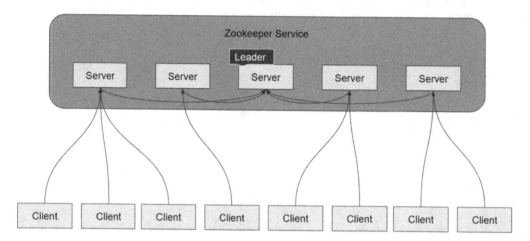

Figure 7-15. *ZooKeeper service*

Clients, meanwhile, connect to a single server. A TCP connection maintains communication with this server (sending heartbeats). If something happens to the server, the client only connects to another server.

Installation

At the time of this writing, the stable version of ZooKeeper was 3.4.6. The installation process is simple. Download the binary file of the latest stable version from this web page:

```
http://zookeeper.apache.org/releases.html
```

The `tar.gz` file for this version has the following size:

```
Mode                LastWriteTime        Length Name
----                -------------        ------ ----
-a----     15/05/2016  08:17 a. m.      17699306 zookeeper-3.4.6.tar.gz
```

Once unzipped, the first is to create a configuration file; the configuration file must be named `zoo.cfg` and it must be located in the `conf/` directory.

By default, the `conf/` directory has as an example file where the parameters to set are described in detail. In short, a `zoo.cfg` file must have at least the following values:

```
/opt/apache/zookeeper/zookeeper-3.4.6/conf%> vi zoo.cfg
tickTime=2000
initLimit=10
syncLimit=5
dataDir=/tmp/zookeeper
clientPort=2181
```

The same directory has a sample file; we can copy its contents to our zoo.cfg file.

Once the zoo.cfg file is configured, to check the status to validate the ZooKeeper configuration file location and execution mode run this command.

```
~/opt/apache/zookeeper/zookeeper-3.4.6/bin%>./zkServer.sh status
JMX enabled by default
Using config: /Users/isaacruiz/opt/apache/zookeeper/zookeeper-3.4.6/bin/../conf/zoo.cfg
Mode: standalone
```

If we run only the zKServer.sh file, we can see the list of tasks that can be used with the ZooKeeper binary (be sure to execute instructions with a user that has enough privileges):

```
~/opt/apache/zookeeper/zookeeper-3.4.6/bin%>./zkServer.sh
Password:
JMX enabled by default
Using config: /users/isaacruiz/opt/apache/zookeeper/zookeeper-3.4.6/bin/../conf/zoo.cfg
Usage: ./zkServer.sh {start|start-foreground|stop|restart|status|upgrade|print-cmd}
{16-05-10 21:24}:~/opt/apache/zookeeper/zookeeper-3.4.6/bin isaacruiz%
```

As you can see, we have the following tasks:

```
start, start-foreground, stop, restart, status, upgrade, print-cmd
```

Now, to start ZooKeeper.

```
~/opt/apache/zookeeper/zookeeper-3.4.6/bin%>./zkServer.sh start
JMX enabled by default
Using config: /users/isaacruiz/opt/apache/zookeeper/zookeeper-3.4.6/bin/../conf/zoo.cfg
Starting zookeeper ... STARTED
{16-05-10 21:24} opt/apache/zookeeper/zookeeper-3.4.6/bin isaacruiz%
```

Chronos

The second component is Chronos, the substitute for the cron sentence in the Mesos context. The home page of this project is at https://mesos.github.io/chronos/.

If you've used a Unix-based operating system, have probably performed the repetitive execution of a process using this operating system utility. Chronos does the same; it is a task scheduler. Only in the Chronos context, it is a distributed task scheduler, and in addition to isolating tasks, it can orchestrate them.

Another advantage of Chronos is to schedule tasks using the ISO 8601 8; the notation offered by this standard is much friendlier in specifying the time intervals to execute tasks. Chronos runs directly on Mesos. It is the first line of interaction with the outside world. Its integration is in both the master and the slave servers, and through this communication manages the records of the jobs to be done.

The Chronos architecture is shown in Figure 7-16.

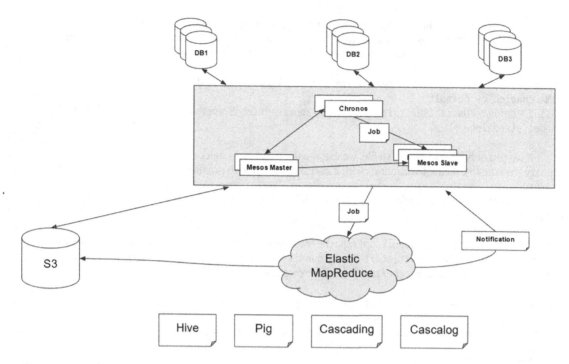

Figure 7-16. *Chronos architecture*

Installation

At the time of this writing, the stable Chronos version was 2.4.0. Having a mature version, the installation process is simple, but it is a little slow for the binary generation of the platform where it is used.

The installation process assumes that you have already installed a version of Mesos (0.20.x) and ZooKeeper. And have also installed Apache Maven 3.x and JDK 1.6 or higher.

The installation process begins by downloading the binary from the home page:[9]

```
curl -0 https://github.com/mesos/chronos/archive/2.3.4.tar.gz
tar xvf 2.3.4.tar.gz
```

Once the file is decompressed, note that the main folder contains the POM files required by Maven to perform their tasks.

The directory contents should be similar to the following:

```
~/opt/apache/chronos/chronos-2.4.0%> ls -lrt
total 104
drwxr-xr-x@  4 isaacruiz  staff    136 Aug 28  2015 src
-rw-r--r--@  1 isaacruiz  staff  17191 Aug 28  2015 pom.xml
drwxr-xr-x@ 14 isaacruiz  staff    476 Aug 28  2015 docs
-rw-r--r--@  1 isaacruiz  staff   2521 Aug 28  2015 changelog.md
```

---

[9]https://mesos.github.io/chronos/docs/

```
-rw-r--r--@  1 isaacruiz  staff   1165 Aug 28  2015 build.xml
drwxr-xr-x@ 13 isaacruiz  staff    442 Aug 28  2015 bin
-rw-r--r--@  1 isaacruiz  staff   3087 Aug 28  2015 README.md
-rw-r--r--@  1 isaacruiz  staff    837 Aug 28  2015 NOTICE
-rw-r--r--@  1 isaacruiz  staff  11003 Aug 28  2015 LICENSE
-rw-r--r--@  1 isaacruiz  staff    470 Aug 28  2015 Dockerfile
```

The only thing remaining is to run the mvn package to generate the .jar file used to start Chronos.

```
~/opt/apache/chronos/chronos-2.4.0%> mvn package
[INFO] Scanning for projects...
[INFO]
[INFO] ------------------------------------------------------------------------
[INFO] Building chronos 2.4.0
[INFO] ------------------------------------------------------------------------
Downloading: https://repo1.maven.org/maven2/org/apache/maven/plugins/maven-antrun-
plugin/1.7/maven-antrun-plugin-1.7.pom
Downloaded: https://repo1.maven.org/maven2/org/apache/maven/plugins/maven-antrun-plugin/1.7/
maven-antrun-plugin-1.7.pom (5 KB at 0.5 KB/sec)
Downloading: https://repo1.maven.org/maven2/org/apache/maven/plugins/maven-antrun-
plugin/1.7/maven
...
...
...
Downloaded: https://repo.maven.apache.org/maven2/org/slf4j/slf4j-api/1.6.1/slf4j-api-
1.6.1.jar (25 KB at 5.9 KB/sec)
[INFO] Dependency-reduced POM written at: /Users/isaacruiz/opt/apache/chronos/chronos-2.4.0/
dependency-reduced-pom.xml
[INFO] Dependency-reduced POM written at: /Users/isaacruiz/opt/apache/chronos/chronos-2.4.0/
dependency-reduced-pom.xml
[INFO] ------------------------------------------------------------------------
[INFO] BUILD SUCCESS
[INFO] ------------------------------------------------------------------------
[INFO] Total time: 03:55 min
[INFO] Finished at: 2016-05-19T01:45:13-05:00
[INFO] Final Memory: 68M/668M
[INFO] ------------------------------------------------------------------------
```

This step can take time, depending on your Internet connection and your machine's characteristics.

Run

Having the .jar file (found in the target directory), it is possible start Chronos with the following line:

```
~/opt/apache/chronos/chronos-2.4.0%> java -cp target/chronos*.jar org.apache.mesos.chronos.
scheduler.Main --master zk://localhost:2181/mesos --zk_hosts localhost:2181

[2016-05-19 01:45:56,621] INFO -------------------- (org.apache.mesos.chronos.scheduler.
                                                      Main$:26)
```

```
[2016-05-19 01:45:56,624] INFO Initializing chronos. (org.apache.mesos.chronos.scheduler.Main$:27)
[2016-05-19 01:45:56,627] INFO -------------------- (org.apache.mesos.chronos.scheduler.Main$:28)
[2016-05-19 01:45:59,109] INFO Wiring up the application (org.apache.mesos.chronos.
scheduler.config.MainModule:39)
...
...
2016-05-19 01:46:01,446:3328(0x700002495000):ZOO_INFO@check_events@1703: initiated
connection to server [::1:2181]
2016-05-19 01:46:01,449:3328(0x700002495000):ZOO_INFO@check_events@1750: session
establishment complete on server [::1:2181], sessionId=0x154c75bb0940008, negotiated
timeout=10000
I0519 01:46:01.451170 16019456 group.cpp:349] Group process (group(1)@192.168.1.5:53043)
connected to ZooKeeper
I0519 01:46:01.452013 16019456 group.cpp:831] Syncing group operations: queue size (joins,
cancels, datas) = (0, 0, 0)
```

Now Apache Chronos is running.

One Chronos advantage is that is already in an advanced version; it has a web interface that allows to manage scheduled jobs. This web interface is available in the following port:

```
http://localhost:8080/
```

Figure 7-17 shows this screen.

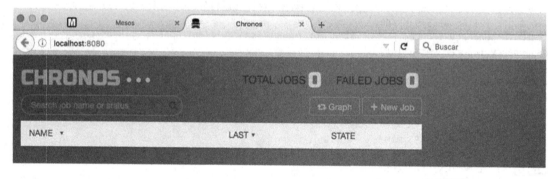

Figure 7-17. *Chronos web interface*

Part of the Chronos power lies in its API,[10] from which you can better interact from other integration points. You can easily try curl, as follows:

```
~/opt/apache/chronos/chronos-2.4.0%> curl -L -X GET http://localhost:8080/scheduler/jobs

[]%
```

Right now, there are no scheduled jobs, so both the web interface and the API report the same thing: no scheduled tasks.

---

[10]https://mesos.github.io/chronos/docs/api.html

Marathon

Marathon is another tool that fits very well with Mesos; although it can be used independently, with Mesos it is even more powerful, and given the integration, it is a lot easier to use.

The Marathon home page is at `https://mesosphere.github.io/marathon/`. From this page we can download the latest stable version; at the time of this writing, the version was 1.1.1.

Figure 7-18 shows the Marathon home page.

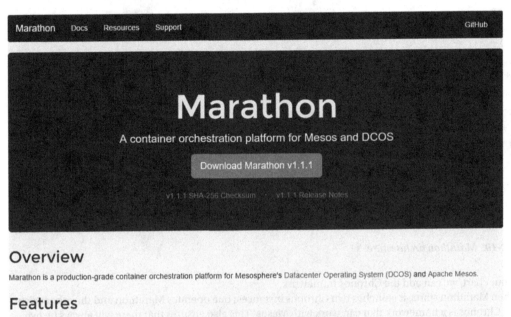

Figure 7-18. Marathon home page

A quick way to understand Marathon is with this phrase: "A self-serve interface to your cluster. Distributed init for long-running services."[11]

Probably you have used the `init` command on any Unix-based operating system that helps us to start tasks and/or processes already defined and configured on the operating system's host.

Marathon has a particular way to manage the tasks execution.[12] Marathon intends to help keep each task executed by Mesos 100% available.

---

[11]Simplifying with Mesos and Marathon. `https://www.youtube.com/watch?v=0gVaQPYEsVo`
[12]`https://mesosphere.github.io/marathon/docs/`

Figure 7-19 shows the Marathon architecture. It is based on official documentation at
https://mesosphere.github.io/marathon/.

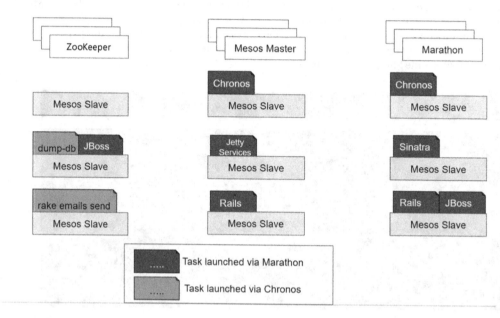

Figure 7-19. *Marathon architecture*

In our chart, we can add the Chronos framework.[13]

When Marathon starts, it launches two Chronos instances: one operates Marathon and the other exists
because Chronos is a framework that can work with Mesos. This also ensures that there will always be two
Chronos instances running and ready to receive tasks.

Installation

The main binary is downloaded directly from the Marathon home page. Once the file is decompressed, we
can start it (Marathon assumes that Mesos and ZooKeeper are already running).

Before running it, be sure to export the MESOS_NATIVE_JAVA_LIBRARY variable pointing to the route
already detected (the Marathon start file will look in /usr/lib). When running it, check if the current os user
has read permission on system directories.

```
opt/apache/marathon/marathon-1.1.1/bin%>./start --master local
MESOS_NATIVE_JAVA_LIBRARY is not set. Searching in /usr/lib /usr/local/lib.
MESOS_NATIVE_LIBRARY, MESOS_NATIVE_JAVA_LIBRARY set to '/usr/local/lib/libmesos.dylib'
[2016-05-15 15:23:22,391] INFO Starting Marathon 1.1.1 with --master local
(mesosphere.marathon.Main$:main)
[2016-05-15 15:23:26,322] INFO Connecting to ZooKeeper... (mesosphere.marathon.Main$:main)
[2016-05-15 15:23:26,346] INFO Client environment:zookeeper.version=3.4.6-1569965, built on
02/20/2014 09:09 GMT (org.apache.zookeeper.ZooKeeper:main)
```

---

[13]https://github.com/mesos/chronos

```
[2016-05-15 15:23:26,347] INFO Client environment:host.name=192.168.1.5
(org.apache.zookeeper.ZooKeeper:main)
[2016-05-15 15:23:26,348] INFO Client environment:java.version=1.8.0_51
(org.apache.zookeeper.ZooKeeper:main)
[2016-05-15 15:23:26,349] INFO Client environment:java.vendor=Oracle Corporation
(org.apache.zookeeper.ZooKeeper:main)
[2016-05-15 15:23:26,349] INFO Client environment:java.home=/Library/Java/
JavaVirtualMachines/jdk1.8.0_51.jdk/Contents/Home/jre (org.apache.zookeeper.ZooKeeper:main)
```

Aurora

Aurora is one of the Mesos frameworks. (Do you remember the diagram?) Mesos requires frameworks to retrieve a scheduler and run a task from it.

Aurora allows to run applications and services through a set of machines. Its primary responsibility is to maintain this state of execution as long as possible; the ideal is "always."

Figure 7-20 shows the Aurora project home page.

Introduction

Apache Aurora is a service scheduler that runs on top of Apache Mesos, enabling you to run long-running services, cron jobs, and ad-hoc jobs that take advantage of Apache Mesos' scalability, fault-tolerance, and resource isolation.

We encourage you to ask questions on the Aurora user list or the #aurora IRC channel on irc.freenode.net .

Getting Started

Information for everyone new to Apache Aurora.

- Aurora System Overview
- Hello World Tutorial
- Local cluster with Vagrant

Features

Description of important Aurora features.

- Containers
- Cron Jobs
- Job Updates
- Multitenancy
- Resource Isolation
- Scheduling Constraints
- Services
- Service Discovery
- SLA Metrics
- Webhooks

Figure 7-20. *Aurora home page http://aurora.apache.org/*

If a machine fails, Aurora is responsible for rescheduling the execution of a task in service if one of the remaining machines is available.

The use of Aurora[14] on Twitter is the most widespread use case. It is used as a reference on the Aurora main page; the introduction[15] is provided by the Twitter senior staff engineer.

Overview

Figure 7-21 shows the components of Aurora; this is based on the official documentation (http://aurora.apache.org/).

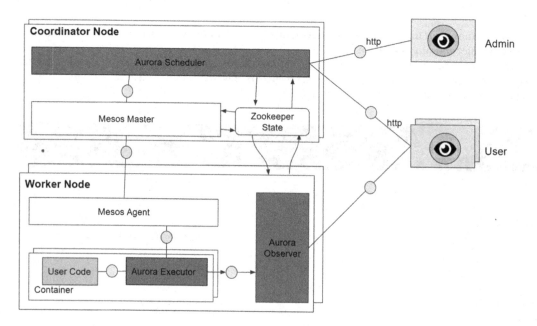

Figure 7-21. *Aurora components*

Aurora is currently at version 0.30.0.

Let's Talk About Clusters

Apache Mesos was designed to work in clusters. These Mesos clusters require a main server named MASTER and several secondary servers called SLAVES. Original, isn't it?

Figure 7-22 shows the relationship between the coordinator and master-slave servers. It is based on official Mesos documentation.

---

[14]Introduction to Apache Aurora. https://www.youtube.com/watch?v=asd_h6VzaJc
[15]Operating Aurora and Mesos at Twitter. https://www.youtube.com/watch?v=E4lxX6epM_U

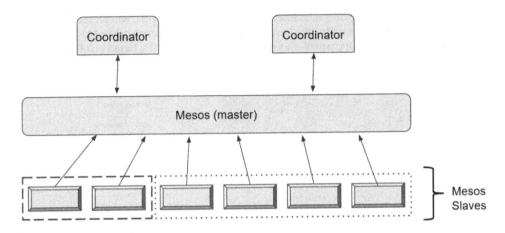

Figure 7-22. *Master and slaves server distribution*

There are already several frameworks available for use by Mesos. The true potential is the ability to create special Mesos frameworks using any of the supported languages: Java, Scala, Python, and C ++.

One of these ready-to-use frameworks is the Apache Kafka framework.

Apache Mesos and Apache Kafka

Apache Kafka is one of the frameworks ready to be used with Mesos. There is a GitHub repository in charge of this project. Figure 7-23 shows the main screen of the project on GitHub.

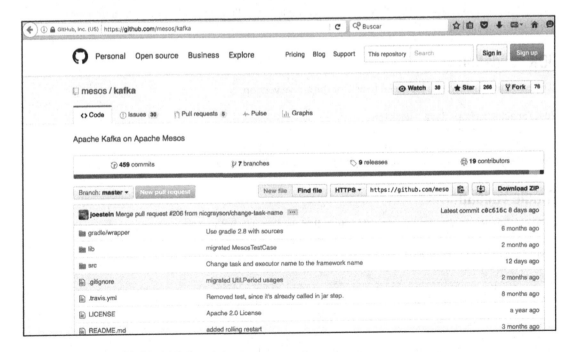

Figure 7-23. *Mesos/Kafka GitHub project*

Like any Mesos framework, Kafka requires schedulers to run tasks. In Figure 7-24, we can see the relationship between the scheduler and executor, the basic components of any framework in Mesos. The figure shows an already known scheme but particularly applied to Apache Kafka; it is based on official documentation.[16]

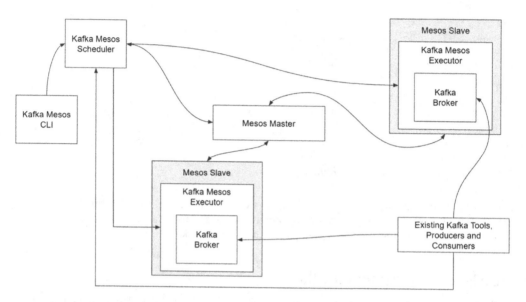

Figure 7-24. *The Apache Kafka framework and its interaction with Apache Mesos*

Before building the binaries, check if you have already installed Java and Gradle (the automated building tool for Java projects).

JDK Validation

JDK validation is easy; you just need to ask for the active version.

```
/opt/apache/kafka> java -version
java version "1.8.0_51"
Java(TM) SE Runtime Environment (build 1.8.0_51-b16)
Java HotSpot(TM) 64-Bit Server VM (build 25.51-b03, mixed mode)
```

Gradle Validation

Gradle validation is easy. In this example is installed the Gradle version 2.9:

```
~/opt/apache/kafka%> gradle -version

------------------------------------------------------------
Gradle 2.9
------------------------------------------------------------
```

---

[16]https://mesosphere.com/blog/2015/07/16/making-apache-kafka-elastic-with-apache-mesos/

```
Build time:    2015-11-17 07:02:17 UTC
Build number: none
Revision:      b463d7980c40d44c4657dc80025275b84a29e31f

Groovy:        2.4.4
Ant:           Apache Ant(TM) version 1.9.3 compiled on December 23 2013
JVM:           1.8.0_51 (Oracle Corporation 25.51-b03)

{16-05-10 17:55}Isaacs-MacBook-Pro-2:~/opt/apache/kafka isaacruiz%
```

Export libmesos Location

Follow the instructions provided in the guide. When compiling Mesos, several native libraries are generated. Find the file called libmesos.so (or libmesos.dylib if you're on a Mac with OS X) and export it or declare it in the file: kafka-mesos.sh

```
# export MESOS_NATIVE_JAVA_LIBRARY=/usr/local/lib/libmesos.so
```

Now start cloning the repository. The console output will be similar to this:

```
~/opt/apache/kafka%> git clone https://github.com/mesos/kafka
Cloning into 'kafka'...
remote: Counting objects: 4343, done.
remote: Total 4343 (delta 0), reused 0 (delta 0), pack-reused 4343
Receiving objects: 100% (4343/4343), 959.33 KiB | 44.00 KiB/s, done.
Resolving deltas: 100% (1881/1881), done.
Checking connectivity... done.
```

Once the repository is cloned, proceed to build the Kafka-Mesos binaries with the command:

```
gradle jar
```

Gradle is characterized by place the artifacts required for compilation in the directories according to the invocation structure, this task may take a while depending on the script dependencies.

```
~/opt/apache/kafka/kafka@master%> ./gradlew jar
Downloading https://services.gradle.org/distributions/gradle-2.8-all.zip
.................................................................
Unzipping /Users/isaacruiz/.gradle/wrapper/dists/gradle-2.8-all/ah86jmo43de9lfa8xg9ux3c4h/
gradle-2.8-all.zip to /Users/isaacruiz/.gradle/wrapper/dists/gradle-2.8-all/
ah86jmo43de9lfa8xg9ux3c4h
Set executable permissions for: /Users/isaacruiz/.gradle/wrapper/dists/gradle-2.8-all/
ah86jmo43de9lfa8xg9ux3c4h/gradle-2.8/bin/gradle
:compileJava UP-TO-DATE
:compileScala
Download https://repo1.maven.org/maven2/org/scala-lang/scala-library/2.10.6/scala-library-
2.10.6.pom
Download https://repo1.maven.org/maven2/org/apache/mesos/mesos/0.25.0/mesos-0.25.0.pom
...
```

```
Download https://repo1.maven.org/maven2/org/scala-lang/scala-reflect/2.10.6/
scala-reflect-2.10.6.jar
:processResources UP-TO-DATE
:classes
:compileTestJava UP-TO-DATE
:compileTestScala
[ant:scalac] Element '/Users/isaacruiz/opt/apache/kafka/kafka/out/gradle/resources/main'
does not exist.
:processTestResources UP-TO-DATE
:testClasses
:test
:jar

BUILD SUCCESSFUL

Total time: 29 mins 54.98 secs

This build could be faster, please consider using the Gradle Daemon: https://docs.gradle.
org/2.8/userguide/gradle_daemon.html
{16-05-10 18:33}Isaacs-MacBook-Pro-2:~/opt/apache/kafka/kafka@master isaacruiz%
```

After the Gradle compilation, you should have a structure similar to the following:

```
~/opt/apache/kafka/kafka@master%> ls -lrt
total 34360
drwxr-xr-x  6 isaacruiz  staff       204 May 10 18:02 src
-rwxr-xr-x  1 isaacruiz  staff      1634 May 10 18:02 quickstart.sh
drwxr-xr-x  3 isaacruiz  staff       102 May 10 18:02 lib
-rwxr-xr-x  1 isaacruiz  staff       307 May 10 18:02 kafka-mesos.sh
-rw-r--r--  1 isaacruiz  staff       422 May 10 18:02 kafka-mesos.properties
-rwxr-xr-x  1 isaacruiz  staff      4971 May 10 18:02 gradlew
drwxr-xr-x  3 isaacruiz  staff       102 May 10 18:02 gradle
-rw-r--r--  1 isaacruiz  staff      1769 May 10 18:02 build.gradle
-rw-r--r--  1 isaacruiz  staff     29334 May 10 18:02 README.md
-rw-r--r--  1 isaacruiz  staff     11325 May 10 18:02 LICENSE
drwxr-xr-x  3 isaacruiz  staff       102 May 10 18:25 out
-rw-r--r--  1 isaacruiz  staff  17522191 May 10 18:33 kafka-mesos-0.9.5.0.jar
```

Now you can use the main shell, use the help command to learn about valid sentences.

```
{16-05-10 19:05}Isaacs-MacBook-Pro-2:~/opt/apache/kafka/kafka> ./kafka-mesos.sh help
Usage: <command>

Commands:
  help [cmd [cmd]] - print general or command-specific help
  scheduler        - start scheduler
  broker           - broker management commands
  topic            - topic management commands

Run `help <command>` to see details of specific command
{16-05-10 21:25}Isaacs-MacBook-Pro-2:~/opt/apache/kafka/kafka%>
```

Or you can start the scheduler directly:

```
{16-05-10 21:25}Isaacs-MacBook-Pro-2:~/opt/apache/kafka/kafka%> ./kafka-mesos.sh scheduler
Loading config defaults from kafka-mesos.properties
2016-05-10 21:25:33,573 [main] INFO  ly.stealth.mesos.kafka.Scheduler$  - Starting
Scheduler$:
debug: true, storage: zk:/mesos-kafka-scheduler
mesos: master=master:5050, user=vagrant, principal=<none>, secret=<none>
framework: name=kafka, role=*, timeout=30d
api: http://192.168.3.5:7000, bind-address: <all>, zk: master:2181, jre: <none>
```

Mesos and Apache Spark

Since its earliest releases, Spark was ready for Mesos. The web page that explains how to perform the integration is http://spark.apache.org/docs/latest/running-on-mesos.html.

It's easy to start Spark to work with Mesos. Just be careful when establishing the libmesos file location (the native library compiled earlier).

First, validate that Mesos is running by opening a browser and validating that your host is active as follows:

```
http://MESOS_HOST:5050/
```

The next step is to locate the file called libmesos.so (or libmesos.dylib if you're on a Mac with OS X) and make it available as an environment variable:

```
export MESOS_NATIVE_JAVA_LIBRARY=<path to libmesos.so>
```

Once this is done, try running this line:

```
~/opt/apache/spark/spark-1.6.1-bin-hadoop2.6/bin%> ./spark-shell --master mesos://MESOS_
HOST:5050
```

If you receive this error:

```
Failed to load native library from Mesos
Failed to load native Mesos library from
/Users/your_user/Library/Java/Extensions:
/Users/your_user/Library/Java/Extensions/Library/Java/Extensions:
/Network/Library/Java/Extensions:
/System/Library/Java/Extensions:
/usr/lib/java:.
```

Copy the libmesos.so file to any of these routes, preferably one within your user directory to avoid conflicts with another version after you compile. If the path does not exist, you must create it.

The following is the successful output. The prompt appears available, and more importantly, Mesos recognizes an active framework.

```
16-05-15 12:47}Isaacs-MacBook-Pro-2:~/opt/apache/spark/spark-1.6.1-bin-hadoop2.6/bin
isaacruiz% ./spark-shell --master mesos://localhost:5050
log4j:WARN No appenders could be found for logger (org.apache.hadoop.metrics2.lib.
MutableMetricsFactory).
```

```
log4j:WARN Please initialize the log4j system properly.
log4j:WARN See http://logging.apache.org/log4j/1.2/faq.html#noconfig for more info.
Using Spark's repl log4j profile: org/apache/spark/log4j-defaults-repl.properties
To adjust logging level use sc.setLogLevel("INFO")
Welcome to


      ____              __
     / __/__  ___ _____/ /__
    _\ \/ _ \/ _ `/ __/  '_/
   /___/ .__/\_,_/_/ /_/\_\   version 1.6.1
      /_/

Using Scala version 2.10.5 (Java HotSpot(TM) 64-Bit Server VM, Java 1.8.0_51)
Type in expressions to have them evaluated.
Type :help for more information.
I0515 12:48:34.810873 62210048 sched.cpp:222] Version: 0.28.1
I0515 12:48:34.842321 57393152 sched.cpp:326] New master detected at master@127.0.0.1:5050
I0515 12:48:34.843389 57393152 sched.cpp:336] No credentials provided. Attempting to
register without authentication
I0515 12:48:34.876587 60612608 sched.cpp:703] Framework registered with 7f7d9b4b-c5e4-48be-
bbb7-78e6fac701ea-0000
Spark context available as sc.
SQL context available as sqlContext.
scala>
```

From the web console, we can see the running frameworks as shown in Figure 7-25.

Figure 7-25. *Apache Spark already appears in the list of active frameworks*

The Best Is Yet to Come

At the beginning of this chapter, we mentioned that Mesos is still in pre-1.0 versions. All of Mesos's versatility and usefulness work and can be achieved in version 0.28.0. (Imagine when we get to version 1.0!) The expectation level is high, and no wonder: on April 2016, *Wired* magazine published an article titled "You want to build an empire like Google's? This is your OS."[17] Among other things, the article mentions that Google runs on architectures similar to Apache Mesos. It also mentions Mesos's history and its creator, Ben Hindman; part of the original design includes creating data centers in the same way that software runs on a mobile device or a laptop.

Through Mesosphere,[18] the company launched by Hindman, any company (and any of us) can build an infrastructure similar to Google's.

If anything is missing to give new impetus to startups, Mesos probably covers it.

At MesosConf-Europe in 2015, Hindman presented the "State of Apache Mesos"[19] and a brief summary with three main indicators of the growing Mesos community:

- New users: Cisco, Apple, Yelp, Ericsson

- New frameworks: Elastic, Kibana, MySQL, rial, CRATE, and Logstash

- New books: This book is among the proof.

Every month and a half, a smaller version (now in 0.28) is released; by the end of 2016, it will likely be at version 0.40 or 0.50. Mesos surely has many surprises ahead—as we say, the best is yet to come.

And if that is not enough, as shown in Figure 7-26, Mesos is designed to run in the cloud as physical machines, so the hardware layer is transparent.

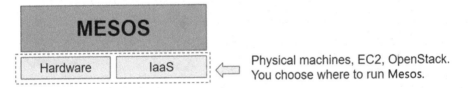

Figure 7-26. Mesos can run both physical machines and cloud

In 2016, presentations at #MesosConf North America[20] highlighted growing interest in Mesos.

Summary

In this chapter, you learned a little more about distributed systems. Now you know how difficult it is to try to build one. You learned that Mesos is a general-purpose cluster manager. You know its architecture and part of its ecosystem. Within this ecosystem, you know about the main frameworks that Mesos interacts with to increase its potential. The chapter also overviewed why Mesos is considered a SDK for distributed environments.

---

[17]http://www.wired.com/2016/04/want-build-empire-like-googles-os/
[18]https://mesosphere.com/
[19]https://www.youtube.com/watch?v=K-x7yOy8Ymk&list=PLGeMO9tlguZS6MhlSZDbf-gANWdKgjeOI
[20]https://www.linux.com/news/mesoscon-north-america-2016-video-sessions

CHAPTER 8

■ ■ ■

The Broker: Apache Kafka

The goal of this chapter is to get you familiar with Apache Kafka and show you how to solve the consumption of millions of messages in a pipeline architecture. Here we show some Scala examples to give you a solid foundation for the different types of implementations and integrations for Kafka producers and consumers.

In addition to the explanation of the Apache Kafka architecture and principles, we explore Kafka integration with the rest of the SMACK stack, specifically with Spark and Mesos. At the end of the chapter, we show how to administer Apache Kafka.

This chapter covers the following topics:

- Kafka introduction

- Kafka installation

- Kafka in cluster

- Kafka architecture

- Kafka producers

- Kafka consumers

- Kafka integration

- Kafka administration

Kafka Introduction

The Apache Kafka author, Jay Kreps, who took a lot of literature courses in the college, if the project is mainly optimized for writing (in this book when we say "optimized" we mean 2 million writes per second on three commodity machines) when he open sourced it, he thought it should have a cool name: Kafka, in honor of Franz Kafka, who was a very prolific author despite dying at 40 age.

Nowadays, real-time information is continuously generated. This data needs *easy* ways to be delivered to multiple types of receivers. Most of the time the information generators and the information consumers are inaccessible to each other; this is when integration tools enter the scene.

In the 1980s, 1990s and 2000s, the large software vendors whose names have three letters (IBM, SAP, BEA, etc.) and more (Oracle, Microsoft, Google) have found a very well-paid market in the integration layer, the layer where live: enterprise service bus, SOA architectures, integrators, and other panaceas that cost several millions of dollars.

Now, all traditional applications tend to have a point of integration between them, therefore, creating the need for a mechanism for seamless integration between data consumers and data producers to avoid any kind of application rewriting at either end.

© Raul Estrada and Isaac Ruiz 2016
R. Estrada and I. Ruiz, *Big Data SMACK*, DOI 10.1007/978-1-4842-2175-4_8

As we mentioned in earlier chapters, in the big data era, the first challenge was the data collection and the second challenge was to analyze that huge amount of data.

Message publishing is the mechanism for connecting heterogeneous applications through sending messages among them. The message router is known as message broker. Apache Kafka is a software solution to *quickly* route real-time information to consumers.

The message broker provides seamless integration, but there are two collateral objectives: the first is to not block the producers and the second is to not let the producers know who the final consumers are.

Apache Kafka is a real-time publish-subscribe solution messaging system: open source, distributed, partitioned, replicated, commit-log based with a publish-subscribe schema. Its main characteristics are as follows:

- **Distributed**. Cluster-centric design that supports the distribution of the messages over the cluster members, maintaining the semantics. So you can grow the cluster horizontally without downtime.

- **Multiclient**. Easy integration with different clients from different platforms: Java, .NET, PHP, Ruby, Python, etc.

- **Persistent**. You cannot afford any data lost. Kafka is designed with efficient O(1), so data structures provide constant time performance no matter the data size.

- **Real time**. The messages produced are immediately seen by consumer threads; these are the basis of the systems called *complex event processing* (CEP).

- **Very high throughput**. As we mentioned, all the technologies in the stack are designed to work in commodity hardware. Kafka can handle hundreds of read and write operations per second from a large number of clients.

Figure 8-1 shows an Apache Kafka messaging system typical scenario.

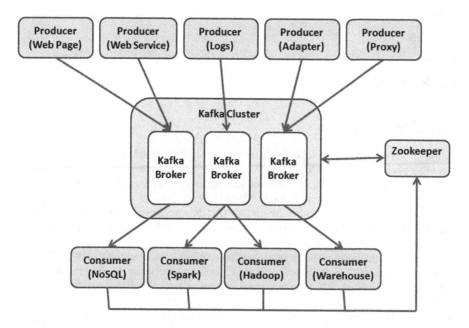

Figure 8-1. *Apache Kafka typical scenario*

On the producers' side, you can find several types of actors, for example:

- **Adapters**. Generate transformation information; for example, a database listener or a file system listener.

- **Logs**. The log files of application servers and other systems, for example.

- **Proxies**. Generate web analytics information.

- **Web pages**. Front-end applications generating information.

- **Web services**. The service layer; generate invocation traces.

You could group the clients on the customer side as three types:

- **Offline**. The information is stored for posterior analysis; for example, Hadoop and data warehouses.

- **Near real time**. The information is stored but it is not requested at the same time; for example, Apache Cassandra, and NoSQL databases.

- **Real time**. The information is analyzed as it is generated; for example, an engine like Apache Spark or Apache Storm (used to make analysis over HDFS).

Born in the Fast Data Era

As we have mentioned, data is the new ingredient of Internet-based systems. Simply, a web page needs to know user activity, logins, page visits, clicks, scrolls, comments, heat zone analysis, shares, and so forth.

Traditionally, the data was handled and stored with traditional aggregation solutions. Due to the high throughput, the analysis could not be done until the next day. Today, yesterday's information often useless. Offline analysis such as Hadoop is being left out of the new economy.

There are several examples of Apache Kafka use cases:

- Web searches based on relevance

- Application security: login analysis, brute force attack detection, systemic denial of service attack detection

- Recommendations based on popularity, correlation

- Sentiment analysis, tendencies, segmentation

- Collecting data from device sensors or sophisticated sensors like surveillance cameras to GPS cell phone sensors; passing through sensors: light, temperature, pressure, humidity

- Real-time merchandising to a huge population

- Collecting logs from business systems such as application server logs, CRM, ERP, and so forth.

In all of these cases, the analysis is done in real time or it is never done, without middle points.

Apache Kafka usually is compared to traditional messaging systems such as ActiveMQ or RabitMQ. The difference is the data volume that Kafka can handle in real time.

Use Cases

Well, you have seen some business scenarios that are solved with Apache Kafka. In which layer in the architecture should you put Kafka? Here are some popular (real examples with real enterprises) use cases:

- **Commit logs**. What happens when your system does not have a log system? In these cases, you can use Kafka. Many times systems do not have logs, simply because (so far) it's not possible to handle such a large data volume. The stories of application servers falling simply because they could not write their logs correctly with the verbosity needed by the business are more common than it seems. Kafka can also help to start and restart fallen log servers.

- **Log aggregation**. Contrary to what people believe, much of the work of the onsite support team is on log analysis. Kafka not only provides a system for log management, but it can also handle heterogeneous aggregation of several logs. Kafka can physically collect the logs and remove cumbersome details such as file location or format. In addition, it provides low latency and supports multiple data sources while making distributed consumption.

- **Messaging**. Systems are often heterogeneous, and instead of rewriting them, you have to translate between them. Often the manufacturer's adapters are unaffordable to a company; for such cases, Kafka is the solution because it is open source and can handle more volume than many traditional commercial brokers.

- **Stream processing**. We could write an entire book on this topic. In some business cases, the process of collecting information consists of several stages. A clear example is when a broker is used not only to gather information but also to transform it. This is the real meaning and success of the Enterprise Service Bus (ESB) architectures. With Kafka, the information can be collected and further enriched; this (very well paid) enrichment process is known as *stream processing*.

- **Record user activity**. Many marketing and advertising companies are interested in recording all the customer activity on a web page. This seems a luxury, but until recently, it was very difficult to keep track of the clicks that a user makes on a site. For those tasks where the data volume is huge, you can use Kafka for real-time process and monitoring.

All of this seems good, but who is using Kafka today? Here are some examples:

- **LinkedIn**.[1] Used for activity stream and operational metrics. We cannot imagine the today's LinkedIn newsfeed without Kafka.

- **Uber**.[2] Relied on Kafka data feeds to bulk-load log data into Amazon S3 to stream change-data logs from the local data centers.

- **Twitter**.[3] Handling five billion sessions a day in real time requires Kafka to handle their stream processing infrastructure.

- **Netflix**.[4] Kafka is the backbone of Netflix's data pipeline for real-time monitoring and event processing.

---

[1] https://engineering.linkedin.com/blog/2016/04/kafka-ecosystem-at-linkedin
[2] http://www.datanami.com/2015/10/05/how-uber-uses-spark-and-hadoop
[3] https://blog.twitter.com/2015/handling-five-billion-sessions-a-day-in-real-time
[4] http://techblog.netflix.com/2013/12/announcing-suro-backbone-of-netflixs.html

- **Spotify.**[5] Kafka is used as part of their log delivery system.

- **Yahoo.** Used by the media analytics team as a real-time analytics pipeline. Their cluster handles 20Gbps of compressed data.

Kafka Installation

Go to the Apache Kafka home page at `http://kafka.apache.org/downloads`, as shown in Figure 8-2.

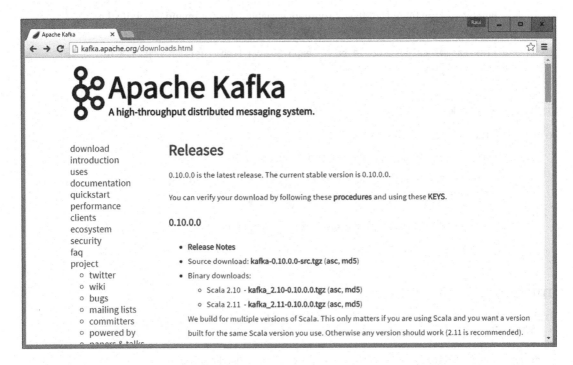

Figure 8-2. *Apache Kafka download page*

The Apache Kafka current version available as a stable release is 0.10.0.0. The major limitation with Kafka since 0.8.x is that it is not backward-compatible. So, you cannot replace this version for one prior to 0.8.
Once you download the available release, let's proceed with the installation.

Installing Java

You need to install Java 1.7 or later. Download the latest JDK from Oracle's web site at `http://www.oracle.com/technetwork/java/javase/downloads/index.html`.
For example, to install in Linux:

1. Change the file mode:

    ```
    [restrada@localhost opt]# chmod +x jdk-8u91-linux-x64.rpm
    ```

---

[5]`http://www.meetup.com/stockholm-hug/events/121628932/`

2. Change the directory in which you want to perform the installation:

   ```
   [restrada@localhost opt]# cd <directory path name>
   ```

3. To install the software in the /usr/java/ directory, type the following command:

   ```
   [restrada@localhost opt]# cd /usr/java
   ```

4. Run the installer using this command:

   ```
   [restrada@localhost java]# rpm -ivh jdk-8u91-linux-x64.rpm
   ```

5. Finally, add the JAVA_HOME environment variable. This command will write the JAVA_HOME environment variable to the /etc/profile file:

   ```
   [restrada@localhost opt]# echo "export JAVA_HOME=/usr/java/jdk1.8.0_91" >>
   /etc/profile
   ```

Installing Kafka

To install in Linux, take the following steps.

1. Extract the downloaded kafka_2.10-0.10.0.0.tgz file:

   ```
   [restrada@localhost opt]# tar xzf kafka_2.10-0.10.0.0.tgz
   ```

2. Add the Kafka bin directory to PATH as follows:

   ```
   [restrada@localhost opt]# export KAFKA_HOME=/opt/kafka_2.10-0.10.0.0
   ```

   ```
   [restrada@localhost opt]# export PATH=$PATH:$KAFKA_HOME/bin
   ```

Importing Kafka

To include Kafka in our programming projects, we include the dependencies.
    With SBT:

```
// https://mvnrepository.com/artifact/org.apache.kafka/kafka_2.10
libraryDependencies += "org.apache.kafka" % "kafka_2.10" % "0.10.0.0"
```

With Maven:

```
<!-- https://mvnrepository.com/artifact/org.apache.kafka/kafka_2.10 -->
<dependency>
    <groupId>org.apache.kafka</groupId>
    <artifactId>kafka_2.10</artifactId>
    <version>0.10.0.0</version>
</dependency>
```

With Gradle:

```
// https://mvnrepository.com/artifact/org.apache.kafka/kafka_2.10
compile group: 'org.apache.kafka', name: 'kafka_2.10', version: '0.10.0.0'
```

Kafka in Cluster

We are ready to program with the Apache Kafka publisher-subscriber messaging system. In Kafka, there are three types of clusters:

- Single node–single broker
- Single node–multiple broker
- Multiple node–multiple broker

A Kafka cluster has five main components:

- **Topic**. A category or *feed name* in which messages are published by the message producers. Topics are partitioned; each partition is represented by an ordered immutable messages sequence. The cluster has a partitioned log for each topic. Each message in the partition has a unique sequential id called an offset.

- **Broker**. A Kafka cluster has one or more physical servers in which each one may have one or more server processes running. Each server process is called a *broker*. The topics live in the broker processes.

- **Producer**. Publishes data to topics by choosing the appropriate partition in the topic. For load balancing, the messages allocation to the topic partition can be done in a round-robin mode or by defining a custom function.

- **Consumer**. Applications or processes subscribed to topics and process the feed of published messages.

- **ZooKeeper**. ZooKeeper is the coordinator between the broker and the consumers. ZooKeeper coordinates the distributed processes through a shared hierarchical name space of data registers; these registers are called *znodes*.

  There are two differences between ZooKeeper and a file system:

  - Every znode has data associated and is designed to store coordination data.
  - Znodes are limited on the amount of data that they can have.

Single Node–Single Broker Cluster

An example diagram of a single node–single broker cluster is shown in Figure 8-3.

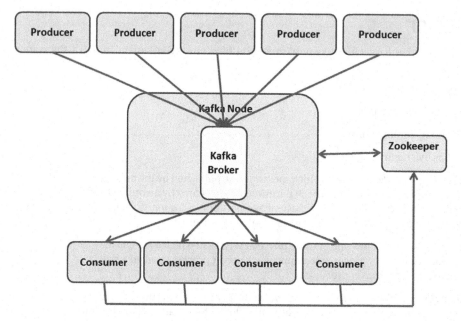

Figure 8-3. *Single node-single broker Kafka cluster example*

First, start the ZooKeeper server. Kafka provides a simple ZooKeeper configuration file to launch a single ZooKeeper instance. To install the ZooKeeper instance, use the following command:

```
[restrada@localhost kafka_2.10.0-0.0.0.0]# bin/zookeeper-server-start.sh config/zookeeper.
properties
```

The following are the main properties defined in zookeeper.properties:

- **dataDir**. The data directory where ZooKeeper is stored:

    ```
    dataDir=/tmp/zookeeper
    ```

- **clientPort**. The listening port for client requests. By default, ZooKeeper listens in the 2181 TCP port:

    ```
    clientPort=2181
    ```

- **maxClientCnxns**. The limit per IP for the number of connections (0 = unbounded):

    ```
    maxClientCnxns=0
    ```

For more information about Apache ZooKeeper, visit the project page at http://zookeeper.apache.org/.

Starting the Broker

After start ZooKeeper, start the Kafka broker with the following command:

```
[restrada@localhost kafka_2.10.0-0.0.0.0]# bin/kafka-server-start.sh config/server.
properties
```

The following are the main properties defined in server.properties:

- **Broker id**. The unique positive integer id for each broker.

  `Broker.id=0`

- **Port**. The port where the socket server listens on:

  `port=9092`

- **Log dir**. The directory to store log files:

  `log.dir=/tmp/kafka10-logs`

- **Num partitions**. The number of log partitions per topic:

  `num.partitions=2`

- **ZooKeeper connect**. The ZooKeeper connection URL:

  `zookeeper.connect=localhost:2181`

Creating a Topic

Kafka has a command to create topics. Let's create a topic called *amazingTopic* with one partition and one replica:

```
[restrada@localhost kafka_2.10.0-0.0.0.0]#bin/kafka-topics.sh --create --zookeeper
localhost:2181 --replication-factor 1 --partitions 1 --topic amazingTopic
```

Obtain the output, as follows:

```
Created topic "amazingTopic".
```

These are the parameters:

- `--replication-factor 1` indicates one replica
- `--partition 1` indicates one partition
- `--zookeeper localhost:2181` indicates the ZooKeeper URL

To obtain the list of topics on any Kafka server, use the following command:

```
[restrada@localhost kafka_2.10.0-0.0.0.0]# bin/kafka-topics.sh --list
--zookeeper localhost:2181
```

Obtain the output:

```
amazingTopic
```

Starting a Producer

Kafka has a command line to start producers. It accepts input from the command line and publishes them as messages. By default, each new line is considered a message.

```
[restrada@localhost kafka_2.10.0-0.0.0.']# bin/kafka-console-producer.sh --broker-list
localhost:9092 --topic amazingTopic
```

Two parameters are required:

- **broker-list**. The URL of the brokers to be connected.

- **topic**. The name of the topic used to send a message to its subscribers.

Now type the following:

```
Valar morghulis [Enter]
Valar dohaeris [Enter]
```

You get this output:

```
Valar morghulis
Valar dohaeris
```

The following are the main properties defined in producer.properties:

- **Metadata broker list**. A list of brokers used for bootstrapping knowledge about the rest of the cluster.

  Format: host1:port1, host2:port2

  ```
  metadata.broker.list=localhost:9092
  ```

- **Compression codec**. The compression codec for data generated.

  Example: none, gzip, snappy

  ```
  compression.codec=none
  ```

Later on this chapter, you see how to write producers.

Starting a Consumer

Kafka has a command line to start a message consumer client. It shows the output at the command line as soon as it subscribes to the topic in the broker:

```
[restrada@localhost kafka_2.10.0-0.0.0.0]# bin/kafka-console-consumer.sh --zookeeper
localhost:2181 --topic amazingTopic --from-beginning
```

As you request from-beginning, you see the following output:

```
Valar morghulis
Valar dohaeris
```

The following is the main property defined in consumer.properties:

- **Group id**. A string that identifies a set of consumers in the same group:

  ```
  group.id=test-consumer-group
  ```

Later on this chapter, you will learn how to write consumers.

Now let's play with the new toy architecture. Open each technology in a different console: ZooKeeper, broker, producer, and consumer. Type the commands in the producer and watch them displayed in the consumer.

If you don't recall how to run producers or consumers, running the command with no arguments will show the possible parameters.

Single Node–Multiple Broker Cluster

An example diagram of a single node–multiple broker cluster is shown in Figure 8-4.

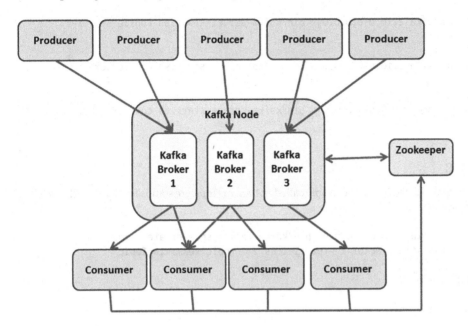

Figure 8-4. *Single node–multiple broker Kafka cluster example*

As usual, start the ZooKeeper server:

```
[restrada@localhost kafka_2.10.0-0.0.0.0]# bin/zookeeper-server-start.sh config/zookeeper.
properties
```

You need a different server.properties file for every broker. Let's call them: server-1.properties, server-2.properties, server-3.properties, and so forth.

In server-1.properties, specify the following:

- broker.id=1

- port=9093

- log.dir=/tmp/kafka-logs-1

Similarly, on server-2.properties, specify the following:

- broker.id=2

- port=9094

- log.dir=/tmp/kafka-logs-2

Follow the same procedure for server-3.properties:

- broker.id=3

- port=9095

- log.dir=/tmp/kafka-logs-3

175

Starting the Brokers

With ZooKeeper running, start the Kafka brokers with the following commands:

```
[restrada@localhost kafka_2.10.0-0.0.0.0]# bin/kafka-server-start.sh config/server-1.
properties

[restrada@localhost kafka_2.10.0-0.0.0.0]# bin/kafka-server-start.sh config/server-2.
properties

[restrada@localhost kafka_2.10.0-0.0.0.0]# bin/kafka-server-start.sh config/server-3.
properties
```

Creating a Topic

Using the command to create topics, create a topic called *reAmazingTopic* (*re* stands for *replicated*). It has two partitions and two replicas:

```
[restrada@localhost kafka_2.10.0-0.0.0.0]#bin/kafka-topics.sh --create --zookeeper
localhost:2181 --replication-factor 2 --partitions 2 --topic reAmazingTopic
```

Obtain the output, as follows:

```
Created topic "reAmazingTopic".
```

Starting a Producer

Now that you know the command to start producers, indicating more brokers in the broker-list is a trivial task:

```
[restrada@localhost kafka_2.10.0-0.0.0.0]# bin/kafka-console-producer.sh --broker-list
localhost:9093, localhost:9094, localhost:9095 --topic reAmazingTopic
```

Yes, our architects always have weird requirements; if we need to run multiple producers connecting to different broker combinations, we need to specify a different broker-list for each producer.

Starting a Consumer

To start a consumer, use the same Kafka command that you already know:

```
[restrada@localhost kafka_2.10.0-0.0.0.0]# bin/kafka-console-consumer.sh --zookeeper
localhost:2181 --from-beginning --topic reAmazingTopic
```

Multiple Node–Multiple Broker Cluster

An example of a multiple node–multiple broker cluster is shown in Figure 8-5.

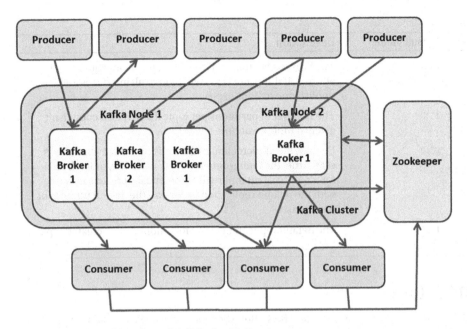

Figure 8-5. *Multiple node–multiple broker Kafka cluster*

Here you are in front of the real power of the cluster. Kafka should be installed in every machine in the cluster. Every physical server could have one or many Kafka brokers. All the nodes on the same cluster should connect to the same ZooKeeper.

But don't worry, all the previous commands remain equal. The commands for ZooKeeper, broker, producer, and consumer don't change.

Broker Properties

To recapitulate the section, Table 8-1 lists the most popular broker properties.[6]

Table 8-1. *Kafka Broker Most Important Properties*

Name	Default value	Description
broker.id	0	Each broker is identified with a positive integer id. This id is the broker's name and allows the broker to be moved to a different host or port without losing consumers.
log.dirs	/tmp/kafka-logs	The directory where the log data is stored. Each new partition created will be placed in the directory with the fewest partitions.
zookeper.connect	localhost:2181	The ZooKeeper's connection string in the hostname:port/chroot form. Here, chroot is the base directory for the path operations (namespace for sharing with other applications on the same ZooKeeper cluster).

(continued)

---

[6]The complete list is in http://kafka.apache.org/documentation.html#brokerconfigs

Table 8-1. (*continued*)

Name	Default value	Description
host.name	null	The broker's hostname. If this is set, it will only bind to this address. If this is not set, it will bind to all interfaces and publish one to ZooKeeper.
num.partitions	1	The number of partitions per topic if a partition count isn't given at topic creation.
auto.create.topics. enable	true	Enables the autocreation of the topic on the server. If this is set to true, the attempts to produce, consume, or fetch data for a non-existent topic will automatically create a new one with the default replication factor and the default number of partitions.
default.replication. factor	1	The default replication factor for automatically created topics.

Kafka Architecture

In its beginning, LinkedIn used Java Message Service (JMS). But when more power was needed (i.e., a scalable architecture), the LinkedIn development team decided to build the project that we know today as Kafka. In 2011, Kafka was an open source Apache project. In this chapter, section we give you some reflections on why things are designed in the way they are.

The following are Kafka's project goals:

- **An API**. Supports custom implementation of producers and consumers.

- **Low overhead**. Low network latency and low storage overhead with message persistence on disk.

- **High throughput**. Publishes and subscribes millions of messages; supports data feeds and real time.

- **Distributed**. Highly scalable architecture to handle low-latency delivery.

- **High availability**. Autobalances consumers in case of failure.

- **Fault tolerant**. Guarantees data integrity in case of failure.

Kafka is more than a queuing platform; the messages are received and enqueued to be delivered to a consumer pool.

Kafka is more than a published-subscriber platform; the messages are not published to all customers. The following describes Kafka's operation in a nutshell:

- Messages are published to a Kafka topic, which is a message queue or a message category.

- The Kafka topic runs in the Kafka broker, which is a server. Kafka brokers do not just run the topics, but also store the messages when required.

- The consumers use the ZooKeeper service to get the information to track the messages (the data about a message state).

Figure 8-6 shows a topic with three partitions. You can see the five Kafka components: ZooKeeper, broker, topic, producer, and consumer.

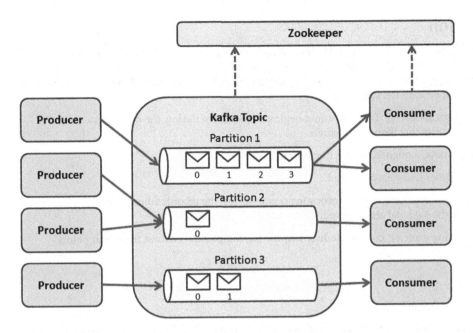

Figure 8-6. *A topic with three partitions*

The following describes parts of the partition.

- **Segment files**. Internally, every partition is a logical log file, represented as a set of segment files with the same size. The partition is a sequence of ordered messages. When a message is published, the broker appends the message to the last segment of the file. When a certain number of messages is reached, the segment file is flushed to the disk. Once the file is flushed, the messages are available for consumption by the consumers.

- **Offset**. The partitions are assigned to a unique sequential number called an *offset*. The offset is used to identify messages inside the partition. The partitions are replicated between the servers for fault tolerance.

- **Leaders**. Inside Kafka, each partition has one Kafka server as it *leader*. The other servers are *followers*. The leader of a partition coordinates the read and write requests for that partition. The followers asynchronously replicate the data from the leader. If the leader fails, another server becomes the new leader. In a cluster, every server has two roles: the leader on some partitions and a follower on other partitions.

- **Groups**. The consumers are organized into groups. Each consumer is represented as a process; one process belongs to only one group.

In Kafka, there are three ways to deliver messages (as a reflection exercise, think about why there are only three):

- Messages are never redelivered but may be lost.

- Messages may be redelivered but never lost.

- Messages are delivered once and only once.

Log Compaction

There are two types of retention: finer-grained (per message) and coarser-grained (time based). Log compaction is the process to pass from time-based to per-message retention.

In Kafka, the retention policy can be set to per-topic (time based), size-based, and log compaction-based. Log compaction ensures the following:

- Reads begin at offset 0; if the consumer begins at the start of the log, the messages are in the order that they were written.

- Messages have sequential offsets that never change.

- Message order is always preserved.

- A group of background threads recopy log segment files; the records whose keys appear in the log head are removed.

As another reflection exercise, can you deduce why the log compaction ensures these four points?

Kafka Design

The following are Kafka design bullet points:

- **Storage**. The purpose of Kafka is to provide message processing. The main functions are caching and storing messages on a file system. The caching and flushing to disk are configurable.

- **Retention**. If a message is consumed, the message is not wasted; it is retained, allowing message reconsumption.

- **Metadata**. In many messaging systems, the message metadata is kept at the server level. In Kafka, the message state is maintained at the consumer level. This prevents the following:

  - Multiple deliveries of the same message

  - Losing messages due to failures

- **OLTP**. Consumers store the state in ZooKeeper, but Kafka also allows the storage in OLTP external systems (online transaction processing).

- **Push and pull**. Producers push the message to the broker and consumers pull the message from the broker.

- **Masterless**. Like Apache Cassandra, Apache Kafka is masterless; you can remove any broker at any time. The metadata is maintained by ZooKeeper and shared with the customers.

- **Synchronous**. Producers have the option to be asynchronous or synchronous when sending messages to the broker.

Message Compression

There are cases where the network bandwidth is the bottleneck. This usually does not happen, but it could. In Kafka, there is a mechanism to compress groups of messages. Note that without being compression experts, we can deduce that it is better to compress a group of messages than compress every message individually.

When a group of messages is compressed, the network overhead is reduced. Before Kafka 0.8.0, groups of messages were compressed and presented to the consumer as a single message; the consumer decompressed it later. But there were issues with decompression that made overhead.

Since Kafka 0.8.0, some changes were introduced to the broker to handle offsets; so the problem was moved to the broker, but the overall performance improved. The lead broker is responsible for compressing messages, which lowers the network overhead but could also increase the load in the broker's CPU.

As you saw, Kafka handles Gzip and Snappy compression protocols. You need to specify this configuration in the producer to use compression.

- **compression.codec**. This parameter indicates the codec for all data generated on the producer. The default value is none. The valid values are none, gzip, and snappy.

- **compressed.topics**. This parameter turns on the compression on particular topics. Note that if the list of compressed topics is empty, then you are enabling the compression for all the topics. If the compression codec is none, the compression is disabled for all the topics.

If there is a mission in your work that does not let you sleep, and it is related to mirror data across data centers, consider using Kafka. Kafka is a good option when you have to transfer huge amounts of data between active and passive data centers in a compressed format with low network bandwidth overhead.

Replication

When you have message partitioning in Kafka, the partitioning strategy decision is made on the broker side. The decision on how the message is partitioned is made at the producer end. The broker stores the messages as they arrive. If you recall, the number of partitions configured for each topic is done in the Kafka broker.

Replication is one of the best features introduced in Kafka 0.8.0. Replication ensures that messages will be published and consumed in the event of broker failure. Both producers and consumers are replication-aware.

In replication, each partition has n replicas of a message (to handle $n-1$ failures). One replica acts as the leader. ZooKeeper knows who the replica leader is. The lead replica has a list of its follower replicas. The replicas store their part of the message in local logs.

Kafka has two replication modes: the synchronous replication process and the asynchronous replication process.

This is the synchronous replication process:

1. The producer identifies the lead replica from ZooKeeper.

2. The producer publishes the message.

3. When the message is published, it is written to the lead replica's log.

4. The followers pull the message.

5. The leader waits for all the followers to acknowledge that the replica was written.

6. Once replications are complete, the leader sends the acknowledgment to the producer.

This is the asynchronous replication process:

1. The producer identifies the lead replica from ZooKeeper.

2. The producer publishes the message.

3. When the message is published, it is written to the lead replica's log.

4. The followers pull the message.

5. Once the message is written on the lead replica, the leader sends the acknowledgment to the consumer.

As you can see, asynchronous mode is faster, but it is not fault tolerant.

Replication ensures strong durability and high availability. It guarantees that any successfully published message will not be lost and will be consumed, even in the event of broker failures.

Kafka Producers

As you saw, producers are applications that create messages and publish them to the broker. Normally, producers are front-end applications, web pages, web services, back-end services, proxies, and adapters to legacy systems. You can write Kafka producers in Java, Scala, C, and Python.

The process begins when the producer connects to any live node and requests metadata about the partitions' leaders on a topic so as to put the message directly to the partition's lead broker.

Producer API

First, you need to understand the required classes to write a producer:

- **Producer**. The class is KafkaProducer <K, V> in org.apache.kafka.clients.producer. KafkaProducer

  KafkaProducer is a type of Java generic written in Scala. K specifies the partition key type and V specifies the message value.

- **ProducerRecord**. The class is ProducerRecord <K, V> in org.apache.kafka.clients. producer.ProducerRecord

  This class encapsulates the data required for establishing the connection with the brokers (broker list, partition, message serializer, and partition key).

  ProducerRecord is a type of Java generic written in Scala. K specifies the partition key type and V specifies the message value.

The Producer API encapsulates all the low-level producer implementations. The default mode is asynchronous, but you can specify in producer.type in the producer configuration.

Scala Producers

Now let's write a simple Scala Kafka producer to send messages to the broker. The SimpleProducer class is used to create a message for a specific topic and to send it using message partitioning. This chapter's examples were tested with Scala version 2.10.

Step 1. Import Classes

Import two classes:

```
import org.apache.kafka.clients.producer.{KafkaProducer, ProducerRecord}
```

Step 2. Define Properties

Define the following properties:

```
val props = new Properties()
props.put("metadata.broker.list",
  "192.168.146.132:9093, 192.168.146.132:9094, 192.168.146.132:9095")

props.put("serializer.class", "kafka.serializer.StringEncoder")

props.put("request.required.acks", "1")

producer = new KafkaProducer(props)
```

As you can see, the properties are as follows:

- **metadata.broker.list**

  Specifies the list of brokers that connect to the producer in the format [node:port, node:port]. As you know, Kafka determines the lead broker of the topic.

- **serializer.class**

  Specifies the serializer used while preparing the message for transmission from the producer to the broker.

  In this example, we use the string encoder provided by Kafka. By default, the serializer for the key and message is the same, but you can also implement the custom serializer class by extending kafka.serializer.Encoder.

- **request.required.acks**

  Indicates to the broker to send an acknowledgment to the producer when a message is received.

  1 means that the producer receives an acknowledgment once the lead replica has received the message. The default mode is "fire and forget," so that it is not informed in the event of message loss.

Step 3. Build and Send the Message

The following code should be self-explanatory:

```
val runtime = new Date().toString
val msg = "Message Publishing Time - " + runtime
val data = new ProducerRecord[String, String](topic, msg)
producer.send(data)
```

Listing 8-1 shows the complete SimpleProducer.

Listing 8-1. SimpleProducer.scala

```scala
package apress.ch08

import java.util.{Date, Properties}

import apress.ch08.SimpleProducer._
import org.apache.kafka.clients.producer.{KafkaProducer, ProducerRecord}

object SimpleProducer {

  private var producer: KafkaProducer[String, String] = _

  def main(args: Array[String]) {
    val argsCount = args.length
    if (argsCount == 0 || argsCount == 1)
      throw new IllegalArgumentException(
        "Provide topic name and Message count as arguments")

    // Topic name and the message count to be published is passed from the
    // command line
    val topic = args(0)
    val count = args(1)

    val messageCount = java.lang.Integer.parseInt(count)
    println("Topic Name - " + topic)
    println("Message Count - " + messageCount)
    val simpleProducer = new SimpleProducer()
    simpleProducer.publishMessage(topic, messageCount)
  }
}

class SimpleProducer {

  val props = new Properties()

  // Set the broker list for requesting metadata to find the lead broker
  props.put("bootstrap.servers",
    "192.168.146.132:9093, 192.168.146.132:9094, 192.168 146.132:9095")

  //This specifies the serializer class for keys
  props.put("key.serializer", "org.apache.kafka.common.serialization.StringSerializer")
  props.put("value.serializer", "org.apache.kafka.common.serialization.StringSerializer")

  // 1 means the producer receives an acknowledgment once the lead replica
  // has received the data. This option provides better durability as the
  // client waits until the server acknowledges the request as successful.
  props.put("request.required.acks", "1")

  producer = new KafkaProducer(props)
```

```
  private def publishMessage(topic: String, messageCount: Int) {
    for (mCount <- 0 until messageCount) {
      val runtime = new Date().toString
      val msg = "Message Publishing Time - " + runtime
      println(msg)

      // Create a message
      val data = new ProducerRecord[String, String](topic, msg)

      // Publish the message
      producer.send(data)
    }

    // Close producer connection with broker.
    producer.close()
  }
}
```

Step 4. Create the Topic

Before running the program, you must create the topic. You can create it using the API (amazing, isn't it?) or from the command line:

```
[restrada@localhost kafka_2.10.0-0.0.0.0]#bin/kafka-topics.sh --create --zookeeper
localhost:2181 --replication-factor 1 --partitions 3 --topic amazingTopic
```

Step 5. Compile the Producer

Compile the program with this command:

```
[restrada@localhost kafka_2.10.0-0.0.0.0]# scalac . apress/ch08/SimpleProducer.scala
```

Step 6. Run the Producer

Run the SimpleProducer with the following command:

```
[restrada@localhost kafka_2.10.0-0.0.0.0]# scala apress.ch08.SimpleProducer amazingTopic 10
```

This program takes two arguments: the topic name and the number of messages to publish.

Step 7. Run a Consumer

As you already saw, you can run the consumer program with the following command:

```
[restrada@localhost kafka_2.10.0-0.0.0.0]# bin/kafka-console-consumer.sh --zookeeper
localhost:2181 --from-beginning --topic amazingTopic
```

Producers with Custom Partitioning

Let's jump to the next level by writing another program that implements customized message partitioning. The example consists of recollecting the IPs visiting a web site, which are recorded and published. The message has three parts: timestamp, web site name, and IP address.

Step 1. Import Classes

Import these classes:

```
import java.util.Date
import java.util.Properties
import java.util.Random
import org.apache.kafka.clients.producer.KafkaProducer
import org.apache.kafka.clients.producer.ProducerRecord
```

Step 2. Define Properties

Define the following properties:

```
val props = new Properties()

props.put("metadata.broker.list",
   "192.168.146.132:9092, 192.168.146.132:9093, 192.168.146.132:9094")

props.put("serializer.class", "kafka.serializer.StringEncoder")

// Defines the class to be used for determining the partition
// in the topic where the message needs to be sent.
props.put("partitioner.class", "apress.ch08.SimplePartitioner")

props.put("request.required.acks", "1")

producer = new KafkaProducer(props)
```

Step 3. Implement the Partitioner class

Write the SimplePartitioner class that extends the Partitioner abstract class. The class takes the key, in this case the IP address, and makes a modulo operation with the number of partitions. Listing 8-2 shows the SimplePartitioner code.

Listing 8-2. SimplePartitioner.scala

```
package apress.ch08

import java.util

import kafka.utils.VerifiableProperties
import org.apache.kafka.clients.producer.KafkaProducer
import org.apache.kafka.clients.producer.Partitioner
```

```scala
import org.apache.kafka.common.Cluster

object SimplePartitioner {

  private var producer: KafkaProducer[String, String] = _
}

class SimplePartitioner extends Partitioner {

  def partition(key: AnyRef, a_numPartitions: Int): Int = {
    var partition = 0
    val partitionKey = key.asInstanceOf[String]
    val offset = partitionKey.lastIndexOf('.')
    if (offset > 0) {
      partition = java.lang.Integer.parseInt(partitionKey.substring(offset + 1)) %
        a_numPartitions
    }
    Partition
  }

  override def partition(topic: String,
                         key: AnyRef,
                         keyBytes: Array[Byte],
                         value: AnyRef,
                         valueBytes: Array[Byte],
                         cluster: Cluster): Int = partition(key, 10)

  override def close() {
  }

  override def configure(configs: util.Map[String, _]) {
  }
}
```

Step 4. Build and Send the Message

Listing 8-3 presents the complete CustomPartitionProducer.scala.

Listing 8-3. CustomPartitionProducer.scala

```scala
package apress.ch08

import java.util.Date
import java.util.Properties
import java.util.Random
import org.apache.kafka.clients.producer.KafkaProducer
import org.apache.kafka.clients.producer.ProducerRecord
import CustomPartitionProducer._

object CustomPartitionProducer {

  var producer: KafkaProducer[String, String] = _
```

```scala
  def main(args: Array[String]) {
    val argsCount = args.length
    if (argsCount == 0 || argsCount == 1)
      throw new IllegalArgumentException(
        "Please provide topic name and Message count as arguments")

    // Topic name and the message count to be published is passed from the
    // command line
    val topic = args(0)
    val count = args(1)
    val messageCount = java.lang.Integer.parseInt(count)
    println("Topic Name - " + topic)
    println("Message Count - " + messageCount)
    val simpleProducer = new CustomPartitionProducer()
    simpleProducer.publishMessage(topic, messageCount)
  }
}

class CustomPartitionProducer {

  val props = new Properties()

  // Set the broker list for requesting metadata to find the lead broker
  props.put("metadata.broker.list",
    "192.168.146.132:9092, 192.168.146.132:9093, 192.168.146.132:9094")

  // This specifies the serializer class for keys
  props.put("serializer.class", "kafka.serializer.StringEncoder")

  // Defines the class to be used for determining the partition
  // in the topic where the message needs to be sent.
  props.put("partitioner.class", "apress.ch08.SimplePartitioner")

  // 1 means the producer receives an acknowledgment once the lead replica
  // has received the data. This option provides better durability as the
  // client waits until the server acknowledges the request as successful.
  props.put("request.required.acks", "1")

  producer = new KafkaProducer(props)

  private def publishMessage(topic: String, messageCount: Int) {
    val random = new Random()
    for (mCount <- 0 until messageCount) {
      val clientIP = "192.168.14." + random.nextInt(255)
      val accessTime = new Date().toString
      val msg = accessTime + ",kafka.apache.org," + clientIP
      println(msg)
      // Create a ProducerRecord instance
      val data = new ProducerRecord[String, String](topic, clientIP, msg)
```

```
        // Publish the message
        producer.send(data)
    }
    producer.close()
  }
}
```

Step 5. Create the Topic

Before running the program, you must create the pageHits topic from the command line:

```
[restrada@localhost kafka_2.10.0-0.0.0.0]#bin/kafka-topics.sh --create --zookeeper
localhost:2181 --replication-factor 3 --partitions 5 --topic pageHits
```

Step 6. Compile the Programs

Compile the programs with the following commands:

```
[restrada@localhost kafka_2.10.0-0.0.0.0]# scalac . apress/ch08/SimplePartitioner.scala
```

```
[restrada@localhost kafka_2.10.0-0.0.0.0]# scalac . apress/ch08/CustomPartitionProducer.
scala
```

Step 7. Run the Producer

Run CustomPartitionProducer with the following command:

```
[restrada@localhost kafka_2.10.0-0.0.0.0]# scala apress.ch08.CustomPartitionProducer
pageHits 100
```

The program takes two arguments: the topic name and the number of messages to publish.

Step 8. Run a Consumer

As you already saw, you can run the consumer program with the following command:

```
[restrada@localhost kafka_2.10.0-0.0.0.0]# bin/kafka-console-consumer.sh --zookeeper
localhost:2181 --from-beginning --topic pageHits
```

Producer Properties

To recapitulate the section, Table 8-2 lists the most popular producer properties.[7]

---

[7]The complete list is in http://kafka.apache.org/documentation.html#producerconfigs

Table 8-2. *Kafka Producer Most Important Properties*

Name	Type	Default	Description
bootstrap.servers	list		The producer uses this property to get metadata about topics, partitions, and replicas. The format is host1:port1,host2:port2.
key.serializer	class		Specifies the serializer class for the messages. The default encoder accepts and returns the same byte.
value.serializer	class		Specifies the serializer value for the messages.
acks	string	1	Controls when the producer request is considered complete and when the producer receives an acknowledgment from the broker:
			0 = producer will never wait for an acknowledgment from the broker; lowest latency, but with weakest durability.
			1 = producer receives an acknowledgment once the lead replica has received the data; better durability as the client waits until the server acknowledges a successful request.
			–1 = producer will receive an acknowledgment once all the in-sync replicas have received the data; the best durability.
buffer.memory	long	33554432	The total bytes of memory that the producer can use to buffer records waiting to be sent to the server.
compression.type	string	none	Specifies the compression codec for all data generated by this producer. The values accepted are none, gzip, and snappy.
retries	int	0	Setting a value greater than zero will cause the client to resend any record whose send fails with a potentially transient error.

Kafka Consumers

As you saw, consumers are applications that consume the messages published by the broker. Normally, producers are real-time analysis applications, near real-time analysis applications, NoSQL solutions, data warehouses, back-end services, and subscriber-based solutions. You can write Kafka producers in Java, Scala, C, and Python.

The consumer subscribes for the message consumption on a specific topic on the Kafka broker. The consumer then makes a fetch request to the lead broker to consume the message partition by specifying the message offset. The consumer works in the pull model and always pulls all available messages after its current position.

Consumer API

In the Kafka 0.8.0 version, there were two API types for consumers: the high-level API and the low-level API. In version 0.10.0, they are unified.

To use the consumer API with Maven, you should import the following dependency:

```
<dependency>
    <groupId>org.apache.kafka</groupId>
    <artifactId>kafka-clients</artifactId>
    <version>0.10.0.0</version>
</dependency>
```

The consumer API classes with SBT are imported, as follows:

```
// https://mvnrepository.com/artifact/org.apache.kafka/kafka-clients
libraryDependencies += "org.apache.kafka" % "kafka-clients" % "0.10.0.0"
```

The consumer API classes with Gradle are imported:

```
// https://mvnrepository.com/artifact/org.apache.kafka/kafka-clients
compile group: 'org.apache.kafka', name: 'kafka-clients', version: '0.10.0.0'
```

Simple Scala Consumers

Let's write a single threaded Scala consumer using the Consumer API for consuming the messages from a topic. This SimpleConsumer is used to fetch messages from a topic and consume them. We assume that there is a single partition in the topic.

Step 1. Import Classes

Import these classes:

```
import java.util
import java.util.Properties
import kafka.consumer.ConsumerConfig
```

Step 2. Define Properties

Define the following properties:

```
val props = new Properties()
props.put("zookeeper.connect", zookeeper)
props.put("group.id", groupId)
props.put("zookeeper.session.timeout.ms", "500")
props.put("zookeeper.sync.time.ms", "250")
props.put("auto.commit.interval.ms", "1000")
new ConsumerConfig(props)
```

Now let's go over the major properties mentioned in the code:

- **zookeeper.connect.** Specifies the ZooKeeper <node:port> connection used to find the ZooKeeper running instance in the cluster. ZooKeeper is used to store offsets of messages consumed for a specific topic and partition by this consumer group.

- **group.id**. Specifies the consumer group name (shared by all the consumers in the group). This is the process name used by ZooKeeper to store offsets.

- **zookeeper.session.timeout.ms**. Specifies the ZooKeeper session timeout in milliseconds. Represents the amount of time Kafka will wait for a ZooKeeper response to a request before giving up and continuing with consuming messages.

- **zookeeper.sync.time.ms**. Specifies the ZooKeeper sync time (in milliseconds) between the leader and the followers.

- **auto.commit.interval.ms**. Defines the frequency (in milliseconds) at which consumer offsets get committed.

Step 3. Code the SimpleConsumer

Write the SimpleConsumer class, as shown in Listing 8-4.

Listing 8-4. SimpleConsumer.scala

```scala
package apress.ch08

import java.util
import java.util.Properties

import kafka.consumer.ConsumerConfig
import SimpleConsumer._

import scala.collection.JavaConversions._

object SimpleConsumer {

  private def createConsumerConfig(zookeeper: String, groupId: String): ConsumerConfig = {
    val props = new Properties()
    props.put("zookeeper.connect", zookeeper)
    props.put("group.id", groupId)
    props.put("zookeeper.session.timeout.ms", "500")
    props.put("zookeeper.sync.time.ms", "250")
    props.put("auto.commit.interval.ms", "1000")
    new ConsumerConfig(props)
  }

  def main(args: Array[String]) {
    val zooKeeper = args(0)
    val groupId = args(1)
    val topic = args(2)
    val simpleHLConsumer = new SimpleConsumer(zooKeeper, groupId, topic)
    simpleHLConsumer.testConsumer()
  }
}
```

```
class SimpleConsumer(zookeeper: String, groupId: String, private val topic: String) {

  private val consumer =
    kafka.consumer.Consumer.createJavaConsumerConnector(createConsumerConfig(zookeeper,
    groupId))

  def testConsumer() {
    val topicMap = new util.HashMap[String, Integer]()
    topicMap.put(topic, 1)
    val consumerStreamsMap = consumer.createMessageStreams(topicMap)
    val streamList = consumerStreamsMap.get(topic)
    for (stream <- streamList; aStream <- stream)
      println("Message from Single Topic :: " + new String(aStream.message()))
    if (consumer != null) {
      consumer.shutdown()
    }
  }
}
```

Step 4. Create the Topic

Before running the program, you must create the amazingTopic topic from the command line:

```
[restrada@localhost kafka_2.10.0-0.0.0.0]#bin/kafka-topics.sh --create --zookeeper
localhost:2181 --replication-factor 1 --partitions 3 --topic amazingTopic
```

Step 5. Compile the Program

Compile the program with the following command:

```
[restrada@localhost kafka_2.10.0-0.0.0.0]# scalac . apress/ch08/SimpleConsumer.scala
```

Step 6. Run the Producer

Run the SimpleProducer with the following command:

```
[restrada@localhost kafka_2.10.0-0.0.0.0]# scala apress.ch08.SimpleProducer amazingTopic 100
```

Step 7. Run the Consumer

Run SimpleConsumer with the following command:

```
[restrada@localhost kafka_2.10.0-0.0.0.0]# scala apress.ch08.SimpleConsumer localhost:2181
testGroup amazingTopic
```

The SimpleConsumer class takes three arguments: the ZooKeeper connection string in <host:port> form, the unique group id, and the Kafka topic name.

Multithread Scala Consumers

A multithreaded consumer API design is based on the number of partitions in the topic and has a one-to-one mapping approach between the thread and the partitions in the topic.

If you don't have the one-to-one relation, conflicts may occur, such as a thread that never receives a message or a thread that receives messages from multiple partitions. Let's program MultiThreadConsumer.

Step 1. Import Classes

Import these classes:

```
import java.util
import java.util.Properties
import java.util.concurrent.ExecutorService
import java.util.concurrent.Executors
import kafka.consumer.ConsumerConfig
```

Step 2. Define Properties

Define the following properties:

```
val props = new Properties()
props.put("zookeeper.connect", zookeeper)
props.put("group.id", groupId)
props.put("zookeeper.session.timeout.ms", "500")
props.put("zookeeper.sync.time.ms", "250")
props.put("auto.commit.interval.ms", "1000")
new ConsumerConfig(props)
```

Step 3. Code the MultiThreadConsumer

Write the MultiThreadConsumer class, as shown in Listing 8-5.

Listing 8-5. MultiThreadConsumer.scala

```
package apress.ch08

import java.util
import java.util.Properties
import java.util.concurrent.ExecutorService
import java.util.concurrent.Executors

import kafka.consumer.ConsumerConfig
import MultiThreadConsumer._

import scala.collection.JavaConversions._

object MultiThreadConsumer {
```

```scala
  private def createConsumerConfig(zookeeper: String, groupId: String): ConsumerConfig = {
    val props = new Properties()
    props.put("zookeeper.connect", zookeeper)
    props.put("group.id", groupId)
    props.put("zookeeper.session.timeout.ms", "500")
    props.put("zookeeper.sync.time.ms", "250")
    props.put("auto.commit.interval.ms", "1000")
    new ConsumerConfig(props)
  }

  def main(args: Array[String]) {
    val zooKeeper = args(0)
    val groupId = args(1)
    val topic = args(2)
    val threadCount = java.lang.Integer.parseInt(args(3))
    val multiThreadHLConsumer = new MultiThreadConsumer(zooKeeper, groupId, topic)
    multiThreadHLConsumer.testMultiThreadConsumer(threadCount)
    try {
      Thread.sleep(10000)
    } catch {
      case ie: InterruptedException =>
    }
    multiThreadHLConsumer.shutdown()
  }
}

class MultiThreadConsumer(zookeeper: String, groupId: String, topic: String) {

  private var executor: ExecutorService = _

  private val consumer = kafka.consumer.Consumer.createJavaConsumerConnector(createConsumer
  Config(zookeeper,
    groupId))

  def shutdown() {
    if (consumer != null) consumer.shutdown()
    if (executor != null) executor.shutdown()
  }

  def testMultiThreadConsumer(threadCount: Int) {
    val topicMap = new util.HashMap[String, Integer]()

    // Define thread count for each topic
    topicMap.put(topic, threadCount)

    // Here we have used a single topic but we can also add
    // multiple topics to topicCount MAP
    val consumerStreamsMap = consumer.createMessageStreams(topicMap)
    val streamList = consumerStreamsMap.get(topic)
```

```scala
    // Launching the thread pool
    executor = Executors.newFixedThreadPool(threadCount)

    // Creating an object messages consumption
    var count = 0
    for (stream <- streamList) {
      val threadNumber = count
      executor.submit(new Runnable() {

        def run() {
          val consumerIte = stream.iterator()
          while (consumerIte.hasNext)
            println("Thread Number " + threadNumber + ": " + new String(consumerIte.next().
            message()))
            println("Shutting down Thread Number: " + threadNumber)
        }
      })
      count += 1
    }
    if (consumer != null) consumer.shutdown()
    if (executor != null) executor.shutdown()
  }
}
```

Step 4. Create the Topic

Before running the program, you must create the amazingTopic topic from the command line:

```
[restrada@localhost kafka_2.10.0-0.0.0.0]#bin/kafka-topics.sh --create --zookeeper
localhost:2181 --replication-factor 2 --partitions 4 --topic amazingTopic
```

Step 5. Compile the Program

Compile the program with the following command:

```
[restrada@localhost kafka_2.10.0-0.0.0.0]# scalac . apress/ch08/MultiThreadConsumer.scala
```

Step 6. Run the Producer

Run SimpleProducer with the following command:

```
[restrada@localhost kafka_2.10.0-0.0.0.0]# scala apress.ch08.SimpleProducer amazingTopic 100
```

Step 7. Run the Consumer

Run MultiThreadConsumer with the following command:

```
[restrada@localhost kafka_2.10.0-0.0.0.0]# scala apress.ch08.MultiThreadConsumer
localhost:2181 testGroup amazingTopic 4
```

MultiThreadConsumer takes four arguments:

- ZooKeeper connection string in <host:port> form
- An unique group id
- Kafka topic name
- Thread count

This program prints all partitions of messages associated with each thread.

Consumer Properties

To recapitulate the section, Table 8-3 lists the most popular consumer properties.[8]

Table 8-3. *Kafka Consumer Most Important Properties*

Name	Default	Type	Description
bootstrap.servers		list	A list of pairs host/port to establishing the initial connection to the cluster. Should be in the form host1:port1,host2:port2, and so forth.
fetch.min.bytes	1	int	The minimum amount of data the server should return for a fetch request. Setting this to something greater than 1 causes the server to wait to accumulate larger data amounts, which improves server throughput a bit at the cost of additional latency.
group.id	""	string	A unique string that identifies the consumer group that this consumer belongs to.
heartbeat.interval.ms	3000	int	The expected time between heartbeats to the consumer coordinator when using Kafka's group management facilities.
key.deserializer		class	A deserializer class for key that implements the Deserializer interface.
max.partition.fetch.bytes	1048576	int	The maximum amount of data per partition that the server will return. The maximum total memory used for a request is #partitions * max.partition.fetch.bytes.
session.timeout.ms	30000	int	Timeout used to detect failures when using Kafka's group management facilities. When a consumer's heartbeat is not received within the session timeout, the broker will mark the consumer as failed and rebalance the group.
value.deserializer		class	Deserializer class for value that implements the Deserializer interface.

---

[8]The complete list is in http://kafka.apache.org/documentation.html#consumerconfigs

Kafka Integration

When processing small amounts of data in real time, it is not a challenge when using Java Messaging Service (JMS); but learning from LinkedIn's experience, you see that this processing system has serious performance limitations when dealing with large data volumes. Moreover, this system is a nightmare when trying to scale horizontally, because it can't.

Integration with Apache Spark

In the next example, you need a Kafka cluster up and running. Also, you need Spark installed on your machine, ready to be deployed.

Apache Spark has a utility class to create the data stream to be read from Kafka. But, as with any Spark project, you first need to create SparkConf and the Spark StreamingContext.

```
val sparkConf = new SparkConf().setAppName("SparkKafkaTest")
val jssc = new JavaStreamingContext(sparkConf, Durations.seconds(10))
```

Create the hash set for the topic and Kafka consumer parameters:

```
val topicsSet = new HashSet[String]()
topicsSet.add("mytesttopic")
```

```
val kafkaParams = new HashMap[String, String]()
kafkaParams.put("metadata.broker.list", "localhost:9092")
```

You can create a direct Kafka stream with brokers and topics:

```
val messages = KafkaUtils.createDirectStream(
        jssc,
        classOf[String],
        classOf[String],
        classOf[StringDecoder],
        classOf[StringDecoder],
        kafkaParams,
        topicsSet)
```

With this stream, you can run the regular data processing algorithms.

1. Create a Spark StreamingContext that sets up the entry point for all stream functionality. Then set up the stream processing batch interval at 10 seconds.

2. Create the hash set for the topics to read from.

3. Set the parameters for the Kafka producer using a hash map. This map must have a value for metadata.broker.list, which is the comma-separated list of host and port numbers.

4. Create the input DStream using the KafkaUtils class.

Once you have the DStream ready, you can apply your algorithms to it. Explaining how to do that is beyond the scope of this book.

Spark Streaming is explained in detail in Chapter 6.

Kafka Administration

There are numerous tools provided by Kafka to administrate features such as cluster management, topic tools, and cluster mirroring. Let's look at these tools in detail.

Cluster Tools

As you already know, when replicating multiple partitions, you can have replicated data. Among replicas, one acts as leader and the rest as followers. When there is no leader, a follower takes leadership.

When the broker has to be shut down for maintenance activities, the new leader is elected sequentially. This means significant I/O operations on ZooKeeper. With a big cluster, this means a delay in availability.

To reach high availability, Kafka provides tools for shutting down brokers. This tool transfers the leadership among the replicas or to another broker. If you don't have an in-sync replica available, the tool fails to shut down the broker to ensure data integrity.

This tool is used through the following command:

```
[restrada@localhost kafka_2.10.0-0.0.0.0]# bin/kafka-run-class.sh kafka.admin.
ShutdownBroker --zookeeper <zookeeper_host:port/namespace> --broker <brokerID> --num.retries
3 --retry.interval.ms 100
```

The ZooKeeper URL and the broker id are mandatory parameters. There are other optional parameters; for example, num.retries (the default value is 0) and retry.interval.ms (the default value is 1000).

When the server is stopped gracefully, it syncs all of its logs to disk to avoid any log recovery when it is restarted again, because log recovery is a time-consuming task. Before shutdown, it migrates the leader partitions to other replicas; so it ensures low downtime for each partition.

Controlled shutdown is enabled in this way:

```
controlled.shutdown.enable=true
```

When there is a big cluster, Kafka ensures that the lead replicas are equally distributed among the broker. If a broker fails in shutdown, this distribution cannot be balanced.

To maintain a balanced distribution, Kafka has a tool to distribute lead replicas across the brokers in the cluster. This tool's syntax is as follows:

```
[restrada@localhost kafka_2.10.0-0.0.0.0]# bin/kafka-preferred-replica-election.sh
--zookeeper <zookeeper_host:port/namespace>
```

This tool updates the ZooKeeper path with a list of topic partitions whose lead replica needs to be moved. If the controller finds that the preferred replica is not the leader, it sends a request to the broker to make the preferred replica the partition leader. If the preferred replica is not in the ISR list, the controller fails the operation to avoid data loss.

You can specify a JSON list for this tool in this format:

```
[restrada@localhost kafka_2.10.0-0.0.0.0]# bin/kafka-preferred-replicaelection.
sh --zookeeper <zookeeper_host:port/namespace> --path-to-jsonfile
topicPartitionList.json
```

The following is the topicPartitionList.json file format:

```
{"partitions":
        [
                {"topic": "AmazingTopic", "partition": "0"},
                {"topic": "AmazingTopic", "partition": "1"},
                {"topic": "AmazingTopic", "partition": "2"},

                {"topic": "reAmazingTopic", "partition": "0"},
                {"topic": "reAmazingTopic", "partition": "1"},
                {"topic": "reAmazingTopic", "partition": "2"},
        ]
}
```

Adding Servers

When you add servers to the cluster, a unique broker id needs to be assigned to the new server. This way, adding a server doesn't assign data partitions. So, a new server won't perform any work until new partitions are migrated to it or new topics are created.

Let's discuss moving partitions between brokers. There is a tool that reassigns partitions in bin/kafka-reassign-partitions.sh. This tool takes care of everything. When migrating, Kafka makes the new server a follower of the migrating partition. This enables the new server to fully replicate the existing data in the partition.

The reassign-partition tool runs in three different modes:

- **--generate**. Moves the partitions based on the topics and the brokers list shared with the tool.

- **--execute**. Moves the partitions based on the user plan specified in --reassignment-json-file.

- **--verify**. Moves the partitions based on the status (successful/failed/in progress) of the last --execute.

The partition reassignment tool could be used to move selected topics form current brokers to new brokers. The administrator provides a list of topics and a target list of new broker ids. This tool distributes the partitions of a given topic among the new brokers. For example:

```
[restrada@localhost kafka_2.10.0-0.0.0.0]# cat topics-for-new-server.json
{"partitions":
        [{"topic": "amazingTopic",
        {"topic": "reAmazingTopic"}],
        "version":1
}

[restrada@localhost kafka_2.10.0-0.0.0.0]# bin/kafka-reassign-partitions.sh --zookeeper
localhost:2181 --topics-to-move-json-file topics-for-new-server.json --broker-list
"4,5" --generate new-topic-reassignment.json
```

This command generates the assignment (new-topic-reassignment.json) plan to move all partitions for topics amazingTopic and reAmazingTopic to the new set of brokers having ids 4 and 5. At the end of this move, all partitions will only exist on brokers 5 and 6. To initiate the assignment with the kafka-reassign-partitions.sh tool, use this:

```
[restrada@localhost kafka_2.10.0-0.0.0.0]# bin/kafka-reassign-partitions. sh --zookeeper
localhost:2181 --reassignment-json-file new-topic-reassignment.json --execute
```

You could use this tool to selectively move the partitions from the existing broker to the new broker:

```
[restrada@localhost kafka_2.10.0-0.0.0.0]# cat partitions-reassignment.json
{"partitions":
        [{"topic": "amazingTopic",
                "partition": 1,
                "replicas": [1,2,4] }],
        }],
        "version":1
}
```

```
[restrada@localhost kafka_2.10.0-0.0.0.0]# bin/kafka-reassign-partitions.sh --zookeeper
localhost:2181 --reassignment-json-file partitions-reassignment.json --execute
```

This command moves some replicas for certain partitions to the new server. Once the reassignment is done, the operation can be verified:

```
[restrada@localhost kafka_2.10.0-0.0.0.0]# bin/kafka-reassign-partitions. sh --zookeeper
localhost:2181 --reassignment-json-file new-topic-reassignment.json --verify
```

```
Status of partition reassignment:
Reassignment of partition [amazingTopic,0] completed successfully
Reassignment of partition [amazingTopic,1] is in progress
Reassignment of partition [amazingTopic,2] completed successfully
Reassignment of partition [reAmazingTopic,0] completed successfully
Reassignment of partition [reAmazingTopic,1] completed successfully
Reassignment of partition [reAmazingTopic,2] is in progress
```

To separate a server from the Kafka cluster, you have to move the replica for all partitions hosted on the server to be detached from the remaining brokers. You can also use the kafka-reassign-partitions.sh tool to increase the partition's replication factor, as follows:

```
[restrada@localhost kafka_2.10.0-0.0.0.0]# cat increase-replication-factor.json {"partitions
":[{"topic":"amazingTopic","partition":0,"replicas":[2,3]}],
"version":1 }
```

```
[restrada@localhost kafka_2.10.0-0.0.0.0]# bin/kafka-reassign-partitions.sh --zookeeper
localhost:2181 --reassignment-json-file increase-replication-factor.json --execute
```

This command assumes that partition 0 of the amazingTopic has a replication factor of 1 (the replica is on broker 2); and now it increases the replication factor to 2 and also creates the new replica on the next server, which is broker 3.

Kafka Topic Tools

When Kafka creates topics, it uses the default number of partitions (1) and the default replication factor (1). In real life, you need to specify these parameters.

```
[restrada@localhost kafka_2.10.0-0.0.0.0]# bin/kafka-topics.sh --create --zookeeper
localhost:2181/chroot --replication-factor 3 --partitions 10 --topic amazingTopic
```

You can interpret this command as follows: replication factor 3 means that up to two servers can fail before data access is lost. Ten partitions are defined for a topic, which means that the full data set will be handled by no more than ten brokers, excluding replicas.

To alter existent Kafka topics, use this command:

```
[restrada@localhost kafka_2.10.0-0.0.0.0]# bin/kafka-topics.sh --alter --zookeeper
localhost:2181/chroot --partitions 20 --topic amazingTopic
```

With this command, we are adding ten more partitions to the topic created in the previous example. To delete a topic, use the following command:

```
[restrada@localhost kafka_2.10.0-0.0.0.0]# bin/kafka-topics.sh --delete --zookeeper
localhost:2181/chroot --topic amazingTopic
```

Using the kafka-topics.sh utility, the configuration can also be added to the Kafka topic, as follows:

```
[restrada@localhost kafka_2.10.0-0.0.0.0]# bin/kafka-topics.sh --alter --zookeeper
localhost:2181/chroot --topic amazingTopic --config <key>=<value>
```

To remove a configuration from the topic, use the following command:

```
[restrada@localhost kafka_2.10.0-0.0.0.0]# bin/kafka-topics.sh --alter --zookeeper
localhost:2181/chroot --topic amazingTopic --deleteconfig <key>=<value>
```

There is a utility to search for the list of topics on the server. The list tool provides a listing of topics and information about partitions, replicas, and leaders by querying ZooKeeper.

The following command obtains a list of topics:

```
[restrada@localhost kafka_2.10.0-0.0.0.0]# bin/kafka-topics.sh --list --zookeeper
localhost:2181
```

The table obtained with this command has the following headers:

- **leader**: A randomly selected node for a specific portion of the partitions; responsible for the reads and writes on this partition.

- **replicas**: The list of nodes that holds the log for a specified partition.

- **isr**: The subset of the in-sync list of replicas that is currently alive and in-sync with the leader.

Cluster Mirroring

Mirroring is used to create a replication of an existing cluster; for example, replicating an active data center into a passive data center. The mirror-maker tool mirrors the source cluster into a target cluster.

To mirror the source cluster, bring up the target cluster and start the mirror-maker processes, as follows:

```
[restrada@localhost kafka_2.10.0-0.0.0.0]# bin/kafka-run-class.sh kafka.tools. MirrorMaker
--consumer.config sourceClusterConsumer.config --num.streams 2 --producer.config
targetClusterProducer.config --whitelist=".*"
```

There are also tools to check the position of the consumer while mirroring or in general. The tool shows the position of all the consumers in a consumer group and how far they are to the log's end; it also indicates how well cluster mirroring is performing. This tool is used as follows:

```
[restrada@localhost kafka_2.10.0-0.0.0.0]#bin/kafka-run-class.sh kafka.tools.
ConsumerOffsetChecker --group MirrorGroup --zkconnect localhost:2181 --topic kafkatopic
```

Summary

During this complete journey through Apache Kafka, we touched upon many important facts. You learned how to install Kafka, how to set up a Kafka cluster with single and multiple brokers on a single node, how to run command-line producers and consumers, and how to exchange some messages. You discovered important Kafka broker settings. You also learned the reason why Kafka was developed, its installation procedures, and its support for different types of clusters.

We explored the Kafka's design approach and wrote a few basic producers and consumers. Finally, we discussed Kafka's integration with technologies, such as Spark. In the next chapter, we review all the enterprise integration patterns.

PART III

Improving SMACK

CHAPTER 9

■ ■ ■

Fast Data Patterns

In this chapter, we examine well-known patterns in developing fast data applications. As you know, there are two approaches: (1) the batch, on disk, traditional approach and (2) the streaming, on memory, modern approach. The patterns in this chapter apply to both approaches.

The chapter has three main sections. In the first, we discuss the concept of *fast data* to differentiate it from big data. In the second section, we discuss the differences between ACID and CAP in order to understand the capabilities and limitations of both in fast data. The third section features recipes with design patterns to write certain types of streaming applications.

The chapter's goal is to make a cookbook with a recipe collection for fast data application development. Of course, there are many more recipes and patterns than revealed here, but recall that the fast data approach is relatively new.

This chapter covers the following:

- Fast data

- ACID vs. CAP

- Integrating streaming and transactions

- Streaming transformations

- Fault recovery strategies

- Tag data identifiers

Fast Data

Lately, some marketing and IT companies have abused some important terms to create great illusions, which only resulted in frustration when it was discovered that these buzzwords were not the panacea that everyone expected; two of these terms were *big data* and *the cloud*.

If you are perceptive, you may have noticed that in this book we try to avoid the term "big data" because although many organizations require data analysis, they do not have large volumes of data. Businesses do not really want big data, they need fast data.

At this moment, we are living in the fast data explosion, driven by mobile-devices proliferation, the Internet of Things (IoT), and machine-to-machine (M2M) communication. In regards to business needs, it is due to close interaction with customers, personalized offers, and reaction recording.

One characteristic of fast data applications is the ingestion of vast amounts of data streams. Note the *big* difference between ingestion and storage. Businesses require real-time analysis and the need to combine transactions on live data with real-time analytics.

© Raul Estrada and Isaac Ruiz 2016
R. Estrada and I. Ruiz, *Big Data SMACK*, DOI 10.1007/978-1-4842-2175-4_9

Fast data applications solve three challenges:

- Data streams analysis

- Data pipelines

- Real-time user interaction

We are too close to this change, so we cannot accurately distinguish the border between big data and fast data. Nor can we precisely identify which one has the greater value for business. All we know so far is that each one brings different values.

Another distinguishing phenomenon is that we have reached the boundaries of traditional models. For example, we consider the model of relational databases a pillar of all modern technological knowledge. We have reached the level where questioning relational model transitions is no longer a far-fetched proposal but a viable recurring option.

NoSQL solutions offer speed and scale in exchange for a lack on transactionality and query capabilities. Today, developers do not use a single technology; they have to use several (a clear example is the SMACK stack) because one technology is no longer enough. The problem with this approach is that it has a steep learning curve, often adds unnecessary complexity, causes duplication of effort, and often sacrifices performance to increase speed.

The question to answer in this chapter (and in the book) is this: How do we combine real-time data stream analysis with a reliable, scalable, and simple architecture?

Many companies have opted for the traditional batch approach, but history has shown that it requires too much infrastructure and both human and computational efforts. Or we can opt for a modern approach, which often involves the challenge of traditional paradigms, such as Batch, SQL, and ACID processing. Although there are many skeptics, this approach simplifies development and increases the performance by reducing infrastructure costs.

Fast Data at a Glance

Today's world is interactive. Information delivery should go to the right person at the right device in the right place at the right moment; or using the correct terms—personalized, ubiquitous, geolocalized, and in real time. That is what you call fast data.

However, building fast data applications requires a tremendous skill set. This chapter is a compendium of some patterns to handle analysis of data streams with operational workloads. A pattern is a recipe; this chapter is a cookbook to overcome the well-known challenges with new and more predictable applications.

Fast data applications must scale across multiple machines and multiple coordinate systems, and above all, reduce the complexity of the issue. Recall that an application must be simple, reliable, and extensible. In order to quickly implement data, you need to understand the structure, the data flow, and the implicit requirements of data management.

Right now fast data styles are being created for developers who are having problems with current development scalability. Many fast data issues far exceed the capabilities of traditional tools and techniques, creating new challenges still unresolved by systems that are slow and don't scale.

Modern problems cannot be solved by traditional approaches. The new tools must be created from thinking differently and using approaches that challenge traditional paradigms. That's how LinkedIn generated Kafka, Facebook generated Cassandra, and the AMPLab generated Spark and Mesos. And in turn, this generated new companies, such as Confluent, DataStax, Databricks, and Mesosphere.

If anything is certain it is that when each technology in the SMACK stack was coded, the thinking and skills of the people involved were vastly different from what they gained from past experiences.

Beyond Big Data

In a world with abundant and mundane discussions on big data, where marketing makes more noise than technology, fast data was born in a work context, midnight calls, and aggressive and excessive competition between companies looking to provide the best service at the lowest cost. Fast data is the agent of change; the engine that defines a new economy.

In a nutshell, you can say that fast data is data on the move. It is the streaming of hundreds of millions of endpoints to applications and servers. Imagine if you can mobile devices, sensors, financial transactions, logs, retail systems, telecommunication routers, authorization systems, and so forth. Everything changes for developers; you can only say that the increase in data is constant. There is Moore's law, which states that each year the amount of data is doubled. As mentioned in earlier chapters, the world was a quiet and peaceful place when data was stored for eternal rest; that's what you call big data, which is stored in Hadoop, in data warehouses, and in *data lakes*.

Fast data, on the other hand, is data arising from turmoil, data in motion, data streaming. An intrinsic feature of fast data is that data streams have to be treated in real time. The big data era is based on the analysis of structured and non-structured data stored in Hadoop and data warehouses through batch processes.

The SMACK stack emerges across verticals to help developers build applications to process fast data streams (note that here you also use the term *fast data stream* instead of *big data stream*). The sole purpose of the SMACK stack is processing data in real time and outputting data analysis in the shortest possible time, which is usually in milliseconds. For example, bank authorizations on credit cards can't delay too long before the client application times out. Although, some applications tolerate responses on minutes, the scenario where the big data analysis is delivered tomorrow is no longer viable.

Fast Data Characteristics

Fast data applications meet several characteristics. As we will discuss later, they influence architecture decisions. There are three main characteristics:

- Fast ingestion

- Analysis streaming

- Per event transactions

Fast Ingestion

The first stage in the data streaming process is data ingestion. The purpose of ingestion is to have a direct interface with data sources in order to make changes and the normalization of input data. Ingestion presents the challenge of extracting value from data and labeling it by assigning key-value pairs.

There are two types of ingestion:

- **Direct ingestion**. Here a system module hooks directly with the API generation. System speed depends on the speed of the API and the network. The analysis engines have a direct adapter. One advantage is that it can be very simple; a disadvantage is that it is not flexible—making changes that don't affect the performance can be a complex process.

- **Message queue**. When you do not have access to the data generation API, you can use a broker such as Apache Kafka. In this case, the data is managed in the form of queues. The advantage, as you know, is that you can partition, replicate, sort, and manage the pipeline in proportion to the pressure over the slower component.

Analysis Streaming

As the data is created, it reaches the analysis engine. Data can come in multiple types and formats. Often the data is enriched with metadata about the transformation process. This information may come through messages or events. Examples include sensor data of all types, user interaction with a web site, transaction data, and so forth.

The increase in the amount of fast data has made analysis move from the backend layer to the streaming layer. Every day there is less analysis in data warehouses. The ability to analyze data streams and make decisions with live transaction is most wanted today.

Per Event Transactions

As analysis platforms have to produce real-time analysis over incoming data, analysis speed far exceeds human speed. Hence, machine learning tools on streaming data are recent trending.

To generate value on streaming data, you must take action in real time. This has two reasons. The first is a technical reason related to the fact that real-time data chunks are "stored" in memory, and you cannot store them on a disk or another storage medium, because you quickly flood large amounts of space and because you likely don't have the money and hardware of Facebook or Twitter to indefinitely store the data. The second is a business reason that has to do with decision making in real time; for example, online authorization charges, real-time user interaction with web site recording, real-time multiplayer game engines, and so forth.

The ability to extract information as it arrives and to combine it with business logic in real time makes possible modern fraud detection systems, trading shares on the stock market, or the Uber operation.

On the data management layer, all the actions must be able to read and write many pieces of data, storing only results, inferences, and recommendations. It is worth noting that online input data is not stored, because there is no space or budget to store this amount of data.

All of this can be summarized as the interaction of the event when it arrives. The streams of high-speed data required to have high-availability schemas are discussed later in a section on the at-least-one schema on event delivery.

The modern challenge for data engineers is the extraction and capture of the value on per-event transactions.

Fast Data and Hadoop

And what if you already have our big data model mounted on Apache Hadoop? Well, the important thing here is to build a front end. The front end of a big data system *must* have every one of the following functions: filter, de-dupe, aggregate, enrich, and denormalize.

If you already have a model like Hadoop, it is important to change the whole paradigm. You can continue using Hadoop, but instead of storing all the information in Hadoop as it arrives, you use an engine like Spark to move all Lambda Architecture to a streaming architecture, and from a batch processing model to an online pipeline processing model.

The associated costs and the time to do common operations, as filter, de-dupe, aggregate, and so forth, in a model such as the Spark is drastically reduced compared if you made it over Apache Hadoop with a next-day batch model. Moreover, a batch model usually has no redundancy and high availability schemas, and if so, they are very expensive.

The batch processing schemas always require the process of cleaning data before storing it. In a pipelined architecture, the cleaning process is part of the ingestion process.

Another modern alternative is to dump the Hadoop Distributed File System (HDFS). An advantage of the pipeline model is that very old and obsolete data can be eliminated as new data arrives. In the pipeline model, no garbage is stored because the data stored is not input data, but those produced by the same engine.

A Hadoop developer's recurring complaint is the difficulty of analysis to scale. With a pipeline model, counting and aggregation reduces the problem by several orders of magnitude. By reducing the size of stored data, you reduce the time to analyze it.

Hadoop developers also complain when they have to send aggregates to HDFS; with a fast data front end, this doesn't happen because the aggregates are sent as they arrive—no batch process and everything is microbatching in Spark.

Data Enrichment

Data enrichment is another advantage of fast data over traditional models. The data always has to be filtered, correlated, and enriched before being stored in the database. Performing the enrichment process at the streaming stage provides the following advantages:

- NoETL process. As you saw, unnecessary latency created by ETL processes is avoided in a streaming model.

- Unnecessary disk I/O is removed. As you saw, as Hadoop solutions are based on disk, everything in fast data is based on memory. Everything is in real time because there is no time for batch processes.

- The use of hardware is reduced. Because you don't have to store everything and you don't have to do very complex analysis over data lakes, the cost of hardware is dramatically reduced; resources (processor, memory, network, and disk) are used more efficiently.

Since fast data entry feeds are information streams, maintaining the semantics between streams is simpler because it creates a consistent and clean system. This can only be achieved if you act in each event individually; here there are no big data windows or handling large data chunks susceptible to errors.

These per event transactions need three capacities:

- **Stream connection oriented**. You need clusters of Kafka, Cassandra, Spark, and Hadoop/HDFS.

- **Fast searches**. To enrich each event with metadata.

- **Contextual filtering**. Reassembles discrete input events in logical events that add more meaning to the business.

In short, transactions per event require the entire system to be stateful; that is, everything is in memory and has to store the minimum in disk.

Queries

Take the example of advertising based on user clicks on a given web page. How do you know which ad the user clicked? How do you know that it wasn't a robot? How do you know the amount to charge the advertising agency at the end of month?

Another example is when you have a security system attack. How do you know when you are being attacked by a denial of service? How do you know that an operation is fraudulent? To find out if another machine is attacking, should you consider only the information from the last hour?

Today all contracts are based on a *service-level agreement* (SLA). In order to verify at the end of the month that you meet those contracts, you need to make queries, sometimes very sophisticated, of the data within your system.

Not meeting an SLA could lead to multimillion-dollar sanctions. Knowing that you met the SLA requires the ability to make queries in your system. This fast data feature allows the user to query at any time and over any time frame.

ACID vs. CAP

Fast data is a transformation process. There are two key concepts in modern data management: the ACID properties and CAP theorem. In both acronyms, the C stands for *consistency*, but it means something different to each. We will discuss the differences between the Cs later.

Let's now delve into transactions. The core concepts of a transaction are semantics and guarantees. The more data a computer handles, more important its function, but also more complex and prone to errors.

At the beginning of the computer age, when two computers had to write the same data at the same time, the academia noted that the process should be regulated to ensure that data was not corrupted or written incorrectly. When computers were exposed to human interaction, the risk of human error in the middle of a calculation became a major concern.

The rules were defined by Jim Gray[1] and published by the Association for Computing Machinery (ACM) in 1976. In the 1980s, IBM and other companies were responsible for popularizing ACID. It was like everything in computer science: on paper things worked perfectly, but in practice strong performance discussions are untied. Today, ACID transactions are a mainstay in any database course.

A transaction consists of one or more operations in a linear sequence on the database state. All modern database engines should start, stop, and cancel (or roll back) a set of operations (reads and writes) as a metadata operation.

Transactional semantics alone do not make the transaction. You have to add ACID properties to prevent developers from being lost when they have concurrent access on the same record.

ACID Properties

ACID means Atomic, Consistent, Isolated, and Durable.

- **Atomic**. All the transaction parts should be treated as a single action. This is the mantra: All parts are completed or none is completed. In a nutshell, if part of the transaction fails, the state of the database remains unchanged.

- **Consistent**. Transactions must follow the rules and restrictions defined by the database (e.g. constraints, cascades, triggers). All data that is written to the database must be valid. No transaction must invalidate the database state. (Note that this is different from the C in the CAP theorem.)

- **Isolated**. To achieve concurrency control, transactions isolation must be the same as if you were running the transactions in serial, sequentially. No transaction should affect another transaction. In turn, any incomplete transaction should not affect another transaction.

- **Durable**. Once the transaction is committed, the change must be persisted and should not change anymore. Likewise, it should not cause conflicts with other operations. Note that this has nothing to do with writing to disk and recent controversies, because many modern databases live on memory or are distributed on the users' mobile devices.

---

[1] http://dl.acm.org/citation.cfm?doid=360363.360369

CAP Theorem

The CAP theorem is a tool to explain the problems of a distributed system. It was presented by Eric Brewer at the 2000 Symposium on Principles of Distributed Computing, and formalized and demonstrated (as good theorem) by Gilbert and Lynch[2] in 2002.

CAP means Consistent, Available, and Partition Tolerant.

- **Consistent**. All replicas of the same data must have the same value across the distributed system.

- **Available**. Each living node in a distributed system must be able to process transactions and respond to queries.

- **Partition Tolerant**. The system will continue to operate even if it has network partitioning.

These are the original sad words of the CAP theorem: "In the face of network partitions, you can't have both perfect consistency and 100% availability. Plan accordingly."

It is a very sad theorem because it does not mention what is possible, but the impossibility of something. The CAP theorem is known as the "You-Pick-Two" theorem; however, you should avoid this conception, because choosing AP does not mean that you will not be consistent, and choosing CP does not mean that you will not be available. In fact, most systems are not any of the three. It means that designing a system is to give preference to two of the three characteristics.

Furthermore, it is not possible to choose CA. There cannot be a distributed system in which the partitions are ignored. By definition, a non-partitioned network means not having a distributed system. And if you don't have a distributed system, the CAP theorem is irrelevant. Thus, you can never exclude the P.

Consistency

The ACID consistency was formulated in terms of databases. Consistency in the CAP theorem is formulated in terms of distributed systems.

In ACID, if a scheme states that a value must be unique, then a consistent system reinforces the uniqueness of that value across all operations. A clear example is when you want to delete a primary key when you have references to other tables using constraints; the database engine will indicate that there are children records and you cannot erase the key.

The CAP consistency indicates that each replica of the original value—spread across the nodes of a distributed system—will always have the same value. Note that this warranty is logical, not physical. Due to network latency (even running over optic fiber at the speed of light), it is physically impossible for a replication of all nodes to take zero seconds. However, the cluster can present a logical view to customers to ensure that everyone sees the same value.

The two concepts reach their splendor when systems offer more than a simple key-value store. When systems offer all ACID properties across the cluster, the CAP theorem makes its appearance, restricting the CAP consistency.

On the other hand, when you have CAP consistency, through repeated readings and full transactions, the ACID consistency should be offered in every node. Thus, the systems that prefer CAP availability over CAP consistency rarely ensure ACID consistency.

---

[2]http://dl.acm.org/citation.cfm?id=564601:

CRDT

To explain *eventual consistency*, consider the example of a cluster with two machines. When the cluster works, the writings are spread equally to both machines and everything works fine. Now suppose that communication between the two machines fails but the service is still active. At the end of the day, you will have two machines with different information.

To rectify this fault, traditional approaches offer very complex rectification processes to examine both servers and try to resynchronize the state.

Eventual consistency (EC) is a process that facilitates the data administrator's life. The original white paper on Dynamo (the Amazon database)[3] formally defined eventual consistency as the method by which several replicas may become temporarily different, but eventually converge to the same value. Dynamo guarantees that the fix process is not complex.

It is worth noting that eventual consistency is not immediate; so two queries may yield different results until synchronization is complete. The problem is that EC does not guarantee that the data converges to the latest information, but to the more correct value. This is where the correctness definition becomes complicated.

Many techniques have been developed to offer an easier solution under these conditions. It's important to mention *conflict-free replicated data types* (CRDTs). The problem with these methods is that in practice, they offer fewer guarantees on the final status of the system than those offered by the CAP theorem. The benefit of CRDT is that under certain partitioning conditions, the high availability offer leaves nodes operating.

The EC Dynamo-style is very different from the log-based rectification methods offered by the bank industry to move money between bank accounts. Both systems can diverge for a period of time, but banks usually take longer and reach a more precise agreement.

Integrating Streaming and Transactions

Imagine the operation of these high-speed transactional applications: real-time payments, real-time authorization, anti-fraud systems, and intelligent alerting. These applications would not be conceived today if there weren't a mix of real-time analysis and transaction processing.

Transactions in these applications require real-time analysis as input. Since it is impossible in real time to redo the analysis based on data derived from a traditional data store, to scale, you must keep streaming aggregation within the transaction. Unlike regular batch operations, aggregation streams maintain the consistency, up-to-dateness, and accuracy of the analysis, which is necessary for the transaction.

In this pattern, you sacrifice the ability to make ad-hoc analyses in exchange for high-speed access to the analysis, which is necessary for the application.

Pattern 1: Reject Requests Beyond a Threshold

Consider a high-volume-requests web page that implements sophisticated usage metrics for groups and individual users as a function of each operation.

The metrics are used for two main purposes:

- Billing charges based on use

- To force the same contracted service quality level (expressed as the number of requests per second, per user, and per group).

In this case, the platform implementation of the policy verification should have counters for every user and group of users. These counters must be accurate (because they are inputs for billing and implementation of service quality policies), and they must be accessible in real time to evaluate and authorize (or deny) new accesses.

---

[3]http://www.allthingsdistributed.com/files/amazon-dynamo-sosp2007.pdf

It is necessary to maintain a balance in real time for each user. To accurately maintain a balance, you need an ACID OLTP system. The same system requires the ability to maintain high-speed aggregations. The scalability of the solution is achieved by combining aggregation transactions with real-time high-speed transmission. Examples of these systems include new credits granting systems and used credit deductions).

Pattern 2: Alerting on Predicted Trends Variation

Imagine an operational monitoring platform where you need to issue warnings or alarms when a threshold predicate is exceeded at a statistically significant level. This system combines two capabilities:

- It keeps the analysis on real time (counters, streaming add-ons, and status summary of current use)

- It compares the analysis with the predicted trend. If the trend is exceeded, the system should raise an alert.

The system records this alarm to suppress other alerts (limiting the intermittency of an alarm for a single event). This is another system that requires the combination of analytical and transactional capabilities.

Analyzed separately, this system needs three independent systems working simultaneously:

- An analysis system that is microdosing real-time analysis

- An application reading these analyses and the trend line predicted to generate alerts on the application

- A transactional system that stores the generated alerts data and that implements suppression logic

The execution of three tightly coupled systems like this (our solution requires the three systems running) reduces the reliability and complicates the operation.

To achieve real time analysis you need to combine the request-response system with event processing streaming applications.

When Not to Integrate Streaming and Transactions

OLAP (online analytical processing) systems offer the benefit of rapid analytical queries without pre-aggregation. These systems can execute complex queries over huge data, but within the threshold, they work in batch, reporting to human analysts in the data workflow. These systems are not compatible with high-speed transactional workloads because they are optimized to batch reporting, not OLTP (online transaction processing) applications.

Aggregation Techniques

Pre-aggregation is a technique with many algorithms and features developed. The following are common techniques for implementing real-time aggregation:

- **Windowed events.** Used to express moving averages or a timeframe summary of a continuous event. These techniques are found in CEP (complex event processing) or microbatching systems like Apache Spark.

- **Probabilistic data structures**. Data is added within a certain margin of error bounded by probability. These algorithms typically exchange precision for space, allowing estimation in a smaller storage space. Examples of probabilistic data structures and algorithms include Bloom filters, as in Apache Cassandra.

- **Materialized views**. A view could define aggregation, partition, filter, or join. Materialized views group the base data and keep a physical copy of the resulting data. Materialized views allow declarative aggregations, which eliminate coding and offer easy, concise, and accurate aggregation. You find examples of this in Oracle DB, Postgres, SQL Server, and MySQL.

Streaming Transformations

Effectively processing big data often requires multiple database engines, each with a special purpose. Usually, systems good at online CEP (complex event processing) are not good at batch processing against large data volumes. Some systems are good for high-velocity problems; others are good for large volume problems. In most cases, you need to integrate these systems to run meaningful applications.

Usually, the data arrives at high-velocity ingest-oriented systems and is processed into the volume-oriented systems. In more advanced cases, predictive models, analysis, and reports are generated on the volume-oriented systems and sent as feedback to the velocity-oriented systems to support real-time applications. The real-time analysis from the fast systems is integrated into downstream applications and operational dashboards that process real-time alerts, alarms, insights, and trends.

In a nutshell, many fast data applications run on top of a set of tools. Usually, the platform components include the following:

- At least one large shared storage pool (e.g., HDFS, Apache Cassandra)

- A high performance BI analytics query tool (e.g., a columnar SQL system, Apache Spark)

- A batch processing system (e.g., Map Reduce, Apache Spark)

- A streaming system (e.g. Apache Kafka)

The input data and processing output move across these systems. The key to solve many big data challenges is the design of this dataflow as a processing pipeline that coordinates these different systems.

Pattern 3: Use Streaming Transformations to Avoid ETL

The new events captured into a long-term repository often require transformation, filtering, or processing before being available for exploitation. For example, an application that captures user sessions consisting of several discrete events, enriching those events with static data to avoid expensive repeated joins in the batch layer, and/or filtering redundant events storing only unique values.

There are (at least) two approaches to run this process:

1. The data can be stored in a long-term repository and then ETLed (extracted, transformed, and loaded) to its final form. This approach trades I/O, storage, and time (results are delayed until the entire ETL process is completed) for a slightly simpler architecture (e.g., move data directly from a queue to HDFS).

2. This approach is referred as *schema on read*. It reduces the choice of back-end systems to those of schema-free systems, removing the non-optimal, depending on your specific reporting requirements.

3. Execute the transformations in a streaming way before the data arrives at the long-term repository. This approach adds a streaming component (Apache Spark) between the source queue (Apache Kafka) and the final repository (Apache Cassandra), creating a continuous processing pipeline.

4. Moving the entire process to a real-time processing pipeline has several advantages. Writing I/O to the back-end system is drastically reduced (in the first model, raw data input is written, and then the ETLed data is written; with this approach only ETLed data is written).

5. You have this comparison between the two approaches:

   - The second model leaves more I/O available for the primary purpose of the back-end repository: data analysis and reporting activities.

   - In the second approach, the operational errors are noticeable nearly in real time. When using ETL, the raw data is not inspected until the entire ETL process runs. This delays operational notifications of corrupt inputs or missing data.

   - In the second model, the time to insight is reduced. For example, when managing data of sessions, a session can participate in batch reporting before being closed. With ETL, you must wait approximately half of the ETL period before the data is available for processing.

Pattern 4: Connect Big Data Analytics to Real-Time Stream Processing

The incoming events from real-time processing applications require back-end systems analysis. The following are some examples:

- On an alerting system that notifies when an interval exceeds historical patterns, the data describing the historical pattern needs to be available.

- Applications managing real-time customer experiences or personalization often use customer segmentation reports generated by statistical analysis running on a batch analytics system.

- Hosting OLAP outputs in a fast, scalable query cache to support operators and applications that need high-speed and highly concurrent access to data.

In all of these cases, the reports, analysis, and models from big data analytics need to be made available to real-time applications. In this case, information flows from the big data–oriented system (batch) to the high velocity system (streaming).

This brings important requirements:

- The fast data, speed-oriented application requires a data management system capable of holding the state generated by the batch system.

- This state needs to be regularly updated or fully replaced. There are a few common ways to manage the refresh cycle. The best trade-off depends on the specific application.

Some applications (e.g., applications based on user segmentation) require per record consistency but can tolerate eventual consistency across records. In these cases, updating state in the velocity-oriented database on a per-record base is sufficient.

Updates will need to do the following:

- Communicate new records (in our example, new customers)

- Update existing records (customers that have been recategorized)

- Delete outdated records (ex-customers)

The records in the velocity system should be timestamped for operational monitoring and alerts generated if stale records persist beyond an expected refresh cycle.

Other applications require the analysis to be strictly consistent. If it is not sufficient for each record to be internally consistent, the records set as a whole requires guaranteed consistency. These cases are often seen in analytic query caches. Often these caches are queried for additional levels of aggregation; aggregations that span multiple records. Producing a correct result therefore requires that the full data set be consistent.

A reasonable approach to transferring this report data from the batch analytics system to the real-time system is to write the data into a shadow table. Once the shadow table is completely written, it can be atomically swapped, with the main table addressed by the application. The application will either see only data from the previous version of the report or only data from the new version of the report, but it will never see a mix of data from both reports in a single query.

Pattern 5: Use Loose Coupling to Improve Reliability

When connecting multiple systems, it is imperative that all systems have an independent administration. Any part of the pipeline could fail, although the other systems remain available and functional. If the (batch) back end is offline, the (high velocity) front end should still operate, and vice versa.

This requires thinking through several design constraints:

- The location of data that cannot be pushed (or pulled) through the pipeline. The components responsible for the durability of stalled data.

- The failure and availability model of each component in the pipeline.

- The system recovery process. The list of the components that have record meaning or can have recovery sources for lost data or interrupted processing.

- When a component fails, the list of the components become unavailable. The time upstream components maintain functionality.

These constraints form the *recovery time objective* (RTO).

In every pipeline, there is a slowest component, the *bottleneck*. When designing a system, you must explicitly choose a component that will be the bottleneck. Having many systems, each with identical performance, a minor degradation on any system will create an overall bottleneck. Operationally, this is a pain. It is better to choose the most reliable component as the bottleneck or the most expensive resource as the bottleneck so that you can achieve a more predictable reliability level.

Points to Consider

Connecting multiple systems is always a complex task. This complexity is not linear with the number of systems. Generally, complexity increases in the function of connections (in the worst-case scenario, you have N*N connections between N systems).

This problem cannot be solved with a single stand-alone monolithic system. However, high velocity and large volume data management scenarios typically require a combination of specialized systems. When combining these systems, you must carefully design dataflow and connections between them.

Make a couple of designs, so each system operates independently of the failure of the others. Use multiple systems to simplify; for example, replace batch ETL processes with continuous processes.

Fault Recovery Strategies

Most streaming applications move data across multiple processing stages.

Often, the events land in a queue and are then read by downstream components. Those components might write new data back to a queue as they process, or might directly stream data to their downstream components. Building a reliable data pipeline always implies designing fault recovery strategies.

When multiple processing components are connected, statistically, one component will fail, or become unreachable or unavailable. When this occurs, the other components should continue receiving data. When the failed component comes back online, it must recover its previous state and then continue processing new events. Here we discuss how to resume processing.

Idempotency is a specific technique to achieve exactly-once semantics.

Additionally, when processing horizontally scaled pipelines, each stage has multiple servers or processes running in parallel. A subset of servers within the cluster can always fail. In this case, the failed servers need to be recovered and their work needs to be reassigned.

There are a few factors that complicate these situations and lead to different trade-offs:

- Usually, it is uncertain to determine what the last processed event was. Typically, it is not feasible to two-phase commit the event processing across all pipeline components.

- Event streams are often partitioned across several processors. Processors and upstream sources can fail in arbitrary combinations. Picturing everything as a single, unified event flow is not recommendable.

Here we discuss three options for resuming processing distinguished by how events near the failure time are handled. The approaches to solving the problem are explained as follows.

Pattern 6: At-Most-Once Delivery

At-most-once delivery allows dropping some events. In this case, the events not processed by an interruption are simply dropped and they don't become part of the input of the downstream system. Note that, this pattern is only accepted when the data itself is low value or loses value if it is not immediately processed.

The following are points to evaluate an at-most-once delivery:

- The historical analytics should show which data is unavailable.

- If the event stream will be eventually stored into an OLAP or data lake, you need reports and data algorithms that detect and manage the missing values.

- It should be clear which data is lost.

Lost data generally is not aligned exactly with session boundaries, time windows, or even data sources. It is also probable that only partial data was dropped during the outage period, so some values are present.

Additional points to be considered include the maximum outage period and the size of largest dropped gap.

If your pipeline is designed to ignore events during outages, you should determine each pipeline component mean recovery time to understand the data volume that will be lost during a typical failure. The maximum allowable data loss is a fundamental consideration when designing an at-most-once delivery pipeline.

Most of the pipelines are shared infrastructure. The pipeline is a platform supporting many applications. You should consider whether all current and expected future applications can detect and support data loss due to at-most-once delivery.

You should not assume that during an outage data is always discarded by upstream systems. When recovering from a failure, many systems (especially queues and checkpoint subscribers) read points and resume event transmission from that checkpoint; this is at-least-once delivery.

It is not correct to assume that at-most-once delivery is the default strategy if another is not explicitly chosen. Designing at-most-once delivery requires explicit choices and implementation.

Pattern 7: At-Least-Once Delivery

At-least-once delivery replays recent events starting from an acknowledged (known processed) event. This approach presents some data more than once to the processing pipeline. The typical implementation returns at-least-once delivery checkpoints to a safe point (so you know that they have been processed).

After a failure, the processing is resumed from the checkpoint. As it is possible that events were successfully processed after the checkpoint, these events will be replayed during recovery. This replay means that downstream components will see each event at least once.

There are a number of considerations when using at-least-once delivery:

- This delivery can lead to an unordered event delivery. Note that regardless of the failure model chosen, you should assume that some events will arrive late, unordered, or not arrive.

- Data sources are not well coordinated and rarely are events from sources delivered end to end over a single TCP/IP connection or some other order guaranteeing protocol.

- If the processing operations are not idempotent, replaying events could corrupt and change the output. When designing at-least-once delivery, you must identify and classify processes as idempotent or not.

- If processing operations are not deterministic, replaying events will produce different outputs. Common examples of nondeterministic operations include querying the current clock time or invoking a remote service that could be unavailable.

- This delivery requires a durability contract with upstream components. In the case of failure, some upstream component must have a durable record of the event from which to replay. You should clearly identify durability responsibility through the pipeline, and manage and monitor durable components appropriately. Test operational behavior when the disks fail or are full.

Pattern 8: Exactly-Once Delivery

This type of processing is the ideal because each event is processed exactly once. It avoids the difficult side effects and considerations raised by the other two deliveries. You have exposed the strategies to achieve exactly-once semantics using idempotency in combination with at-least-once delivery.

The following are the fundamental aspects of designing distributed recovery schemas:

- Input streams are usually partitioned across multiple processors

- Inputs can fail on a per partition basis

- Events can be recovered using different strategies

Tag Data Identifiers

When dealing with data streams facing a possible failure, processing each datum exactly once is extremely difficult. If the processing system fails, it may not be easy to determine which data was successfully processed and which was not.

The traditional approaches to this problem are complex, because they require strongly consistent processing systems and smart clients to determine thorough introspection of which data was processed and which was not.

The strongly consistent systems have become scarcer and throughput needs have skyrocketed. This approach has become hard and impractical. Many have failed on precise answers and opted for answers that are as correct as possible under certain circumstances.

As you saw, the Lambda Architecture proposes doing all calculations twice, in two different ways, to provide cross-checks. CRDTs have been proposed as a way to add data structures that can be reasoned when using eventually consistent data stores.

These are not the best options, but idempotency offers another path.

By definition, an *idempotent* operation is an operation that has the same effect no matter how many times it is applied. The simplest example is setting a value. If you set $x = 3.1416$, and then you set $x = 3.1416$ again, the second action doesn't have any effect.

The relation with exactly-once processing is as follows: for idempotent operations, there is no effective difference between at-least-once processing and exactly-once processing. And you know that at-least-once processing is easier to achieve.

One of the core tools used to build robust applications on these platforms is leveraging the idempotent setting of values in eventually consistent systems. Setting individual values is a weaker tool than the twentieth-century ACID transactional model. CRDTs offer more, but come with rigid constraints and restrictions. It is very dangerous to build something without a deep understanding of the offer and how it works.

The advent of consistent systems that truly scale gives a broader set of supported idempotent processing, which can improve and simplify past approaches dramatically. ACID transactions can be built to read and write multiple values based on business logic, while offering the same effects if repeatedly executed.

Pattern 9: Use Upserts over Inserts

An upsert is shorthand for describing a conditional insert. In a nutshell, if the row exists, don't insert it. If the row doesn't exist, insert it.

Some SQL systems have specific syntax for upserts, an ON CONFLICT clause, a MERGE statement, or even a straightforward UPSERT statement. Some NoSQL systems have ways to express the same thing. For key-value stores, the default PUT behavior is an upsert.

When dealing with rows that can be uniquely identified, through a unique key or a unique value, upsert is an idempotent operation.

When the status of an upsert is unclear, often due to the client server or network failure, you can see that it's safe to send it repeatedly until its success can be verified. Note that this type of retry often takes a lot of time to reverse.

Pattern 10: Tag Data with Unique Identifiers

The idempotent operations are difficult when data is not uniquely identifiable. For example, imagine a digital ad application that tracks clicks on a web page. Let's say that an event arrives as a three-value tuple that says user U clicked on spot S at time T with a resolution in seconds. The upsert pattern simply can't be used because it would be possible to record multiple clicks by the same user in the same spot in the same second. This leads to the first subpattern.

Subpattern: Fine-Grained Timestamps

One solution to this click problem is to increase the timestamp resolution to a point at which clicks are unique. If the timestamp allows milliseconds, it is reasonable to assume that the user couldn't click faster than once per millisecond. This enables upsert and idempotency.

It is always critical to verify on the client side that generated events are in fact unique. Trusting a computer's time API to reflect real-world time is a common dangerous mistake. There is a lot of hardware and software that offer milliseconds values, but just on 100ms resolutions. Moreover, the NTP (network time protocol) is able to move clocks backward in many default configurations. Virtualization software is a common example for messing with guest operating system clocks.

To implement it well, you must always check the client side to make sure that the last event and new event have different timestamps before sending them to the server.

Subpattern: Unique IDs at the Event Source

If you can generate a unique id at the client, send that value with the event to ensure that it is unique. If events are generated in one place, it is possible that a simple incrementing counter can uniquely identify events. The trick with a counter is to ensure that you do not use values again after restarting some service.

The following are unique ids approaches:

- Use a central server distributing block of unique ids. A database with strong consistency (e.g., Apache Cassandra) or an agreement system such as ZooKeeper (as you saw on Apache Kafka) can be used to assign blocks. If the event producer fails, then some ids are wasted; 64 bits are enough ids to cover any loss.

- Combine timestamps with ids for uniqueness. If you use millisecond timestamps but want to ensure uniqueness, you start an every-millisecond counter. If two events share a millisecond, give one counter the value 0 and another counter the value 1. This ensures uniqueness.

- Combine timestamps and counters in a 64-bit number. Some databases generate unique ids, dividing 64-bit integers into sections, using 41 bits to identify a millisecond timestamp, 10 bits as a millisecond counter, and 10 bits as an event source id. This leaves one bit for the sign, avoiding issues mixing signed and unsigned integers. Note that 41 bits of milliseconds is about 70 years. Obviously, you can play with the bit sizes for each field, but be careful to anticipate the case where time moves backward.

In case you need something simpler than getting incrementing ids correct, try a universally unique identifier (UUID) library to generate universally unique ids. These work in different ways, but often combine machine information, such as a MAC address, with random values and timestamp values, similar to what was described earlier. The upside is that you can safely assume that UUIDs are unique; the downside is that they often require 16 or more bytes to store.

Pattern 11: Use Kafka Offsets as Unique Identifiers

As you already saw, Apache Kafka has built-in unique identifiers. Combining the topic id with the offset in the log can uniquely identify the event. This sounds like a panacea, but there are reasons to be careful:

- Inserting items into Kafka has the same problems as any other distributed system. Managing exactly-once insertion into Apache Kafka is not easy and it doesn't offer the right tools (at the time of this writing) to manage idempotency when writing to a topic.

- If the Kafka cluster is restarted, topic offsets may no longer be unique. It may be possible to use a third value (e.g., a Kafka cluster id) to make the event unique.

When to Avoid Idempotency

Idempotency can add storage overhead as it stores extra ids for uniqueness. It can add complexity, depending on many factors, such as whether your event processor has certain features or whether your app requires complex operations to be idempotent.

You must evaluate the effort to build an idempotent application against the cost of having imperfect data once in a while. Keep in mind that some data has less value than other data, and spending developer time ensuring that it is perfectly processed may be poor project management.

Another reason to avoid idempotent operations is that the event processor or data store makes it very hard to achieve.

Example: Switch Processing

Consider a phone switch support calls with two events:

1. A request is put on hold (or starts a request).

2. A request is attended.

The system must ingest these events and compute the average hold time.

Case 1: Ordered Requests

In this case, events for a given customer always arrive in the order in which they are generated. Event processing in this example is idempotent, so a request may arrive multiple times, but you can always assume that events arrive in the order they happened.

State schema contains a single tuple containing the total hold time and the total number of hold occurrences. It also contains a set of ongoing holds.

When a request is put on hold (or a request is started), upsert a record into the set of ongoing holds. You use one of the methods described earlier to assign a unique id. Using an upsert instead of an insert makes this operation idempotent.

When a request is attended, you look up the corresponding ongoing hold in the state table. If the ongoing hold is found, you remove it, calculate the duration based on the two correlated events, and update the global hold time and global hold counts accordingly. If this message is seen repeatedly, the ongoing hold record will not be found; the second time it will be processed and can be ignored at that point.

This works quite well, is simple to understand, and is efficient. Guaranteeing order is certainly possible, but it is backstage work. Often it's easier to break the assumption on the processing end, where you may have an ACID consistent processor that makes dealing with complexity easier.

Case 2: Unordered Requests

In this case, requests may arrive in any order. The problem with unordered requests is that you cannot delete from the outstanding holds table when you get a match. What you can do, in a strongly consistent system, is keep one row per hold and mark it as matched when its duration is added to the global duration sum. The row must be kept around to catch repeated messages.

You must hold the events until you are sure that another event for a particular hold could not arrive. This may be minutes, hours, or days, depending on the situation.

This approach is also simple, but requires an additional state. The cost of maintaining an additional state should be weighed against the value of perfectly correct data. It is also possible to drop event records early and allow data to be slightly wrong, but only when events are delayed abnormally. This is a decent compromise between space and correctness in some scenarios.

Summary

In this chapter ...

- You read a fast data cookbook.

- You reviewed the fast data concept and compared it with big data and traditional data models.

- You also saw the differences between ACID properties and the CAP theorem. You saw the differences in the term *consistency* in both concepts.

- You reviewed how to integrate modern streaming analytics techniques with transactions.

- You saw how to make streaming transformations to achieve data pipelines processing.

- You learned about fault recovery strategies: at-most-once, at-least-once and exactly-once.

- You learned how to use tag data identifiers.

In the next chapter, you apply these concepts to data pipeline patterns.

CHAPTER 10

■ ■ ■

Data Pipelines

Well, we have reached the chapter where we have to connect everything, especially theory and practice. This chapter has two parts: the first part is an enumeration of the data pipeline strategies and the second part is how to connect the technologies:

- Spark and Cassandra
- Akka and Kafka
- Akka and Cassandra
- Akka and Spark
- Kafka and Cassandra

Data Pipeline Strategies and Principles

The following are data pipeline strategies and principles:

- Asynchronous message passing
- Consensus and gossip
- Data locality
- Failure detection
- Fault tolerance / no single point of failure
- Isolation
- Location transparency
- Parallelism
- Partition for scale
- Replay for any point of failure
- Replicate for resiliency
- Scalable infrastructure
- Share nothing
- Dynamo systems principles

© Raul Estrada and Isaac Ruiz 2016

R. Estrada and I. Ruiz, *Big Data SMACK*, DOI 10.1007/978-1-4842-2175-4_10

It is important to mention that not all technologies implement SMACK stack strategies; this is because some technologies are not designed to take this strategy into consideration or the strategy is doesn't fit its design. In this section, we try to define concepts and explain how technologies meet. Note that we don't cover Apache Mesos, because it is more implicit to the infrastructure than the pipeline architecture.

Asynchronous Message Passing

Technologies: Akka, Kafka, Spark

An actor sends a message to a process (another actor) and relies on the process and the supporting system to select and invoke the actual code to run. Asynchronous message passing is implemented, so all the complexities that naturally occur when trying to synchronize actors and data are handled by an intermediary level of software, called *middleware*. The most common middleware to support asynchronous message passing is called *message-oriented middleware* (MOM).

Consensus and Gossip

Technologies: Akka, Cassandra

The Paxos protocol is a family of protocols for solving consensus. In Paxos, followers send commands to a leader. During normal operation, the leader receives a client's command, assigns it a new command number (n), and then begins the nth instance of the consensus algorithm by sending messages to a set of acceptor processes.

A gossip protocol occurs when one node transmits information about the new instances to only some of their known colleagues, and if one of them already knows from other sources about the new node, the first node's propagation is stopped. Thus, the information about the node is propagated in an efficient and rapid way through the network.

Data Locality

Technologies: Cassandra, Kafka

Related storage locations are frequently accessed, depending on the memory access pattern. There are two types of locality: temporal and spatial. Temporal locality refers to the reuse of specific data and/ or resources within a short duration of time. Spatial locality refers to the use of data within relatively close storage locations. In practice, latency and throughput are affected by the efficiency of the cache, which is improved by increasing the locality of reference.

Failure Detection

Technologies: Cassandra, Spark, Akka, Kafka

In Kafka, upon successfully registering a consumer, the coordinator adds the consumer to the ping request scheduler's queue, which then tries to keep track of whether the consumer is still alive.

In Cassandra, *failure detection* is a method for locally determining (from the gossip state and the history) if another node in the system is up or down. Cassandra uses this information to avoid routing client requests to unreachable nodes whenever possible.

In Akka and Spark, you use three Spark properties related to network variables: spark.akka.heartbeat. pauses, spark.akka.failure-detector.threshold, and spark.akka.heartbeat.interval.

Fault Tolerance/No Single Point of Failure

Technologies: Spark, Cassandra, Kafka

A single point of failure (SPOF) is the part of a system that, if it fails, stops the entire system from working. SPOFs are not desirable in any system using high availability or reliability.

Isolation

Technologies: Spark, Cassandra, Kafka

Cassandra is at the opposite end of the ACID properties used in most relational databases, because it uses BASE (Basically Available Soft-state Eventual consistency). Cassandra's weak consistency comes in the form of *eventual consistency*, which means that the database eventually reaches a consistent state. As the data is replicated, the latest version is sitting on a particular node, but older versions are still out there on other nodes; yet eventually all nodes will see the latest version.

In Spark, each application gets its own executor processes, which stays up for the duration of the entire application and runs tasks in multiple threads. This has the benefit of isolating applications from each other.

Location Transparency

Technologies: Akka, Spark, Cassandra, Kafka

In Spark, Cassandra, and Kafka, location transparency allows reading and writing to any node in a cluster, and the system replicates the information to the entire cluster.

One of Akka's key contributions to the actor model is the concept of location transparency. An actor's mailing address can actually be a remote location but the location is "transparent" to the developer. Akka abstracts away the transmission of the message over the network; the actor's mailing address is always accessed the same way.

Parallelism

Technologies: Spark, Cassandra, Kafka, Akka

In Kafka, there is parallelism of the partition within the topic. Kafka is able to provide ordering, which guarantees load balancing over a pool of consumer processes.

In Cassandra and Spark, there is *data parallelism*, a form of distributing data across multiple processors in a cluster environment and different parallel computing nodes. It contrasts *task parallelism*, another form of parallelism.

In Spark and Akka, task parallelism focuses on distributing tasks (performed by individual processes or threads) across different processors.

Partition for Scale

Technologies: Cassandra, Spark, Kafka, Akka

A *network partition* refers to the failure of a network device that causes a network to split. If you recall the CAP theorem, the partition tolerance in this context means a data processing system's ability to continue processing data even if a network partition causes communication errors between subsystems. All the SMACK technologies are *network topology aware*.

Replay for Any Point of Failure

Technologies: Spark, Cassandra, Kafka, Akka

In Spark there is *checkpointing*, the computation to recover, the streaming computation (i.e., the DStreams set up with the streaming context) periodically checkpoints to another set of files in the same fault-tolerant file system.

For Kafka and Cassandra, there is the ZooKeeper operation (see Chapters 5 and 8, respectively).

For Akka, there is the Akka persistence (see Chapter 4).

Replicate for Resiliency

Technologies: Spark, Cassandra, Kafka

Kafka replicates the log for each topic's partitions across a configurable number of servers. This allows automatic failover to these replicas when a server in the cluster fails, so messages remain available in the presence of failures.

Cassandra stores replicas on multiple nodes to ensure reliability and fault tolerance. A replication strategy determines the nodes where replicas are placed. The total number of replicas across the cluster is referred to as the *replication factor*. All replicas are equally important; there is no primary or master replica.

If you recall, Spark does not implement replication. Spark uses HDFS implementations, which implement replication. Spark can recompute chunks of data as a function of input data in HDFS, so if a node crashes, the results for those input shards are computed again in the cluster. Spark can checkpoint computed data back to HDFS, so it saves the results of expensive computations. Spark also makes checkpoints on streams (DStream instances).

Scalable Infrastructure

Technologies: Spark, Cassandra, and Kafka

For Spark, recall that you can use either the stand-alone deploy mode, which only needs Java installed on each node, or the Mesos and Yarn cluster managers.

In Kafka, adding servers to a cluster is done simply by assigning them unique broker ids and then starting Kafka on the new servers. However, these new servers are not automatically assigned any data partitions, so unless partitions are moved to them, they won't do any work until new topics are created. Usually when you add machines to your cluster, you need to move some existing data to these machines.

Cassandra allows you to add capacity to a cluster by introducing new nodes to the cluster in stages or by adding an entire data center.

Share Nothing/Masterless

Technologies: Cassandra, Akka

In shared nothing architecture, each node is independent and self-sufficient, and there is no single point of contention across the system. More specifically, none of the nodes shares memory or disk storage.

The architecture of Cassandra is *masterless*, meaning all nodes are the same. Cassandra provides automatic data distribution across all nodes that participate in a ring or database cluster. Since Cassandra is masterless, a client can connect with any node in a cluster. Clients can interface with a Cassandra node using CQL on any node.

Dynamo Systems Principles

Dynamo is a set of techniques that when applied together make a highly available key-value distributed data store or structured storage system. Its principles are as follows:

- **Incremental scalability**: Dynamo should be able to scale out one storage host (referred to as a *node*) with minimal impact on both the system's operators and the system itself.

- **Symmetry**: Every node in Dynamo has the same set of responsibilities as its peers; there is no distinguished node that takes a special role or an extra set of responsibilities.

- **Decentralization**: The Dynamo design favors decentralized peer-to-peer techniques over centralized control.

- **Heterogeneity**: The Dynamo system is able to exploit heterogeneity in the infrastructure it runs on. For example, the work distribution must be proportional to each individual server's capabilities. This is fundamental and powerful when adding new nodes with higher capacity and it doesn't have to upgrade all hosts at once.

Spark and Cassandra

To work with Apache Spark and Apache Cassandra together, you need to work with the Spark-Cassandra connector. If you recall the history, Cassandra was created on Facebook, but as it became a bigger project, it needed one enterprise to support it. Although Apache Cassandra is an open source project, the company responsible for making decisions with Cassandra is DataStax.

DataStax developed the Spark-Cassandra connector, which is a wonderful library that lets you do three fundamental but powerful tasks:

- Expose Cassandra tables as Spark RDDs

- Write Spark RDDs to Cassandra

- Execute CQL queries in your Spark applications

The following are some Apache-Cassandra connector features:

- Compatible with Apache Cassandra version 2.0 or higher

- Compatible with Apache Spark versions 1.0 through 1.5

- Compatible with Scala versions 2.10 and 2.11

- Exposes Cassandra tables as Spark RDDs

- Maps table rows to `CassandraRow` objects or tuples

- Maps rows to objects of user-defined classes

- Saves RDDs back to Cassandra by an implicit `saveToCassandra` call (nice, with one instruction)

- Makes joins with a Cassandra data subset using `joinWithCassandraTable` call

- Allows RDDs partition according to Cassandra replication using `repartitionByCassandraReplica` call

- Converts data types between Cassandra and Scala

- Supports all the Cassandra data types, including collections

- Filters rows on server side via the CQL `WHERE` clause

- Allows the `for` execution on arbitrary CQL statements

- Plays with Cassandra virtual nodes

- Works with PySpark DataFrames

It is very important to emphasize that the development of the connector is performed after versions of Apache Spark, Apache Cassandra, and Scala are released; typically, the most current versions are not supported. Connector version compatibility is shown in Table 10-1.

Table 10-1. *Spark Cassandra Connector Version Compatibility*

Connector	Spark	Cassandra	Cassandra Java Driver
1.6	1.6	2.1.5, 2.2, 3.0	3.0
1.5	1.5, 1.6	2.1.5, 2.2, 3.0	3.0
1.4	1.4	2.1.5	2.1
1.3	1.3	2.1.5	2.1
1.2	1.2	2.1, 2.0	2.1
1.1	1.1, 1.0	2.1, 2.0	2.1
1.0	1.0, 0.9	2.0	2.0

Spark Streaming with Cassandra

As you know, Spark Streaming extends the core API to allow high throughput and fault-tolerant processing of live data streams. Data can be ingested from many sources, such as Akka, Apache Kafka, Apache Flume, ZeroMQ, TCP sockets, and so forth. The results are stored in Cassandra.

If you didn't know, there is support for Akka within Spark streaming. Chapter 8 has an example of how to use Apache Kafka with Spark Streaming, for which we also show an embedded Kafka and ZooKeeper server for quick user prototyping.

Setting up Spark Streaming

Let's revisit the classic example of word count with Spark Streaming, which writes to the console with `wordCounts.print()`.

1. Create a StreamingContext with a SparkConf configuration.

   ```
   val ssc = new StreamingContext(sparkConf, Seconds(1))
   ```

2. Create a DStream that connects to the server at IP and port.

   ```
   val lines = ssc.socketTextStream(serverIP, serverPort)
   ```

3. Count each word in each batch.

   ```
   val words = lines.flatMap(_.split(" "))
   val pairs = words.map( word => (word, 1) )
   val wordCounts = pairs.reduceByKey(_ + _)
   ```

4. Print a few of the counts to the console (don't forget the `start()` method).

   ```
   wordCounts.print()
   ssc.start()
   ```

Setting up Cassandra

Let's add the Cassandra-specific functions on the StreamingContext and RDD into scope. To do this, you simply replace the print to console with pipe the output to Cassandra (the Spark-Cassandra connector does all the magic):

```
import com.datastax.spark.connector.streaming._
wordCounts.saveToCassandra("streaming_test", "words")
```

Setting up SparkContext

The following explains how to set up the SparkContext.

1. As usual, start by importing Spark:

```
import org.apache.spark._
```

2. Before creating the SparkContext, set the `spark.cassandra.connection.host` property to the address of one of the Cassandra nodes:

```
val conf = new SparkConf(true).set("spark.cassandra.connection.host", "127.0.0.1")
```

3. Create a SparkContext. Substitute 127.0.0.1 with the actual address of your Spark master (or use `"local"` to run in local mode):

```
val sc = new SparkContext("spark://127.0.0.1:7077", "test", conf)
```

4. Enable Cassandra-specific functions on the SparkContext, RDD, and DataFrame:

```
import com.datastax.spark.connector._
```

Create a Streaming Context

The second parameter in the streaming context is the `batchDuration`, which sets the interval that streaming data will be divided into batches. Note that the Spark API supports milliseconds, seconds, and minutes, all accepted as duration. Try not to confuse this duration with `scala.concurrent.duration.Duration`.

```
val ssc = new StreamingContext(conf, Seconds(n))
```

Creating a Stream

We can create a stream with any stream type available or with a custom Spark stream. The Spark-Cassandra connector supports Akka actor streams, subsequently it will support many more stream types. We can also extend the types already provided.

```
import com.datastax.spark.connector.streaming.TypedStreamingActor
```

Kafka Stream

The Kafka stream creates an input stream that pulls messages from a Kafka broker:

```
val stream = KafkaUtils.createStream[String, String, StringDecoder, StringDecoder]( ssc, kafka.kafkaParams, Map(topic -> 1), StorageLevel.MEMORY_ONLY)
```

Actor Stream

The following is an actor stream:

```
val stream = ssc.actorStream[String](Props[TypedStreamingActor[String]], "stream", StorageLevel.MEMORY_AND_DISK)
```

Enable Spark Streaming with Cassandra

Do the following to enable Cassandra-specific functions on the StreamingContext, DStream, and RDD:

```
import com.datastax.spark.connector.streaming._
```

In our example, streaming_test is the keyspace name and words is the table name.

Saving Data

This shows how to save data:

```
val wc = stream.flatMap(_.split("\\s+"))
        .map(x => (x, 1))
        .reduceByKey(_ + _)
        .saveToCassandra("streaming_test", "words", SomeColumns("word", "count"))
```

This starts the computation:

```
sc.start()
```

Reading the StreamingContext from Cassandra

To read the StreamingContext from Cassandra, we use something like this:

```
val rdd = ssc.cassandraTable("streaming_test", "key_value")
        .select("key", "value").where("foo = ?", 3)
```

Loading and Analyzing Data from Cassandra

Use the sc.cassandraTable method to view this table as a Spark RDD:

```
val rdd = sc.cassandraTable("test", "kv")
println(rdd.count)
println(rdd.first)
println(rdd.map(_.getInt("value")).sum)
```

Saving data from a RDD to Cassandra

The following shows how to add two more rows to the table:

```
val collection = sc.parallelize(Seq(("key3", 3), ("key4", 4)))
collection.saveToCassandra("test", "kv", SomeColumns("key", "value"))
```

Saving Datasets to Cassandra

It's possible to save any RDD to Cassandra, not just a CassandraRDD. The requisite is that the object class of RDD is a tuple and has property names corresponding to Cassandra column names.

It's also possible to save an RDD to an existing Cassandra table, as well as to let the connector create the appropriate table automatically, based on the definition of the RDD item class.

To save an RDD to an existing table, you need to import com.datastax.spark.connector._ and call the saveToCassandra method with the keyspace name, the table name, and the list of columns. It is important to include at least all the primary key columns. To save an RDD into a new table, instead of calling saveToCassandra, you have to call saveAsCassandraTable or saveAsCassandraTableEx with the name of the table you want to create.

Saving a Collection of Tuples

Assume the following table definition:

```
CREATE TABLE ks.words (word text PRIMARY KEY, count int);
save( "bar", 20);
save("foo",10);
```

You have the following Spark code:

```
val collection = sc.parallelize(Seq(("cat", 30), ("dog", 40)))
collection.saveToCassandra("ks", "words", SomeColumns("word", "count"))

cqlsh:test> select * from words;

 word | count
------+-------
  bar |    20
  foo |    10
  cat |    30
  dog |    40

(4 rows)
```

With tuples, the use of a custom mapper is also supported, as shown here:

```
val collection = sc.parallelize(Seq((30, "cat"), (40, "dog")))
collection.saveToCassandra("ks", "words", SomeColumns("word" as "_2", "count" as "_1"))

cqlsh:test> select * from words;

 word | count
------+-------
  bar |    20
  foo |    10
  cat |    30
  dog |    40

(4 rows)
```

Saving a Collection of Objects

When saving a collection of objects of a class defined by the user, the items to be saved must provide appropriately named public property accessors to get every column to be saved. This example provides more information on property column naming conventions.

```
case class WordCount(word: String, count: Long)
val collection = sc.parallelize(Seq(WordCount("fox", 50), WordCount("cow", 60)))
collection.saveToCassandra("ks", "words", SomeColumns("word", "count"))

cqlsh:test> select * from words;
```

```
 word | count
------+-------
  bar |    20
  foo |    10
  cat |    30
  dog |    40
  fox |    50
  cow |    60
```

You can specify custom columns to property mapping with SomeColumns. If the property names in the objects to be saved don't correspond to the column names in the destination table, use the "as" keyword on the column names that you want to override. The parameter order uses the table column name first, and then the object property name.

For example, let's say that you want to save WordCount objects to a table that has word (TEXT) and num (INT) columns. This is the table definition in Cassandra:

```
CREATE TABLE ks.words (word text PRIMARY KEY, count int);
```

This is the Spark code:

```
case class WordCount(word: String, count: Long)
val collection = sc.parallelize(Seq(WordCount("fox", 50), WordCount("cow", 60)))
collection.saveToCassandra("ks", "words2", SomeColumns("word", "num" as "count"))
```

Modifying CQL Collections

The default behavior of the Spark-Cassandra connector is to overwrite collections when inserted into a Cassandra table. To override this behavior, you can specify a custom mapper with instructions on how to treat the collection.

The following are the operations supported:

- append/add (lists, sets, maps)
- prepend (lists)
- remove (lists, sets) not supported for maps
- overwrite (lists, sets, maps): default

Let's take the elements from rddSetField and remove them from the corresponding "a_set" C* column, and then take elements from rddMapField and add them to the "a_map" C* column, where the key == key C* column is in the RDD elements.

("key", "a_set" as "rddSetField" remove , "a_map" as "rddMapField" append)

The following is an example schema:

```
CREATE TABLE ks.collections_mod (
     key int PRIMARY KEY,
     list_col list<text>,
     map_col map<text, text>,
     set_col set<text>
  )
```

The following are appending and prepending lists:

```
val listElements = sc.parallelize(Seq(
  (1,Vector("One")),
  (1,Vector("Two")),
  (1,Vector("Three"))))

val preElements = sc.parallelize(Seq(
  (1,Vector("PreOne")),
  (1,Vector("PreTwo")),
  (1,Vector("PreThree"))))

listElements.saveToCassandra("ks", "collections_mod", SomeColumns("key", "list_col" append))
preElements.saveToCassandra("ks", "collections_mod", SomeColumns("key", "list_col" prepend))

cqlsh> select * from ks.collections_mod where key = 1;
```

```
key  | list_col                                      |map_col | set_col
------+-----------------------------------------------+--------+----------
   1  | ['PreThree', 'PreTwo', 'PreOne', 'One', | null   | null
         'Two', 'Three']
(1 rows)
```

Saving Objects of Cassandra User-Defined Types

To save structures consisting of many fields, use a case class or a com.datastax.spark.connector.UDTValue class. An instance of this class can be easily obtained from a Scala map by calling the fromMap method.

Take the following table definition as an example:

```
CREATE TYPE ks.address (city text, street text, number int);
CREATE TABLE ks.companies (name text PRIMARY KEY, address FROZEN<address>);
CREATE TABLE ks.udts (key text PRIMARY KEY, name text, addr FROZEN<address>);
```

You can use a case class to insert into the UDT:

```
case class Address(street: String, city: String, zip: Int)
val address = Address(city = "San Jose", zip = 95126, street = "Santa Clara")
val col = Seq((1, "Raul", address))
sc.parallelize(col).saveToCassandra(ks, "udts", SomeColumns("key", "name", "addr"))
```

Or use the fromMap of UDTValue to create the UDT:

```
import com.datastax.spark.connector.UDTValue
case class Company(name: String, address: UDTValue)
val address = UDTValue.fromMap(Map("city" -> "Palo Alto", "street" -> "Infinite Loop",
"number" -> 1))
val company = Company("Apple", address)
sc.parallelize(Seq(company)).saveToCassandra("ks", "companies")
```

Converting Scala Options to Cassandra Options

To convert Cassandra options to Scala options, you use an implemented implicit. This means that Cassandra options can be dealt with as if they were normal Scala options. For the reverse transformation (from a Scala option into a Cassandra option), you need to define the None behavior. This is done via CassandraOption. deleteIfNone and CassandraOption.unsetIfNone.

```
import com.datastax.spark.connector.types.CassandraOption

//Setup original data (1, 1, 1) ... (6, 6, 6)
sc.parallelize(1 to 6).map(x => (x,x,x)).saveToCassandra(ks, "tab1")

//Setup options Rdd (1, None, None) (2, None, None) ... (6, None, None)
val optRdd = sc.parallelize(1 to 6).map(x => (x, None, None))

//Deleting second column, but ignore the third column
optRdd.map{ case (x: Int, y: Option[Int], z: Option[Int]) =>
    (x, CassandraOption.deleteIfNone(y), CassandraOption.unsetIfNone(z))
  }.saveToCassandra(ks, "tab1")

val results = sc.cassandraTable[(Int, Option[Int], Option[Int])](ks, "tab1").collect
```

The following shows the results:

```
(1, None, Some(1)),
(2, None, Some(2)),
(3, None, Some(3)),
(4, None, Some(4)),
(5, None, Some(5)),
(6, None, Some(6))
```

Saving RDDs as New Tables

As mentioned, you use the saveAsCassandraTable method to automatically create a new table with the given name and save the RDD into it. The keyspace that you are saving to must exist. The following code creates a new words_new table in the test keyspace with word and count columns, where word becomes a primary key:

```
case class WordCount(word: String, count: Long)
val collection = sc.parallelize(Seq(WordCount("dog", 50), WordCount("cow", 60)))
collection.saveAsCassandraTable("test", "words_new", SomeColumns("word", "count"))
```

To customize the table definition, call saveAsCassandraTableEx. The following code demonstrates how to add another column of int type to the table definition, creating a new words_new_2 table:

```
import com.datastax.spark.connector.cql.{ColumnDef, RegularColumn, TableDef}
import com.datastax.spark.connector.types.IntType

case class WordCount(word: String, count: Long)
val table1 = TableDef.fromType[WordCount]("test", "words_new")
val table2 = TableDef("test", "words_new_2", table1.partitionKey, table1.clusteringColumns,
table1.regularColumns :+ ColumnDef("additional_column", RegularColumn, IntType))
val collection = sc.parallelize(Seq(WordCount("dog", 50), WordCount("cow", 60)))
collection.saveAsCassandraTableEx(table2, SomeColumns("word", "count"))
```

The following is example code to create a table with a custom definition. It defines which columns are partition and clustering column keys:

```
import com.datastax.spark.connector.cql.{ColumnDef, RegularColumn, TableDef,
ClusteringColumn, PartitionKeyColumn}
import com.datastax.spark.connector.types._

// 1. Define the RDD structure
case class outData(col1:UUID, col2:UUID, col3: Double, col4:Int)

// 2. Define columns
val p1Col = new ColumnDef("col1",PartitionKeyColumn,UUIDType)
val c1Col = new ColumnDef("col2",ClusteringColumn(0),UUIDType)
val c2Col = new ColumnDef("col3",ClusteringColumn(1),DoubleType)
val rCol = new ColumnDef("col4",RegularColumn,IntType)

// 3. Create table definition
val table = TableDef("test","words",Seq(p1Col),Seq(c1Col, c2Col),Seq(rCol))

// 4. Map RDD into custom data structure and create the table
val rddOut = rdd.map(s => outData(s._1, s._2(0), s._2(1), s._3))
rddOut.saveAsCassandraTableEx(table, SomeColumns("col1", "col2", "col3", "col4"))
```

Akka and Kafka

A connector is available for Scala 2.11 at Maven Central in the following coordinates:

```
libraryDependencies += "com.typesafe.akka" %% "akka-stream-kafka" % "0.11-M4"
```

This is a producer settings example:

```
import akka.kafka._
import akka.kafka.scaladsl._
import org.apache.kafka.common.serialization.StringSerializer
import org.apache.kafka.common.serialization.ByteArraySerializer
val producerSettings = ProducerSettings(system, new ByteArraySerializer, new
StringSerializer).withBootstrapServers("localhost:9092")
```

The following is a produce messages example:

```
Source(1 to 10000)
  .map(_.toString)
  .map(elem => new ProducerRecord[Array[Byte], String]("topic1", elem))
  .to(Producer.plainSink(producerSettings))
```

This is an example of produce messages in a flow:

```
Source(1 to 10000).map(elem => ProducerMessage.Message(new ProducerRecord[Array[Byte],
String]("topic1", elem.toString), elem))
    .via(Producer.flow(producerSettings))
    .map { result =>
      val record = result.message.record
      println(s"${record.topic}/${record.partition} ${result.offset}: ${record.value}
(${result.message.passThrough}")
      result
    }
```

This is a consumer settings example:

```
import akka.kafka._
import akka.kafka.scaladsl._
import org.apache.kafka.common.serialization.StringDeserializer
import org.apache.kafka.common.serialization.ByteArrayDeserializer
import org.apache.kafka.clients.consumer.ConsumerConfig

val consumerSettings = ConsumerSettings(system, new ByteArrayDeserializer, new
StringDeserializer)
  .withBootstrapServers("localhost:9092")
  .withGroupId("group1")
  .withProperty(ConsumerConfig.AUTO_OFFSET_RESET_CONFIG, "earliest")
```

The following database example shows consumer messages and stores a representation, including offset:

```
db.loadOffset().foreach { fromOffset =>
      val subscription = Subscriptions.assignmentWithOffset(new TopicPartition("topic1", 1)
      -> fromOffset)
    Consumer.plainSource(consumerSettings, subscription)
     .mapAsync(1)(db.save)}
```

This is a consume messages at-most-once example:

```
Consumer.atMostOnceSource(consumerSettings.withClientId("client1"), Subscriptions.
topics("topic1"))
    .mapAsync(1) { record =>
     rocket.launch(record.value)
    }
```

This is a consume messages at-least-once example:

```
Consumer.committableSource(consumerSettings.withClientId("client1"), Subscriptions.
topics("topic1"))
    .mapAsync(1) { msg =>
     db.update(msg.value).flatMap(_ => msg.committableOffset.commitScaladsl())
    }
```

This is a connect a consumer to a producer example:

```
Consumer.committableSource(consumerSettings.withClientId("client1"))
    .map(msg =>
     ProducerMessage.Message(new ProducerRecord[Array[Byte], String]("topic2", msg.value),
msg.committableOffset))
    .to(Producer.commitableSink(producerSettings))
```

This is a consume messages at-least-once and commit in batches example:

```
Consumer.committableSource(consumerSettings.withClientId("client1"), Subscriptions.
topics("topic1"))
    .mapAsync(1) { msg =>
     db.update(msg.value).map(_ => msg.committableOffset)
    }
    .batch(max = 10, first => CommittableOffsetBatch.empty.updated(first)) { (batch, elem)
=>
     batch.updated(elem)
    }
    .mapAsync(1)(_.commitScaladsl())
```

Here is a reusable Kafka consumer example:

```
//Consumer is represented by actor
//Create new consumer
val consumer: ActorRef = system.actorOf(KafkaConsumerActor.props(consumerSettings))
```

```
//Manually assign topic partition to it
val stream1 = Consumer
    .plainExternalSource[Array[Byte], String](consumer, Subscriptions.assignment(new
TopicPartition("topic1", 1)))
    .via(business)
    .to(Sink.ignore)

//Manually assign another topic partition
val stream2 = Consumer
    .plainExternalSource[Array[Byte], String](consumer, Subscriptions.assignment(new
TopicPartition("topic1", 2)))
    .via(business)
    .to(Sink.ignore)
```

This is a consumer group example:

```
//Consumer group represented as Source[(TopicPartition, Source[Messages])]
val consumerGroup = Consumer.committablePartitionedSource(consumerSettings.
withClientId("client1"), Subscriptions.topics("topic1"))
  //Process each assigned partition separately
  consumerGroup.map {
    case (topicPartition, source) =>
      source
        .via(business)
        .toMat(Sink.ignore)(Keep.both)
        .run()
  }.mapAsyncUnordered(maxPartitions)(_._2)
```

Here is a use case:

```
import akka.actor.ActorSystem
import akka.stream.ActorMaterializer
import akka.stream.scaladsl.{Sink, Source}
import com.softwaremill.react.kafka.KafkaMessages._
import org.apache.kafka.common.serialization.{StringSerializer, StringDeserializer}
import com.softwaremill.react.kafka.{ProducerMessage, ConsumerProperties,
ProducerProperties, ReactiveKafka}
import org.reactivestreams.{ Publisher, Subscriber }

implicit val actorSystem = ActorSystem("ReactiveKafka")
implicit val materializer = ActorMaterializer()

val kafka = new ReactiveKafka()
val publisher: Publisher[StringConsumerRecord] = kafka.consume(ConsumerProperties(
 bootstrapServers = "localhost:9092",
 topic = "lowercaseStrings",
 groupId = "groupName",
 valueDeserializer = new StringDeserializer()
))
val subscriber: Subscriber[StringProducerMessage] = kafka.publish(ProducerProperties(
  bootstrapServers = "localhost:9092",
```

```
  topic = "uppercaseStrings",
  valueSerializer = new StringSerializer()
))

Source.fromPublisher(publisher).map(m => ProducerMessage(m.value().toUpperCase))
  .to(Sink.fromSubscriber(subscriber)).run()
```

Akka and Cassandra

Let's use the DataStacks Cassandra driver and Akka to build an application that downloads tweets and then stores their id, text, name, and date in a Cassandra table. This shows you how to build a simple Akka application with just a few actors, how to use Akka I/O to make HTTP requests, and how to store the data in Cassandra.

Let's begin by constructing the core of our system. It contains three actors: two that interact with the database and one that downloads the tweets. TwitterReadActor reads from the cluster, TweetWriteActor writes into the cluster, and TweetScanActor downloads the tweets and passes them to TweetWriteActor to be written.

```
class TweetReadActor(cluster: Cluster) extends Actor {   ... }

class TweetWriterActor(cluster: Cluster) extends Actor {   ... }

class TweetScanActor(tweetWrite: ActorRef, queryUrl: String => String) extends Actor { ... }
```

The constructor parameter of the read and write actors is Cassandra's Cluster instance. The scan actor takes an ActorRef of the write actor and a function that, given a String query, can construct the query URL to download the tweets. To construct our application, we have to instantiate the actors in the right sequence, as follows:

```
val system = ActorSystem()
def queryUrl(query: String): String = ???
val cluster: Cluster = ???
val reader  = system.actorOf(Props(new TweetReaderActor(cluster)))
val writer  = system.actorOf(Props(new TweetWriterActor(cluster)))
val scanner = system.actorOf(Props(new TweetScannerActor(writer, queryUrl)))
```

Writing to Cassandra

Now that we have the structure, we can take a look at TwitterWriterActor. It receives instances of Tweet and writes to the tweets keyspace in Cassandra.

```
class TweetWriterActor(cluster: Cluster) extends Actor {
  val session = cluster.connect(Keyspaces.akkaCassandra)
  val preparedStatement = session.prepare("INSERT INTO tweets(key, user_user, text,
createdat) VALUES (?, ?, ?, ?);")

  def receive: Receive = {
    case tweets: List[Tweet] =>
    case tweet: Tweet        =>
  }
}
```

To store the tweets, we need to connect to the correct keyspace, which gives us the Cassandra session. Trying to be as efficient as possible, we will take advantage of Cassandra's PreparedStatements and BoundStatements. The PreparedStatement is a pre-chewed CQL statement, a BoundStatement is a prepared statement whose parameter values are set.

```scala
class TweetWriterActor(cluster: Cluster) extends Actor {
  val session = cluster.connect(Keyspaces.akkaCassandra)
  val preparedStatement = session.prepare("INSERT INTO tweets(key, user_user, text,
createdat) VALUES (?, ?, ?, ?);")

  def saveTweet(tweet: Tweet): Unit =
    session.executeAsync(preparedStatement.bind(tweet.id.id, tweet.user.user, tweet.text.
text, tweet.createdAt))

  def receive: Receive = {
    case tweets: List[Tweet] =>
    case tweet: Tweet        =>
  }
}
```

The only thing that remains to be done is to use it in the `receive` function.

```scala
class TweetWriterActor(cluster: Cluster) extends Actor {
  val session = cluster.connect(Keyspaces.akkaCassandra)
  val preparedStatement = session.prepare("INSERT INTO tweets(key, user_user, text,
createdat) VALUES (?, ?, ?, ?);")

  def saveTweet(tweet: Tweet): Unit =
    session.executeAsync(preparedStatement.bind(tweet.id.id, tweet.user.user, tweet.text.
text, tweet.createdAt))

  def receive: Receive = {
    case tweets: List[Tweet] => tweets foreach saveTweet
    case tweet: Tweet        => saveTweet(tweet)
  }
}
```

We now have the code that saves instances of Tweet to the keyspace in our Cassandra cluster.

Reading from Cassandra

Reading the data is ever so slightly more complex. We need to be able to construct Cassandra queries; then, given a Cassandra row, we need to be able to turn it into our Tweet object. We want to take advantage of the asynchronous nature of the Cassandra driver.

```scala
object TweetReaderActor {
  case class FindAll(maximum: Int = 100)
  case object CountAll
}
```

```scala
class TweetReaderActor(cluster: Cluster) extends Actor {
  val session = cluster.connect(Keyspaces.akkaCassandra)
  val countAll  = new BoundStatement(session.prepare("select count(*) from tweets;"))

  def receive: Receive = {
    case FindAll(maximum)  =>
      // reply with List[Tweet]
    case CountAll =>
      // reply with Long
  }
}
```

We have defined the FindAll and CountAll messages that our actor will react to. We have also left in the code that gives us the session and then used the session to construct a BoundStatement that counts all rows. Next up, we need to be able to construct an instance of Tweet given a row.

```scala
class TweetReaderActor(cluster: Cluster) extends Actor {
  ...
  def buildTweet(r: Row): Tweet = {
    val id = r.getString("key")
    val user = r.getString("user_user")
    val text = r.getString("text")
    val createdAt = r.getDate("createdat")
    Tweet(id, user, text, createdAt)
  }
  ...
}
```

We simply pick the values of the columns in the row and use them to make an instance of Tweet. We would like to asynchronously execute some query, map the rows returned from that query execution to turn them into the tweets, and then pipe the result to the sender.

```scala
class TweetReaderActor(cluster: Cluster) extends Actor {
  val session = cluster.connect(Keyspaces.akkaCassandra)
  val countAll  = new BoundStatement(session.prepare("select count(*) from tweets;"))

  import scala.collection.JavaConversions._
  import cassandra.resultset._
  import context.dispatcher
  import akka.pattern.pipe

  def buildTweet(r: Row): Tweet = {...}

  def receive: Receive = {
    case FindAll(maximum)  =>
      val query = QueryBuilder.select().all().from(Keyspaces.akkaCassandra, "tweets").
limit(maximum)
      session.executeAsync(query) map(_.all().map(buildTweet).toList) pipeTo sender
    case CountAll =>
      session.executeAsync(countAll) map(_.one.getLong(0)) pipeTo sender
  }
}
```

We construct the query using Cassandra's QueryBuilder. We call the executeAsync method on the session, which returns ResultSetFuture. Using implicit conversion in cassandra.resultset._, we turn the ResultSetFuture into Scala's Future[ResultSet]. This allows us to use the Future.map method to turn the ResultSet into List[Tweet].

Calling the session.executeAsync(query) map expects as its parameter a function from ResultSet to some type B. In our case, B is List[Tweet]. The ResultSet contains the all() method, which returns java.util. List[Row]. To be able to map over java.util.List[Row], we need to turn it into the Scala List[Row]. To do so, we bring in the implicit conversions in scala.collection.JavaConversions. And now, we can complete the parameter of the Future.map function.

session.executeAsync gives us Future[List[Tweet]], which is tantalizingly close to what we need. We do not want to block for the result, and we don't use the onSuccess function, because all that it would do is pass on the result to the sender. So, instead, we pipe the success of the future to the sender. That completes the picture, explaining the entire session.executeAsync(query) map(_.all().map(buildTweet).toList) pipeTo sender line.

Connecting to Cassandra

We need to explain where the cluster value comes from. Thinking about the system you are writing, you may need to have different values of cluster for tests and for the main system. Moreover, the test cluster will most likely need some special setup. You simply define that there is a CassandraCluster trait that returns the cluster and to give implementations that do the right thing: one that loads the configuration from the ActorSystem's configuration and one that is hard-coded to be used in tests.

```
trait CassandraCluster {
  def cluster: Cluster
}
```

The configuration-based implementation and the test configuration differ only in the values they use to make the Cluster instance.

```
// in src/scala/main
trait ConfigCassandraCluster extends CassandraCluster {
  def system: ActorSystem

  private def config = system.settings.config

  import scala.collection.JavaConversions._
  private val cassandraConfig = config.getConfig("akka-cassandra.main.db.cassandra")
  private val port = cassandraConfig.getInt("port")
  private val hosts = cassandraConfig.getStringList("hosts").toList

  lazy val cluster: Cluster =
    Cluster.builder().
      addContactPoints(hosts: _*).
      withCompression(ProtocolOptions.Compression.SNAPPY).
      withPort(port).
      build()
}

// in src/scala/test
trait TestCassandraCluster extends CassandraCluster {
  def system: ActorSystem
```

```
  private def config = system.settings.config

  import scala.collection.JavaConversions._
  private val cassandraConfig = config.getConfig("akka-cassandra.test.db.cassandra")
  private val port = cassandraConfig.getInt("port")
  private val hosts = cassandraConfig.getStringList("hosts").toList

  lazy val cluster: Cluster =
    Cluster.builder().
      addContactPoints(hosts: _*).
      withPort(port).
      withCompression(ProtocolOptions.Compression.SNAPPY).
      build()

}
```

This allows you to mix in the appropriate trait and get the properly configured cluster. You want to have the cluster in a well-known state, so you create the CleanCassandra trait that resets the cluster given by a CassandraCluster.cluster.

```
trait CleanCassandra extends SpecificationStructure {
  this: CassandraCluster =>

  private def runClq(session: Session, file: File): Unit = {
    val query = Source.fromFile(file).mkString
    query.split(";").foreach(session.execute)
  }

  private def runAllClqs(): Unit = {
    val session = cluster.connect(Keyspaces.akkaCassandra)
    val uri = getClass.getResource("/").toURI
    new File(uri).listFiles().foreach { file =>
      if (file.getName.endsWith(".cql")) runClq(session, file)
    }
    session.shutdown()
  }

  override def map(fs: => Fragments) = super.map(fs) insert Step(runAllClqs())
}
```

When you mix in this trait into your test, it registers the runAllClqs() steps to be executed before all other steps in the test.

Scanning Tweets

Now that you know that you can safely store and retrieve the tweets from Cassandra, you need to write the component that is going to download them. In our system, this is the TweetScannerActor that receives a message of type String, and it performs the HTTP request to download the tweets.

```scala
class TweetScannerActor(tweetWrite: ActorRef, queryUrl: String => String)
  extends Actor with TweetMarshaller {

  import context.dispatcher
  import akka.pattern.pipe

  private val pipeline = sendReceive ~> unmarshal[List[Tweet]]

  def receive: Receive = {
    case query: String => pipeline(Get(queryUrl(query))) pipeTo tweetWrite
  }
}
trait TweetMarshaller {
  type Tweets = List[Tweet]

  implicit object TweetUnmarshaller extends Unmarshaller[Tweets] {

    val dateFormat = new SimpleDateFormat("EEE MMM d HH:mm:ss Z yyyy")

    def mkTweet(status: JsValue): Deserialized[Tweet] = {
      val json = status.asJsObject
      ...
    }

    def apply(entity: HttpEntity): Deserialized[Tweets] = {
      val json = JsonParser(entity.asString).asJsObject
      ...
    }
  }
}
```

The typeclass instance is the TweetUnmarshaller singleton, which extends Unmarshaller[Tweets]. Notice that we have also defined a type alias, Tweets = List[Tweet], by extending Unmarshaller[Tweets]. We must implement the apply method, which is applied to HttpEntity. It should return deserialized tweets or indicate an error.

Testing TweetScannerActor

To test the scanner fully, we would like to use a well-known service. But where do we get it? We can't really use the live service, because the tweets keep changing. It seems that the only way is to implement a mock service and use it in our tests.

```scala
class TweetScanActorSpec extends TestKit(ActorSystem())
  with SpecificationLike with ImplicitSender {

  sequential

  val port = 12345
  def testQueryUrl(query: String) = s"http://localhost:$port/q=$query"

  val tweetScan = TestActorRef(new TweetScannerActor(testActor, testQueryUrl))
```

```
"Getting all 'typesafe' tweets" >> {

  "should return more than 10 last entries" in {
    val twitterApi = TwitterApi(port)
    tweetScan ! "typesafe"
    Thread.sleep(1000)
    val tweets = expectMsgType[List[Tweet]]
    tweets.size mustEqual 4
    twitterApi.stop()
    success
  }
}
}
```

When constructing TweetScannerActor, we give it the testActor and a function that returns URLs on localhost on some port. In the body of the example, we start the mock TwitterApi on the given port, and use TweetScannerActor to make the HTTP request. Because we gave the testActor the writer ActorRef, we should now be able to see the List[Tweet] that would have been sent to TweetWriterActor.

Because our mock tweet set contains four tweets, we can make the assertion that the list indeed contains four tweets.

Since the components in the system work as expected, we can therefore assemble the App object, which brings everything together in a command-line interface.

```
object Main extends App with ConfigCassandraCluster {
  import Commands._
  import akka.actor.ActorDSL._

  def twitterSearchProxy(query: String) = s"http://twitter-search-proxy.herokuapp.com/
search/tweets?q=$query"

  implicit lazy val system = ActorSystem()
  val write = system.actorOf(Props(new TweetWriterActor(cluster)))
  val read = system.actorOf(Props(new TweetReaderActor(cluster)))
  val scan = system.actorOf(Props(new TweetScannerActor(write, twitterSearchProxy)))

  // we don't want to bother with the ``ask`` pattern, so
  // we set up sender that only prints out the responses to
  // be implicitly available for ``tell`` to pick up.
  implicit val _ = actor(new Act {
    become {
      case x => println(">>> " + x)
    }
  })

  @tailrec
  private def commandLoop(): Unit = {
    Console.readLine() match {
      case QuitCommand                 => return
      case ScanCommand(query)          => scan ! query.toString
```

```
        case ListCommand(count)        => read ! FindAll(count.toInt)
        case CountCommand              => read ! CountAll

        case _                         => return
    }

    commandLoop()
  }

  // start processing the commands
  commandLoop()

  // when done, stop the ActorSystem
  system.shutdown()

}
```

We have the main commandLoop() function, which reads the line from standard input, matches it against the commands, and sends the appropriate messages to the right actors. It also mixes in the "real" source of the Cassandra cluster values and specifies the live function that constructs the URL to retrieve the tweets.

Akka and Spark

We start developing Spark Streaming application by creating a SparkConf that's followed by a StreamingContext.

```
val conf = new SparkConf(false) // skip loading external settings
  .setMaster("local[*]") // run locally with enough threads
  .setAppName("Spark Streaming with Scala and Akka") // name in Spark web UI
  .set("spark.logConf", "true")
  .set("spark.driver.port", s"$driverPort")
  .set("spark.driver.host", s"$driverHost")
  .set("spark.akka.logLifecycleEvents", "true")
val ssc = new StreamingContext(conf, Seconds(1))
```

This gives a context to access the actor system that is of type ReceiverInputDStream.

```
val actorName = "helloer"
val actorStream: ReceiverInputDStream[String] = ssc.actorStream[String](Props[Helloer],
actorName)
```

DStream lets you define a high-level processing pipeline in Spark Streaming.

```
actorStream.print()
```

In the preceding case, the print() method is going to print the first ten elements of each RDD generated in this DStream. Nothing happens until start() is executed.

```
ssc.start()
```

With the context up and running, the code connects to an Akka remote actor system in Spark Streaming that hosts the helloer actor and sends messages that, as the preceding code shows, display them all to standard output.

```scala
import scala.concurrent.duration._
val actorSystem = SparkEnv.get.actorSystem
val url = s"akka.tcp://spark@$driverHost:$driverPort/user/Supervisor0/$actorName"
val timeout = 100 seconds
val helloer = Await.result(actorSystem.actorSelection(url).resolveOne(timeout), timeout)
helloer ! "Hello"
helloer ! "from"
helloer ! "Apache Spark (Streaming)"
helloer ! "and"
helloer ! "Akka"
helloer ! "and"
helloer ! "Scala"
```

Kafka and Cassandra

We need to use kafka-connect-cassandra, which is published by Tuplejump on Maven Central. It is defined as a dependency in the build file. Let's looking at the following example, with SBT:

```scala
libraryDependencies += "com.tuplejump" %% "kafka-connect-cassandra" % "0.0.7"
```

This code polls Cassandra with a specific query. Using this, data can be fetched from Cassandra in two modes:

- bulk
- timestamp based

The modes change automatically based on the query, for example:

```sql
SELECT * FROM userlog ; //bulk

SELECT * FROM userlog WHERE ts > previousTime() ; //timestamp based

SELECT * FROM userlog WHERE ts = currentTime() ; //timestamp based

SELECT * FROM userlog WHERE ts >= previousTime() AND  ts <= currentTime() ; //timestamp based
```

Here, previousTime() and currentTime() are replaced before fetching the data.

CQL Types Supported

CQL Type	Schema Type
ASCII	STRING
VARCHAR	STRING
TEXT	STRING
BIGINT	INT64
COUNTER	INT64
BOOLEAN	BOOLEAN
DECIMAL	FLOAT64
DOUBLE	FLOAT64
FLOAT	FLOAT32
TIMESTAMP	TIMESTAMP

The following types are not currently supported: BLOB, INET, UUID, TIMEUUID, LIST, SET, MAP, CUSTOM, UDT, TUPLE, SMALLINT, TINYINT, DATE, and TIME.

Cassandra Sink

Cassandra Sink stores Kafka SinkRecord in Cassandra tables. Currently, only the STRUCT type is supported in the SinkRecord. The STRUCT can have multiple fields with primitive field types. We assume one-to-one mapping between the column names in the Cassandra sink table and the field names.

The SinkRecords has this STRUCT value:

```
{
    'id': 1,
    'username': 'user1',
    'text': 'This is my first tweet'
}
```

The library doesn't create the Cassandra tables; users are expected to create them before starting the sink.

Summary

This chapter reviewed the connectors among all the SMACK stack technologies. The Spark and Kafka connection was explained in the Chapter 8. Apache Mesos integration was explained in Chapter 7. We end this book with a brief fast data glossary for you to consult if you need the definition of a specific term.

CHAPTER 11

Glossary

This glossary of terms and concepts aids in understanding the SMACK stack.

ACID

The acronym for Atomic, Consistent, Isolated, and Durable. (See Chapter 9.)

agent

A software component that resides within another, much larger, software component. An agent can access the context of the component and execute tasks. It works automatically and is typically used to execute tasks remotely. It is an extension of a software program customized to perform tasks.

API

The acronym for *application programming interface*. A set of instructions, statements, or commands that allow certain software components to interact or integrate with one another.

BI

The acronym for *business intelligence*. In general, the set of techniques that allow software components to group, filter, debug, and transform large amounts of data with the aim of improving a business processes.

big data

The volume and variety of information collected. *Big data* is an evolving term that describes any large amount of structured, semi-structured, and unstructured data that has the potential to be mined for information. Although big data doesn't refer to any specific quantity, the term is often used when speaking about petabytes and exabytes of data. Big data sy stems facilitate the exploration and analysis of large data sets.

CAP

The acronym for Consistent, Available, and Partition Tolerant. (See Chapter 9.)

© Raul Estrada and Isaac Ruiz 2016
R. Estrada and I. Ruiz, *Big Data SMACK*, DOI 10.1007/978-1-4842-2175-4_11

CEP

The acronym for *complex event processing*. A technique used to analyze data streams steadily. Each flow of information is analyzed and generates events; in turn, these events are used to initiate other processes at higher levels of abstraction within a workflow/service.

client-server

An application execution paradigm formed by two components that allows distributed environments. This consists of a component called the *server*, which is responsible for first receiving the requests of the *clients* (the second component). After receiving requests, they are processed by the server. For each request received, the server is committed to returning an answer.

cloud

Systems that are accessed remotely; mainly hosted on the Internet. They are generally administrated by third parties.

cluster

A set of computers working together through a software component. Computers that are part of the cluster are referred to as *nodes*. Clusters are a fundamental part of a distributed system; they maintain the availability of data.

column family

In the NoSQL world, this is a paradigm for managing data using tuples—a key is linked to a value and a timestamp. It handles larger units of information than a key-value paradigm.

coordinator

In scenarios where there is competition, the coordinator is a cornerstone. The coordinator is tasked with the distribution of operations to be performed and to ensure the execution thereof. It also manages any errors that may exist in the process.

CQL

The acronym for *Cassandra Query Language*. A statements-based language very similar to SQL in that it uses SELECT, INSERT, UPDATE, and DELETE statements. This similarity allows quick adoption of the language and increases productivity.

CQLS

A Cassandra-owned CLI tool to run CQL statements.

concurrency

In general, the ability to run multiple tasks. In the world of computer science, it refers to the ability to decompose a task into smaller units so that you can run them separately while waiting for the union of these isolated tasks that represent the execution the total task.

commutative operations

A set of operations are said to be *commutative* if they can be applied in any order without affecting the ending state. For example, a list of account credits and debits is considered commutative because any ordering leads to the same account balance. If there is an operation in the set that checks for a negative balance and charges a fee, however, then the order in which the operations are applied does matter, so it is not commutative.

CRDTs

The acronym for *conflict-free replicated data types*. A collection data structures designed to run on systems with weak CAP consistency, often across multiple data centers. They leverage commutativity and monotonicity to achieve strong eventual guarantees in a replicated state. Compared to strongly consistent structures, CRDTs offer weaker guarantees, additional complexity, and can require additional space. However, they remain available for writes during network partitions that would cause strongly consistent systems to stop processing.

dashboard

A graphical way for indicators to report certain processes or services. Mainly used for monitoring critical activities.

data feed

An automated mechanism used to retrieve updates from a source of information. The data source must be structured to read data in a generic way.

DBMS

The acronym for *database management system*. A software system used to create and manage databases. It provides mechanisms to create, modify, retrieve, and manage databases.

determinism

In data management, a deterministic operation always has the same result given a particular input and state. Determinism is important in replication. A deterministic operation can be applied to two replicas, assuming the results will match. Determinism is also useful in log replay. Performing the same set of deterministic operations a second time will give the same result.

dimension data

Infrequently changing data that expands upon data in fact tables or event records. For example, dimension data may include products for sale, current customers, and current salespeople. The record of a particular order might reference rows from these tables so as not to duplicate data. Dimension data not only saves space, but it also allows a product to be renamed and have that new name instantly reflected in all open orders. Dimensional schemas also allow the easy filtering, grouping, and labeling of data. In data warehousing, a single fact table, a table storing a record of facts or events, combined with many dimension tables full of dimension data, is referred to as a *star schema*.

distributed computing.

A physical and logical model that allows communication between computers distributed across a network. Its goal is to keep the computers together as a single computer, thus achieving resource utilization. This is a complex issue in the world of computer science.

driver

In a general sense, a driver is a connection between two heterogeneous pieces of hardware or software. A driver connects the software of two separate systems and provides an interface that allows interaction between them.

ETL

An acronym for *extract, transform, load*. The traditional sequence by which data is loaded into a database. Fast data pipelines may either compress this sequence, or perform analysis on or in response to incoming data before it is loaded into the long-term data store.

exabyte

(EB) Equivalent to 1024^6 bytes.

exponential backoff

A way to manage contention during failure. During failure, many clients try to reconnect at the same time, overloading the recovering system. Exponential backoff is a strategy of exponentially increasing the timeouts between retries on failure. If an operation fails, wait one second to retry. If that retry fails, wait two seconds, then four seconds, and so forth. This allows simple one-off failures to recover quickly, but for more complex failures, there will eventually be a load low enough to successfully recover. Often the growing timeouts are capped at some large number to bound recovery times, such as 16 seconds or 32 seconds.

failover

Also known as *fault tolerance*, this is the mechanism by which a system is still operating despite failure.

fast data

The processing of streaming data at real-time velocity, enabling instant analysis, awareness, and action. Fast data is data in motion, streaming into applications and computing environments from hundreds of thousands to millions of endpoints—mobile devices, sensor networks, financial transactions, stock tick feeds, logs, retail systems, telco call routing and authorization systems, and more. Systems and applications designed to take advantage of fast data enable companies to make real-time, per-event decisions that have direct, real-time impact on business interactions and observations. Fast data operationalizes the knowledge and insights derived from "big data" and enables developers to design fast data applications that make real-time, per-event decisions. These decisions may have direct impact on business results through streaming analysis of interactions and observations, which enables in-transaction decisions to be made.

gossip

(Protocol) The protocol that Cassandra uses to maintain communication between nodes that form a cluster. Gossip is designed to quickly spread information between nodes and thereby quickly overcome the failures that occur, thus achieving the reliability of the data.

graph database

In the NoSQL world, a type of data storage based on graph theory to manage it. This basically means that nodes maintain their relationships through edges; each node has properties and the relationship between properties that can work with them.

HDSF

The acronym for Hadoop Distributed File System. A distributed file system that is scalable and portable. Designed to handle large files and used in conjunction TCP/IP and RPC protocols. Originally designed for the Hadoop framework, today it is used by a variety of frameworks.

HTAP

The acronym for Hybrid Transaction Analytical Processing architectures. Enables applications to analyze live data as it is created and updated by transaction processing functions. According to the Gartner 2014 Magic Quadrant, HTAP is described as follows: "...they must use the data from transactions, observations, and interactions in real time for decision processing as part of, not separately from, the transactions."[1]

IaaS

The acronym for *Infrastructure as a Service*. Provides the infrastructure of a data center on demand. This includes (but not limited to) computing, storage, networking services, etc. The IaaS user is responsible for maintaining all software installed.

---

[1]Gartner, Inc., "Hybrid Transaction/Analytical Processing Will Foster Opportunities for Dramatic Business Innovation," January 2014, https://www.gartner.com/doc/2657815/hybrid-transactionanalytical-processing-foster-opportunities.

idempotence

An idempotent operation is an operation that has the same effect no matter how many times it is applied. See Chapter 9 for a detailed discussion on idempotence, including an example of idempotent processing.

IMDG

The acronym for *in-memory data grid*. A data structure that resides entirely in RAM and is distributed across multiple servers. It is designed to store large amounts of data.

IoT

The acronym for the *Internet of Things*. The ability to connect everyday objects with the Internet. These objects generally get real-world information through sensors, which take the information to the Internet domain.

key-value

In the NoSQL world, a paradigm for managing data using associative arrays; certain data related to a key. The key is the medium of access to the value to update or delete it.

keyspace

In Apache Cassandra, a keyspace is a logical grouping of column families. Given the similarities between Cassandra and an RDBMS, think of a keyspace as a database.

latency

(Net) The time interval that occurs between the source (send) and the destination (receive). Communication networks require physical devices, which generate the physical reasons for this "delay."

master-slave

A communication model that allows multiple nodes (slaves) to maintain the data dependency or processes of a master node (master). Usually, this communication requires that slaves have a driver installed to communicate with the master.

metadata

Data that describes other data. Metadata summarizes basic information about data, which make finding and working with particular instances of data easier.

NoSQL

Data management systems that (unlike RDBMS systems) do not use scheme, have non-relational data, and are "cluster friendly," and therefore are not as strict when managing data. This allows better performance.

operational analytics

(Another term for operational BI). The process of developing optimal or realistic recommendations for real-time, operational decisions based on insights derived through the application of statistical models and analysis against existing and/or simulated future data, and applying these recommendations to real-time interactions. Operational database management systems (also referred to as OLTP, or *online transaction processing* databases) are used to manage dynamic data in real time. These types of databases allow you to do more than simply view archived data; they allow you to modify that data (add, change, or delete) in real time.

RDBMS

The acronym for *relational database management system*. A particular type of DBMS that is based on the relational model. It is currently the most widely used model in production environments.

real-time analytics

An overloaded term. Depending on context, "real time" means different things. For example, in many OLAP use cases, "real time" can mean minutes or hours; in fast data use cases, it may mean milliseconds. In one sense, "real time" implies that analytics can be computed while a human waits. That is, answers can be computed while a human waits for a web dashboard or a report to compute and redraw. "Real time" also may imply that analytics can be done in time to take some immediate action. For example, when someone uses too much of their mobile data plan allowance, a real-time analytics system notices this and triggers a text message to be sent to that user. Finally, "real time" may imply that analytics can be computed in time for a machine to take action. This kind of real time is popular in fraud detection or policy enforcement. The analysis is done between the time a credit or debit card is swiped and the transaction is approved.

replication

(Data) The mechanism for sharing information with the aim of creating redundancy between different components. In a cluster, data replication is used to maintain consistent information.

PaaS

The acronym for *Platform as a Service*. Offers integration with other systems or development platforms, which provides a reduction in development time.

probabilistic data structures

Probabilistic data structures are data structures that have a probabilistic component. In other words, there is a statistically bounded probability for correctness (as in Bloom filters). In many probabilistic data structures, the access time or storage can be an order of magnitude smaller than an equivalent non-probabilistic data structure. The price for this savings is the chance that a given value may be incorrect, or it may be impossible to determine the exact shape or size of a given data structure. However, in many cases, these inconsistencies are either allowable or can trigger a broader, slower search on a complete data structure. This hybrid approach allows many of the benefits of using probability, and also can ensure correctness of values.

SaaS

The acronym for Software as a Service. Allows the use of hosted cloud applications. These applications are typically accessed through a web browser. Its main advantages are to reduce initial cost and to reduce maintenance costs. It allows a company to focus on their business and not on hardware and software issues.

scalability

A system property to stably adapt to continued growth; that is, without interfering with the availability and quality of the services or tasks offered.

shared nothing

A distributed computing architecture in which each node is independent and self-sufficient. There is no single point of contention across the system. More specifically, none of the nodes share memory or disk storage.

Spark-Cassandra Connector

A connector that allows an execution context Spark and to access an existing keyspace on a Cassandra server.

streaming analytics

Streaming analytics platforms can filter, aggregate, enrich, and analyze high-throughput data from multiple disparate live data sources and in any data format to identify simple and complex patterns to visualize business in real time, detect urgent situations, and automate immediate actions. Streaming operators include Filter, Aggregate, Geo, Time windows, temporal patterns, and Enrich.

synchronization

Data synchronization. In a cluster that consists of multiple nodes, you must keep data synchronized to achieve availability and reliability.

unstructured data

Any information that is not generated from a model or scheme or is not organized in a predefined manner.

Index

Get the eBook for only $5!

Why limit yourself?

Now you can take the weightless companion with you wherever you go and access your content on your PC, phone, tablet, or reader.

Since you've purchased this print book, we're happy to offer you the eBook in all 3 formats for just $5.

Convenient and fully searchable, the PDF version enables you to easily find and copy code—or perform examples by quickly toggling between instructions and applications. The MOBI format is ideal for your Kindle, while the ePUB can be utilized on a variety of mobile devices.

To learn more, go to www.apress.com/companion or contact support@apress.com.

Printed in the United States
By Bookmasters